PREFACE

At the start of 2020, the year that would go on to change the world, the COVID-19 pandemic swept across the globe. What started off as a few contained cases in China, soon spread rapidly, sending the world into chaos. People flocked to supermarkets to stock up on groceries, like it was an apocalypse. Families relaxing on the beach, to get away from home, eventually cried to try and get back home. Basically, everyone panicked. No one had any idea that such a catastrophe would occur, and what they would do in the face of it. Humans became mindless, falling prey to the base instinct of survival, doing everything they needed to in order to survive.

Similar to this, is the search for happiness. I prefer not to use the word *search*, because, we shouldn't be searching for it—but unfortunately we do—in objects, people, places, and experiences. In fact, every human act has two motives: to get rid of pain, or, to attain happiness. Aristotle said that happiness is the greatest good, and that every human strives for happiness. Despite striving, why do we never achieve permanent happiness?

Exploring the evolving concepts of happiness, we will venture on a journey together. From the ancient sages of millennia, to the modern-day self-help and scientific industries, we delve into this seemingly never-ending quest for happiness. I present this book in front of you after thousands of hours of research, interviews, reading, and experiments. Yes, I am spiritual, and so throughout this book I refer to ancient wisdom. But, I am also a scientist who *needs* to see everything backed up with data, and so, that is exactly what I have done.

To make this book a reality, I studied multiple works of ancient texts, primarily from the three great parts of the world with classical thought: India (The Vedas, The Upanishads, Shrimad Bhāgavatam, Bhagavad Gitā, Vachanāmrut, Swāmini Vāto, and the teachings of Buddha), China (Tao te Ching, The Analects, Mencius, and other philosophers and thinkers), and also the cultures of the Mediterranean (both the Old and New Testaments, the Greek and Roman philosophers, the Stoics, and the Quran). I also reviewed philosophical literature from the last five centuries, as well as a number of scientific studies of the past century. Throughout this research, I collated the coherent ideas to form this book. The aim was to see how differing concepts come together, building upon one another, on this continuous, yet ever-changing, search for happiness by humankind.

There are many out there who talk, write, and preach about peace and happiness. Many of them may also practice the teachings and concepts that they share with others. But my goal in writing this book is different. This book started of as a personal project in exploring the life of my gurus, on *my* search for meaning and happiness. Words have merely become a medium.

This book brings practical concepts together that I believe we should all practice in our daily lives. These concepts and ideas have stemmed from my direct interactions, experiences, and observations with my spiritual gurus, HH Pramukh Swami Maharaj (Pramukh Swami) and HH Mahant Swami Maharaj (Mahant Swami).

Pramukh Swami (1921-2016) lived amongst us, with us, and for us for ninety-four years. Despite leading a worldwide socio-spiritual organisation with thousands of centres, millions of followers, and hundreds of activities, he remained in a continuous state of bliss, joy, and contentment. He remained constantly fulfilled and at peace, in each and every moment of his life, regardless of joy or misery. He was the living embodiment of *param ānanda* (everlasting bliss).

Pramukh Swami inspired his successor, my current guru, Mahant Swami (b. 1933), to also lead a life filled with bliss and inner peace. To live in the state of *param ānanda*. Today, at the tender age of eighty-seven, Mahant Swami helms the worldwide activities of the same organisation, presiding as the spiritual guru to millions of individuals around the world. Yet, he too, is able to remain fulfilled; in a state of total equilibrium. Why is it that they experience this state of *param ānanda* continuously and naturally? Surely, it is not a facade, nor can it be a mere act. Agreed, one can act happy, but for ninety-four or eighty-seven years? I don't think so. This got me questioning and exploring their lives further, realising that it was reality. They are the living proof and sole inspiration behind *The Keshav Way*.

ABOUT THE BOOK

This book is split into four parts.

Part 1 introduces the main characters of this journey.

Part 2 explores the evolving concepts of happiness, as we look at how culture and society has shaped changing beliefs and ideas. We look at how modern-day man's search for happiness could potentially be heading in the wrong direction. We learn, through a number of backed-up studies, where we think happiness lies, and the truth about these *things*. Basically, we try and touch upon almost every aspect of happiness, face the hard facts of life, and look at how we all *could* be completely wrong.

Part 3 outlines five principles that form the basis of *The Keshav Way*. I would suggest you familiarise yourself with these principles first.

Part 4 details how you can transform your life. This is done through habits, or as I prefer to call them, *ways*. Different ways that you can practice, to live a life filled with more joy and fulfilment, and increase your overall well-being. I have broken it down into six key areas of thought, from the acronym of Keshav:

Know Thyself

Engagement

Social Living

Health & Well-being

Ambition, Purpose & Meaning

Voluntary Actions

Although I expand on ancient wisdom from various parts of the world, particularly from the Vedas, it does not demand you to have any prior background knowledge of these schools of thought.

WHAT YOU WILL LEARN

I am certain that this book will open your mind to thoughts you will never have considered before; it will make you see life from another perspective, your personality will change, your performance in areas of your life will improve, your confidence will shoot up, you will be better positioned to handle anxiety, you will mould your relationships, and most importantly, you will learn the truth about happiness, purpose, and meaning.

I know that you've probably heard all of these promises before in many motivational and self-help books, but this book is different. A normal self-help book repackages the same usual stuff about self-belief, confidence, following passion, finding purpose, persevering, and throwing in a couple of nice exercises here and there. In fact, the economic uncertainty across the globe over the last few years, as well as the global pandemic of 2020, has led to the emergence of a growing number of motivational, self-help geniuses. In this book, I bring you the wisdom of spirituality, psychology, philosophy, physical sciences, human biology, and practical habits, that have been around for a while, in an easy to understand and simple-to-read format. Even passively reading this book can be beneficial.

HOW TO READ THIS BOOK

If you are reading this book for this first time, I recommend reading it cover to cover. Most of the ideas presented in this book are best understood if read in order. When you have read the book in this way once, you are free to delve into any section of your choice.

This book is neither a novel nor a textbook—it is your companion. I am hoping that the book will introduce you to a huge amount of mental shifts and unique thought processes. Don't try and complete it in one night; let it grow. Read a section at a time, revisit one if you need to. Just take your time to understand the different thoughts and ideas. Most importantly, please keep an open mind.

You will notice throughout the read that I often switch between 'I' and 'we'. This may seem annoying, but I have done so deliberately. The Vedic tradition teaches us to expand above 'I', and see 'I' in everything; becoming 'we'. Please don't distribute this book as a free copy to anyone, as that will taint the purpose of the book. The book is nominally priced, and by encouraging others to purchase this book, they are giving to a worthwhile cause.

This book is not too technical or difficult, and I have made every effort in using simple language. The thoughts and ideas are clear. I won't spoon-feed you self-help wisdom, or just throw you bog-standard quotes, and so at times, I will leave you with open-ended thoughts without a conclusion. Your mind will have to deal with some ambiguity and prepare to think, or, be irritated by vague thoughts. Hopefully this will ignite thoughts and emotions that take you through a process described in this book.

Certain ideas may be repeated or emphasised more than once, and you may wonder why there are so many commonly heard clichés. I have done so deliberately, and so, I request you to keep progressing and work with me. Research has shown that the repetition of thoughts and ideas lead to neural patterns being formed within your brain.

Finally, whilst reading this book, if you like any thoughts or ideas (or just generally wish to share them), please do! Post pictures of your favourite pages, images, quotes, and experiences from this book, on social media using the **#TheKeshavWay**. This way I can like them and feature them on my social media pages.

With my sincere prayers and wishes, I hope that you enjoy reading this book. I am so glad you have taken the first step on this journey. The journey that I call, *The Keshav Way*.

Vinay

Vinay Sutaria
07 December 2020

CONTENTS

PART FOUR

KESHAV

INTRODUCTION

It was an early morning in the hottest month of the Indian summer, when I sat in front of the *smruti mandir* (memorial shrine) of my guru Pramukh Swami Maharaj, who had left his mortal body two years back. A fellow *swāmi* (ordained monk) called out to me from the neighbouring canopies. I got up and made my way towards him slowly, tired from a restless night.

"Vinay, the morning rituals are about to begin and you're still down here? Why don't you head up?" He spoke in his gentle, yet authoritative voice.

"Sure Swami… I was just got lost in memories, and my tiredness of course, that I didn't even hear the bell ring!" I replied, gesturing my hand towards the *smruti mandir*.

He smiled and said, "I understand. Don't we all? Just go up for now, have breakfast, and then you wanted to come and meet me in the gardens, right?"

I nodded in agreement, as I proceeded up the stairs of the hundred-year-old, magnificent three-storey *mandir* (temple). As the rituals commenced to the beatings of drums, the ringing of bells, and the sounds of conch shells, I sat and observed as hundreds of *swāmis* and *sādhaks* (training monks) were fully engrossed in the prayers. They seemed full of joy, peace, and serenity.

Something was different here; in fact, everything was different here.

Lying on the border of the district, approximately 150km away from Ahmedabad, India, is the small and serene village of Sarangpur. The word *sārang* means peacock, and so this beautiful village is known as the 'land of peacocks'. It is home to the second-highest temple in Gujarat, and the village holds great significance to millions across the globe. It is also the hub for training *swāmis* (from now on I will just use swami[s]), who spend approximately ten years in this remote village, to turn over a new leaf of their life. I knew countless individuals here, who had left their lives of comfort, earning six-figure salaries, and driving the best cars, to discover something greater and bigger than themselves.

It seemed impossible to me that hundreds of youth in their mid-twenties, some from the poorest villages of India, others from the metropolitan mega-cities of the world, could live together in harmony and as one. How could you just give up your Mercedes, five-bed homes, and six-figure salaries, to come to a remote village of India?

The swamis at this *āshram* (monastery) lead a very disciplined lifestyle. They practically denounce all of their belongings, including their family, to go on to accept the entire world as their family. They meditate five times a day, some often for hours, for self-discovery, self-esteem, and to gain self-control. They fast for days on stretch, often even without water. They sleep on cold, hard floors, awaking daily by 4 a.m. to shower with cold water. They don't watch television (including Netflix), nor do they use mobile phones or iPads. They eat simple vegetarian food, which they always mix with water in a bowl before eating. Basically, they reject all pleasures and comforts of this world and their body, to discover something deeper and greater than themselves. They receive no salary or source of income, treading this new life to serve society. Let me remind you, this is a personal choice that they make after years of contemplation and a certain level of self-realisation. Not anyone and everyone is able to tread this new path. It is an extremely difficult, and for them, a one-way path. It was in this tiny, remote village of Sarangpur, amongst the swamis, that my journey began. A journey of discovery—that is, discovering something greater than 'I', 'me' and 'you'. A journey that I am on the path of learning and practicing. A journey that I now wish to share with you all.

Today, more and more people are dissatisfied with life. One in every eight US adults report taking pills to help them sleep at night, and I am almost certain that this number will increase. We are continuously stressed and anxious. We worry and fear the past, present, and the future. We seem to find little to no meaning and purpose in our lives, and so we preoccupy our entire lives on a seemingly endless chase for happiness. Global culture and media are fuelling this further, setting expectations about who and what you should be, not only as individuals, but as a collective too. Many seek happiness through the likes of fame, money, beauty, and other pleasures. All fleeting, yet we seek more and more. We continue to run for these objects and experiences, like hamsters on a wheel which leads only to frustration, anxiety, exhaustion, dissatisfaction, and ultimately unhappiness. Both mentally and physically.

Living *The Keshav Way* isn't just a possibility, now it is a necessity. And so, I am glad that you have picked up this book, and hope that you continue to join me on this journey. Believe me that there is no other choice, that is, if you want to find true peace, purpose, joy, and learn the truth about happiness.

PART ONE

CHARACTERS

THE ANALOGY

Throughout this book I will use and refer to the analogy of 'The Monkey, Tesla & Passenger'. Before I share what exactly this analogy is with you, let me first tell you how it came to mind. It is obvious that the way in which the human mind thinks and understands new and complex ideas is dependent on what we already know. Our minds are easily able to apply metaphors and analogies that it can relate to into our daily lives. I learnt this from some of the primary sources of my research, namely the Vachanāmrut and Upanishads.

In the Vachanāmrut, Bhagwān Shri Swāminārāyan uses countless analogies and metaphors to help his audience relate to his teachings. In one such analogy he describes the state of anger to be like a rabid dog. We've all heard of the popular phrase, 'happiness is a journey'. Now, it would be difficult to understand happiness on its own, but this metaphor helps us to understand that in this journey, that we call life, we need some form of direction. There will be some unfamiliar obstacles, but we should enjoy the trip, and hope that there is something great for us at the end of the journey.

Similarly, to help you understand the different topics addressed in this book, my analogy aims to differentiate some key concepts and guide your thinking. In Buddhism, the mind is compared to monkeys swinging from branch to branch, aimless and uncontrollable. In Hinduism, the body is compared to a vehicle, and the soul to the driver of that vehicle. Similarly, the likes of Plato, Freud, and other Western philosophers have also given metaphors to describe the mind-body-soul relationship. Taking all of these examples into account, I have formed my own analogy, **The Monkey, Tesla & Passenger**.

The monkey refers to the mind. We all have a mind; sometimes we are able to tame it and keep it under our control. But for the most part, it seems uncontrollable to us, as though it works on its own.

The Tesla refers to the body. The majority of the processes that occur within us, and from us, are automatic. Sometimes, the monkey grabs the steering wheel and takes control of the Tesla, but usually it's fine running on autopilot.

The passenger is your soul—a silent observer—literally the passenger in the Tesla. It is seeking its journey to some destination that only it seems to knows. It has inputted it into the SatNav system, and has probably told the monkey where to go a hundred times, but the monkey has paid no attention. Either that, or it isn't able to comprehend the language of the passenger. Of course, the soul itself can take full control over the vehicle, but it can only do so if the monkey learns to work with it, instead of against it. The monkey prefers to keep full power to itself. That is it, it's simple. The monkey is the mind, the Tesla is the body, and the passenger is the soul. In this book, I refer to the word 'soul' by its Sanskrit meaning, *ātmā*.

ALEXANDER

Alexander the Great was the king of the ancient Greek kingdom of Macedon, around 350 BC. He had conquered most of the known world in a brief span of just eleven years. To understand just how much he had conquered, take his wealth as an example. His approximate wealth was 180,000 talents of gold. Adding all the lands and empires he conquered, it is actually impossible to quantify his net worth.

Yet, when he lay on his deathbed at the young age of thirty-two, he came to a self-realisation that he had actually achieved nothing in his life. How is this possible? Alexander had conquered the world. He had acquired so much wealth that he literally had the world at his feet. So how can he say that he had achieved nothing?

Well, on his return home after his fierce, last battle, he fell severely ill in Babylon and regretted that he would not get to see the face of his mother one last time. With this constant thought eating him up, he lay there waiting to breathe his last. Calling upon his generals, he said, "Soon, I will depart this earth. I have three wishes, please ensure they are fulfilled." With tears in their eyes, the generals agreed to abide by the last wishes of their king. Obviously, you will be wondering what his three wishes were, so let's first look at them.

> **Wish 1:** My physicians (doctors) alone must carry my coffin.
> **Wish 2:** Scatter the path to the graveyard with my treasures.
> **Wish 3:** Keep my hands open and dangling out from the coffin.

Some strange requests for sure, but who would dare question such a powerful king? Only his favourite general built up the courage and dared to speak. He asked out of curiosity, "Your majesty! We assure you that we will fulfil these wishes of yours. But tell us, why do you make such strange wishes?"

Taking a deep breath, Alexander shared the secret behind his strange requests, "I want the world to know the three most important lessons that I have just come to realise. The reason I want my physicians to carry my coffin, is so that people realise that *no doctor can really cure any illness or stop death*. They are powerless and cannot save a person from the clutches of death. So, **never take life for granted**. My second wish for strewing my treasures, is to show people that not even a fraction of this wealth is coming with me. *I spent my entire life acquiring wealth, but I won't be taking anything with me*. Let people realise that **it is a sheer waste of time to chase wealth**. And as for my third wish, I want people to know that *I came empty-handed into this world, and I am leaving empty-handed too*. Bury my body, do not build any monument, and keep my hands out, so that the whole world can know that **the king who conquered the world had nothing in his hands when he died**."

The story of Alexander is just one of many, where history has slapped humanity in the face and continues to do so again and again. Even for the likes of King Solomon, Napoleon, and Princess Diana. Alexander didn't die at thirty-two in Babylon. He lives on today. Every one of us is Alexander. Not in the literal sense, but through our lifestyles. In all of us, a part of Alexander lives on. Just take a look around you, and at yourself too, we are all chasing after similar pleasures. Whether that be by competing to beat our friends in school, or a promotion or pay rise at our workplace, we are constantly chasing after our desires to acquire more and more. To get the attention and validation from those around us; to find love; and to eventually build our own *empires*. But the question still remains, when will we truly be happy or content? And, does attaining more make us happy?

I want you to try something. Read the scenario below, then pause from reading the book, and picture yourself in it.

IMAGINE

You are sunbathing on the balcony of your penthouse villa, on an island in the Maldives. Your beautiful partner is beside you, and you can smell the aroma of mouthwatering cuisines that your chef is preparing for you. A butler stands next to you, with an array of fresh, exotic fruit juices from across the world. Your children are happily playing on the beach that overlooks the vast Indian Ocean. Your helicopter is docked on the neighbouring helipad, and your yacht is docked at the shore of the island. You have several investments, and your bank account holds £1 million in savings. Would you now say that you are content and complete in life?

Repeated studies have shown that humans have this innate nature to always want more. When we don't get *more*, we get frustrated and depressed. We are programmed in this way that no matter how much we get in life, we will never be content, and will always want more. Every object and experience that humankind seeks satisfaction in is temporary and fleeting. Think about all your experiences. Like the time when you first got your hands on the phone you have right now. At the time, you felt overjoyed knowing that you had something that made you 'happy'. One year later, when a newer model came out, or when someone else had a model better than yours, where did that happiness go? Why is it that you no longer experience the same joy that you did initially? You can put this thought to use against everything you have, or that you want to have in your life—your car, your home, your wife (sorry, marriage), or anything else for that matter. The desire to want more, this inner wish to crave for more and more is one of the many reasons we are not satisfied in life. It has been proved time and time again (we will talk about this later), not just by studies but, through history too. Until we eliminate this delusion, we will never truly feel content. The idea is not to let everything and everyone go; it isn't to denounce the world and go live in the seclusion of the Himalayan mountains, or the solidarity of a village hut. Instead, we need to learn to be content with what we have, to attain a state of equilibrium.

That is probably the reason you are holding this book. We will be taking a step towards a journey of transforming ourselves. To practice a new approach in our lives and not to stay as *Alexander*, but to transform ourselves into *Keshav*. I hope that by the time you put this book down, you are able to see your life from a fresh perspective. That you will appreciate more, and apply the ideas and concepts shared in this book into your life. Recall Alexander's last realisation:

We are born with nothing, and we will leave with nothing.

KESHAV

After reading the story of Alexander, you will probably understand how you (and I) all mimic Alexander. We can accept this from now, I don't think any of us can even deny this truth. But it's not all bad. So, I now want to introduce you to *Keshav*.

Keshav is abstract. Keshav is metaphysical. It isn't any one particular object, nor is it any one particular person. But, it isn't a mere concept either. I want you to create your own Keshav. Of course, Keshav could be your inspiration; the source of all faith and courage, in the form of a true guru, or even God himself. Keshav could also be the passenger, your *self*. You may have picked up this book to learn how to overcome the negative tendencies of your mind, or to gain control over your thoughts and emotions, and so, Keshav could also be the end goal for you. What you want to eventually achieve, or the state that you want to reach, can be Keshav too. It could be the inner peace, happiness, contentment, or satisfaction you can derive from living the good life. Basically, I want you to decide what you want your Keshav to be. Your God, your guru, your mind, the final state, anything. Put simply, Keshav should be the driving force for you.

For me, Keshav is the *ātmā*, the passenger in this journey called life. I see Keshav as the ultimate state of bliss and happiness— equivalent to the state of *param ānanda*—the natural state of the *ātmā*. According to ancient Vedic concepts, the *ātmā* has travelled through countless births, and we will talk more about this later. But, to bring the passenger back to its default, original, and blissful state. That is Keshav to me.

Keshav is contentment.

Keshav is bliss.

Keshav is peace.

Keshav is happiness.

In fact, Keshav is the epitome of happiness.

Keshav is *param ānanda*—the ultimate state of spontaneous bliss and contentment, also known as *sahaj ānanda*.

The first step to reaching this state begins by following a lifestyle. The lifestyle I call *The Keshav Way*. It isn't an instant change; it is actually a lifelong journey. A journey that presents you with different ways to approach the turbulences of life.

- A journey to find purpose and meaning;
- A journey to eliminate anxiety and stress;
- A journey to mould relationships;
- A journey to achieve your goals;
- A journey to discover inner calm;
- A journey to master your mind;
- A journey to reach the true state of bliss and happiness.

Don't worry if this still seems confusing. As you progress, I am sure that this will become clearer to you. Continue to have faith throughout the process. Not just in me, but in yourself too. Read this book in peace, do not rush through it, just take your time. You now hold the guide to discovering Keshav.

In Sanskrit, 'The Life of Keshav', that we aspire to achieve, translates nicely into my two favourite words: *Keshav Jivan*. Our lives need to become Keshav. I want to make my life Keshav. The important question is, are you willing to do the same?

THE WARS WITHIN

Progress is impossible without change.
Those who cannot change their minds, cannot change anything.
George Bernard Shaw

Until today, you probably identified yourself as one, as a whole. You are *you*. We think of ourselves as a single soldier, battling through this struggle-filled journey of life. But you are terribly wrong. To be precise, there are opposing soldiers within you, constantly fighting with each other in their own duels. I call them *The Wars Within*. Now let's briefly analyse the battlefield.

BATTLE 1: MIND VS. BODY

I presume that the majority of you who have picked up this book, will be open to the fact that the mind and body operate distinctly. You may have also heard people say things like, "My mind has a body of its own!" This is actually true. The French philosopher and writer, Michel de Montaigne, elaborates this distinction, particularly with the bowels in the digestive system. He refers to the bowels as having a brain of their own. He mentions how our intestines are lined by a vast network of more than a 100 million neurons; handling all the computations required to run the gut factory, processing and extracting the nutrients from the food we consume.[1] The gut brain runs

---

[1] Gershon, 1998.

separately to the brain in our heads; it carries out its own management. Studies have shown that when the vagus nerve that connects the two brains together, is cut, the gut continues to function as normal. This is one of the reasons why experts say that looking after your gut is very important. It is able to trigger anxiety in the normal brain when it encounters an infection, alerting you to act with caution now that you are sick. This is also one of the primary reasons that many initial side effects of common drugs, like selective serotonin reuptake inhibitors (SSRIs), comprise of nausea and changes in bowel function. This could be contributing to the popular Vedic theory of the chakras being distinct, and the gut chakra being the source of intuitions, that is, ideas appearing outside of our own mind. This is the first main battle.

BATTLE 2: LEFT VS. RIGHT

The second battle was stumbled upon by accident in the 1960s, by a surgeon named Joe Bogen, who was cutting people's brains in half. He wasn't doing it for fun, don't worry. He was trying to aid those whose lives were being ruined by episodes of persistently dangerous epileptic seizures. Basically, your brain is split into two separate hemispheres (which you have probably learnt at school). The two halves are joined by a huge clump of nerves called the *corpus callosum*. Seizures can begin in any part of the brain and then spread to surrounding tissue. But, if a seizure comes in contact with the corpus callosum, it can very quickly spread to the entire brain, making a person lose consciousness, fall down, and suffer uncontrollably. What Bogen wanted to do was to take away the corpus callosum to prevent seizures spreading to it. How can seizures spread to it, if it wasn't even there? Initially, this seemed crazy, how could you just cut out the largest chunk of nerves? At first, there seemed to be little difference in the patients. But later on, when they brought a young psychologist, Michael Gazzaniga, onboard to study the after-effects of the procedure, the findings were very interesting. The findings are very detailed, but in essence, Gazzaniga discovered the two halves of the brain, as well as the separate modules that work independently, and cross-platform too. He also showed that people fabricate reasons for their behaviours. The battle ensues.

BATTLE 3: NEW VS. OLD

Through evolution, our brains have expanded. It is thought to have started off with just three clusters of neurons: the *hindbrain* (connected to the spinal column), the *midbrain*, and the *forebrain* (connected to the sensory organs). But with time, as bodies and behaviours evolved, the brain too evolved—primarily the forebrain. It developed an outer shell comprising of the *hypothalamus* (for the coordination of basic drives and motivations), the *hippocampus* (for memory), and the *amygdala*. The amygdala is the problem-scanning machine; constantly scanning the world around you for worries. Now, don't worry about remembering these, I am just giving you an overview of this complex battle. These structures are commonly known as the limbic system, as they wrap around the rest of the brain, forming a type of protective border.

As mammals continued to grow and diversify, so did the brain. The mammals that socialised formed a new layer of neural tissue, which spread to surround the limbic system. This was the *neocortex*, which houses the most interesting parts of the brain—the parts that allow us to make new associations and to engage in thinking, planning, and decision-making. This helped in the growth of the *frontal cortex*, believed to be the seat for reasoning (where the monkey sits). The frontal cortex plays an important role in suppressing or inhibiting certain behavioural impulses. It also enables the expansion of emotionality in humans. The lower third of the prefrontal cortex (responsible for rational thought) is called the *orbitofrontal cortex* because it is just above the eyes (*orbit* is Latin for the eye socket). This area is particularly active during emotional reactions, playing a key role when you look at reward and punishment of a given situation.

In the 1990s, neurologist Antonia Damasio found that when certain parts of the orbitofrontal cortex are damaged, patients lose the majority of their emotional lives. They begin to report that they feel nothing when they should. But it doesn't affect any other part of their brain, such as reasoning or logical thinking. They perform normally in intelligence and knowledge tests, as well as in following social and moral principles.[2]

---

[2] Damasio, 1994, Damasio, Tranel, and Damasio, 1990.

BATTLE 4: AUTOMATIC VS. CONTROLLED

In the past thirty odd years, psychologists have started to understand that there are actually two processing systems at work within our brains, at all times. These are the controlled system and the automatic system.

Automatic processes happen unconsciously, but may show up sometimes in consciousness. Basically, it is when we notice our unconscious actions. Say for example, you had to catch a flight to New York at 10:30 a.m, what time would you leave from home? Obviously, you would think consciously about this, choosing how you will get to the airport, considering traffic, the weather, and roadworks. You can't just guess, can you? But if you choose to take the train to the airport, almost everything you do throughout your journey is automatic—blinking, breathing, and even moving about.

The automatic system has been shaped by natural selection to trigger quick, reliable actions, including parts of the brain that make you feel pleasure and pain (orbitofrontal cortex), and that trigger survival motivations (hypothalamus). The automatic system is the one that flicks the dopamine switch, whereas the controlled system is like your advisor. For us, the monkey is meant to work hand-in-hand with the passenger to form the controlled system, but it is more uncontrolled than that. It tends to do what it wants and doesn't like seeking *advice* from the passenger. Both the monkey and the passenger are conscious, whereas the Tesla represents everything else—gut feelings, visceral reactions, emotions, and intuitions from the automatic system. They all have their separate intelligence, but when they all work together, they can create marvels. That is one of the goals, But when, and will, these battles ever end?

BEGIN WITH THE END IN MIND

Remembering that I will be dead soon is the most important tool I've ever encountered to help me make the big choices in life. It was almost everything: all external expectations, all pride, all fear of embarrassment or failure – these things just fall away in the face of death, leaving only what is truly important. Remembering that you are going to die is the best way I know to avoid the trap of thinking you have something to lose. You are already naked. There is no reason not to follow your heart.

Steve Jobs

Before we venture on, I want you to accept the truth about death. Of course, it is a very sensitive topic for some, yet, I feel it needs to be addressed before we begin anything else. But please, only progress with reading this section if you are ready to confront this reality.

In the Hindu epic of the Mahābhārata, Yaksha (a celestial being) asked Yudhishthira a question, "What is the greatest wonder of this world?" Yudhishthira didn't reply by mentioning the Great Pyramid of Giza or the Hanging Gardens of Babylon. Instead, he revealed an astonishing answer saying, "Although before his very eyes, man witnesses people perishing and dying every day, he never, for once feels that death shall also befall him in the same way." This answer is a truth very relatable to us. The majority of you won't have thought extensively about death, unless you happen to be gripped by morbid thoughts. It's not your fault though. Nothing in our current culture recommends that we keep death present in our peripheral vision—in the forefront of our lives. When you are young, you have no reason to think about it. As you grow older, you may think about it more frequently, but for the most part it remains a subject that is mostly avoided. If you are in your twenties, you will probably be seeking your own place in the world. You will only be beginning to discover who the real *you* is, and as a part of that, you will be looking for fresh role models to replace your parents. In your thirties, you will begin to want to do something more worthwhile in the world. You might have started a family. These are the times of interesting discoveries and new beginnings. I was hesitant in writing this section at the start of the book, but today, more and more young people like myself, are actively aware of the deep issues of life. The funny thing is, we are all fully aware that the epiphany of death is looming over us. You know this, but for a moment consider what it means. The world you know is built upon your experiences. All the way from your childhood; the first pet you had, your first day at school, the picture on your bedroom wall, your fifth birthday party. Remember the times you got severely told off. The times of trauma, old toys and TV shows, holidays, and your first friends at school.

Then, as you remember how you grew up, trace your experiences up until now. Notice areas of your relationship with your parents that have shaped your behaviour today. Your struggles through college, getting your degree, falling in love. Maybe you've discovered some way of connecting with something bigger than yourself—through religion, sports, music, arts, or the like. All of this has made *your* world unique. It has shaped *your* beliefs, *your* behaviour, *your* priorities and *your* values. If you have children, then consciously or unconsciously, you will be passing some of these values on to them.

All of this, and more, makes up *your* world. Now for a moment consider the harsh reality that it will all amount to nothing. Everything that you have ever strived for, or intend to strive for, will cease to be. Your friends, family, and children will disappear along with your world. Your story in this world will amount to nothing and will probably remain untold, with little to no significance. Those who remember your name or face will themselves one day breathe their last, and the final wisps of your presence will disappear, within seconds, along with all recollection of you. Don't you know that there will come a day when you will be either be ill in your bed at home, unable to walk, or in the hospital with the beeping of machines and wires attached to you? At that time, I guarantee you will look back at your life and think to yourself "What have I been doing?" In our minds, there is always a part of us that knows we won't go on forever. We have all experienced loss in one way or another, but why do we forget than one day we will also meet the same fate?

Czech writer Milan Kundera said, "What terrifies us most about death is not the loss of the future, but the loss of the past. In fact, the act of forgetting is a form of death always present within life."

I recently watched a short film on YouTube about Philip Gould, called *When I Die: Lessons from the Death Zone*. Gould was a prominent political consultant for Labour, who advised on electoral strategy for nearly twenty years, and a key figure in the modernisation of the party. Unfortunately, he developed cancer of the oesophagus and was eventually told he had three months to live. In the short film, and his small book with the same title, Gould describes his remaining time, very memorably, as the *Death Zone*. When he was informed of his miserable prognosis, he said in a 2011 BBC interview:

> *This time it was clear. I was in a different place, a death zone, where there was such an intensity, such a power. And apparently this is normal. And so, even though obviously I'd, you know, rather not be in this position, it is the most extraordinary time of my life, certainly the most important time of my life.*

The eight-minute YouTube film is really worth watching. It delivers a powerful message that the thing we fear most might not have to be frightening after all. I know it is easier said than done, and even the strongest have proved too weak. We already know of our wonderful friend Alexander, whose death disposed of him with the ease of a spider gorging on a trapped fly. Similarly, the likes of Napoleon, Stalin, and Churchill were all great and powerful. Yet, the power of death was still greater.

In November 1978, 909 people in the remote settlement of the Jonestown project in Guyana committed suicide. The suddenness and freakishness of this incident baffled the world. A third of these were children! No one could have possibly prophesied this. But, none of these individuals had a chance to even say goodbye. For the most part, no one ever does. You must understand the truths about death.

> **Death is predetermined; no one can escape it.**
> **Death can arrive at any time.**
> **Death is too complex to be understood.**
> **Death remains unaffected by scientific/worldly influences.**

If our own body cannot accompany us after death, where even is the question of the possessions we own? Why do we spend our entire lives trying to gain things that we will eventually have to leave behind?

We slog our entire lives working in a continuous routine, till our bodies give up, or we choose to retire. Towards the end, we have much of what we have always wanted around us, but our bodies are shattered to make the most of what we have accumulated over our lifetimes. We sit there in the armchair, probably alone and shaking, when our own children come and visit us once in a while. Of course, now they are busy with their own family and commitments to make time for us, they need to focus on themselves, right? But what happened to us? What about our happiness? All that we aspired to achieve throughout our life? Can you say that you will be content then? Before it is too late, you must change things. You still can; but you have to act fast. Sadly, death can befall any of us, at any time. Even at this very moment (god-forbid) something could happen, and it'll all be over within a blink of an eye.

FACING DEATH

Steve McQueen—The King of Cool—was known as a Hollywood phenomenon of his time. For years of his life, he remained at No. 1. He was a proud, rigid man, disillusioned by his success. Steve relentlessly despised the idea of a higher power. That was until, aged forty-two, the doctors signed him off as a patient of terminable cancer. When the

reality of death stood in front of him, fear struck. He c
changed, struggling to play a role he had never played be
career was on the line, his dreams were shattering, and he des
sought help. How could such a star put his ego aside and seek out
help? What would happen to his past successes and publicity that he
had built upon until now? At last, he realised that in order to reach a
state of inner peace, he had to put aside his painful ego. He did so by
turning towards a higher power, saying in his own words, "I have
touched God. He has given me more courage than I have ever had in
my life."

Unfortunately, McQueen never recovered, but he died a different
death. He had experienced that throughout his entire life, although he
was drowning in fame and wealth, it all summed up to nothing at the
time of death. See the story of Alexander here? This understanding
transformed him. He sought a higher power during his final months,
and fought hard in the last of his limited time. We could say that
Alexander and Steve were lucky, in that they were well aware of death
looming in front of them. This may not be the case for all of us. We
may not get a chance to put things right towards the end, so shouldn't
we start now?

In his principle scripture called the Vachanāmrut, Bhagwān Shri
Swāminārāyan, addressing the truth of death says, "I also constantly
feel as if death is imminent at this moment for myself, as well as for
others. In fact, I constantly regard each and every object to be
perishable and insignificant."

Whatever happiness we know of in this world, never completes us;
it never lasts. For ninety-four years of his life, Pramukh Swami
repeatedly stressed upon this fact. He once said, "Everything is
perishable; one day everything, including every one of us, will perish
and get destroyed. Always remain conscious of this fact."

Death is a concept beyond us, and we can only really have faith that
it is in the hands of a higher power. I am not saying you necessarily
have to believe in *God*; but there is something greater, something in
control. Accepting this will make the process easier, whatever you
choose to call the *Higher Power*.

THE TWINS IN THE WOMB

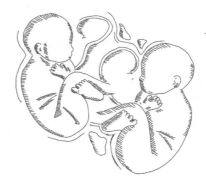

In his book, *Your Sacred Self*, Dr. Wayne Dyer shares a very imaginative story of two twin babies in their mother's womb.

One asked the other, "Hey! Do you believe in life after delivery?"

The other replied, "Obviously! There has to be something after delivery. Maybe we are here to prepare ourselves for what's after."

"That's just silly," said the first, "there is no life after delivery, what kind of life would that even be?"

The second thought for a minute and then said, "I don't know about that, but there will be more light than there is here. Maybe we will walk with our legs and eat with our mouths. Maybe we will have other senses that we yet haven't yet understood!"

The first replied, "That is insane! Walking is not even possible. Eating from our mouths? Are you joking? The umbilical cord supplies our nutrition and everything we need! The umbilical cord is so short too. Life after delivery is not even something to consider."

The second insisted, "Well... I think there is something after, and maybe it differs from what is here. Maybe we won't need this physical cord attached to us anymore."

The first continued, "If there is life, then why has no one ever come back from there? Delivery is the end of life, and in the after-delivery there is nothing but darkness, silence, and oblivion. It takes us nowhere. It is the end."

"Well, I don't know about that..." said the second, "but I am certain we will meet mother and she will take care of us."

The first laughed, "Mother! You believe in mother? That's hilarious! If mother exists, then where is she right now?"

The second answered, "She is here, all around us. She surrounds us. We are of her. It is in her that we live. Without her, this world would not, and could not, exist!"

"Well, I don't see her, so it is only logical that she doesn't even exist." responded the first.

The second continued, "Sometimes, when you're in silence and you focus and listen with attention, you can perceive her presence. You can hear her loving voice, calling down from above..."

I think you get the idea. Believing in a higher power is not a sign of weakness. It is a sign of strength. It is what truly helps us through the journey of life, and we will explore this soon.

But, if even the happiest in the world are interrupted by death, the question arises, is there something more to life? Why has humankind continuously strived to *find* happiness?

PART TWO

HAPPINESS

ĀNANDA

Happiness is a state of mind;
It has nothing to do with the external world.
Shri Vasudev Krishna

In Sanskrit (the oldest documented Indo-European language), the word *ānanda* refers to a state of bliss and happiness. But, *ānanda* differs from happiness. We usually define happiness as the accumulation of wealth, material objects, or fleeting pleasures. On the other hand, *ānanda* refers to a state of complete contentment and composure, distinct from all material objects and pleasures. The word has been repeatedly used in the Vedas, which are considered to be amongst the oldest, if not the oldest, religious texts in the world. But, *ānanda* should not be confused with pleasure, joy, or serenity.

There is pleasure in having a scoop of ice-cream. But, if you keep eating more and more, the pleasure soon turns into pain. Pleasure is *flawed*. Then there is *joy*. There is joy in listening to beautiful music. But, sit next to someone with whom you don't get along with, and the joy slowly fades away. Joy is *conditional*. There is also *serenity*. A few moments of deep breathing and meditative mindfulness surely brings serenity. But, open your eyes, and you are back to the day-to-day struggles of life. Serenity can be *fleeting*.

Ānanda transcends pleasure, joy and serenity. Then there is *param ānanda* - ultimate and eternal *ānanda*. An eternal state of bliss and happiness. It is not momentary, it is forever. It is a far-reaching, all-encompassing stability even in moments of turmoil and struggle.

Param ānanda is not conditional. Rain or shine, fame or shame, win or lose, eyes open or shut, *param ānanda* is a continuous state of contentment and composure—total equilibrium. This state exists not only in our imagination, nor is it a mere dream or experience that is reserved only for the life that follows.

To reach *param ānanda*, you have to live within limits; learn to let go; untangle your ego; tame your mind; give more and take less. To make this a reality, you must be willing to make changes within. These changes, that we explore together in this book, form what I call 'The Keshav Way'. You must understand that you won't achieve happiness or contentment by merely reading this book. You must imbibe the ideas, principles, and concepts shared into your own life. And with time, this journey that we call life will reveal itself to us. Remember, *happiness is not a destination, it is a journey.*

General human happiness is believed to lie on a numerical scale, a continuum ranging from very low to very high. *Ānanda* is different. It is a state, that upon reaching, one never looks back. We will understand how philosophers like Socrates and Aristotle, as well as other writers and thinkers, have offered varying definitions of happiness.

Aristotle said, "Happiness is an expression of the soul in considered actions." Sigmund Freud used the words *lieben und arbeiten*—to love and work. Happiness has always meant different things to different people. You and I too, will have different definitions for happiness.

After reading this book, some of you may still choose to find happiness in pleasures, and who am I to judge that? That is why I prefer to use the word *ānanda*, referring to a state where we experience a state of joy, contentment, or positive well-being, combined with a sense of a meaningful, worthwhile and good life. The Keshav Way presents *ways* to begin experiencing *ānanda*. When you live and breathe these ways in your everyday life,, you begin to experience *sahaj ānanda* —spontaneous bliss. In every thing you do, you will remain at this state; one that can only be known when we instinctively experience it. This is probably why researchers tend to use the term *subjective well-being* to describe happiness. I use the words happiness, well-being and *ānanda* interchangeably, but ultimately we want to experience *ānanda*.

THE BRIEF HISTORY

Throughout history numerous philosophers, prophets, priests, and even ordinary people like you and me, have tried to define happiness. Humankind has been on the eternal search for happiness from when they first appeared on Earth. Regardless of whether you are rich or poor, man or woman, young or old, it doesn't matter. Where you come from, where you live, what language you speak, what you do for a living, what tragedies and struggles you've endured—none of this matters when it comes to happiness. Why? Because wherever you are, or whoever you are, **you want to be happy.** It is the most essential human desire, as natural as it is to the body to blink or breathe. But it is an issue. More on this later, but first let's delve into a very brief history of happiness. Believe me, it is very brief and concise, but it is important that we understand it before we move on further.

SOCRATES AND PLATO

I'm sure you will have heard of the phrase 'Know Thyself'. That is from Socrates, the original one I mean. Because there is another one looming around on all of these quote pages on Instagram. No one has any idea who it is, but they just slap random quotes onto a nice-coloured background, and stick his name underneath. So yes, not that one, we're talking about the original Socrates.

Basically, he was around some 2500 years ago, in Athens, Greece. He is revered in the West as the first thinker to bring philosophy into everyday life and raise the question of an 'examined life'. Note that I mention 'in the West', because a quest sprang almost 2500 years before him in the East. He presented the desire for happiness as something quite natural to humanity. Surprisingly, he wrote nothing down. There are no known writings of his, except those that were written by Plato, his main student. Plato had some very interesting ideas about happiness. In one of his famous analogies, he described the things and qualities of our everyday world as if they were shadows cast on the back wall of a cave. We look at the shadows and mistake them for real things, but we miss the fact that they are nothing more than shapes and silhouettes. Plato believed it to be the job of philosophers to direct our attention towards the light and reveal the *true* objects that are creating the shadows.

Cutting the story short, the important point is that the foundation of Socratic happiness was about self-questioning and about appreciating the reality of an unseen world that lies beyond our physical realm. This idea actually stuck around for a very long time.

ARISTOTLE

After the death of Socrates (a very surprising one if you look into it) the idea of happiness was developed and expanded further by Aristotle. He was Plato's most famous pupil, and tutored Alexander the Great—our friend who we've just met.

Just like Plato, he saw the natural aim of human life, in the best condition of the soul, as *eudemonia*, which is roughly synonymous with happiness, or more accurately *flourishing*. He had a different way of reaching there.

He thought, "What is it that we should have in place in our lives to secure this state?' He believed, and taught, that success of being human would amount to the best use of reason. *Flourishing* is 'an activity of the soul in accordance with virtue'. Basically, the thought that there is an aim to human life, and that happiness is not a state to experience, but instead an activity.

NOBODY WANTS YOU HAPPY

After Aristotle, philosophers wanted to break away from this model and find their own ways of bringing happiness to more people. One of the most famous being Epicurus, who gave some controversial beliefs. He explained that happiness was the one and only, sole purpose of human life. For him, the pursuit of happiness was more of a personal quest. But today, most modern thinkers see it as a collective project.

Skipping to the end of the eighteenth century, the British philosopher Jeremy Bentham declared that the supreme good is 'the greatest happiness of the greatest number', and concluded that the sole worthy aim of the state, the market, and the scientific community is to increase global happiness.[3]

During the nineteenth and twentieth centuries, governments, corporations and scientific laboratories began focussing more on immediate and well-defined aims. Countries began to measure success by the size of their territory, the increase in their population and the growth of their GDP (gross domestic product)—but not by the happiness of their people. Industrialised nations like Germany, France and Japan established large systems of education, health, and welfare, but even then, they weren't aimed to ensure individual well-being or happiness, but instead to strengthen the nation.

Schools were opened to produce skilful, law-abiding citizens who would serve their beloved nation loyally. When you completed school, if you were a boy, you were expected to not only be patriotic, but also literate, so that you could read the order of the army, and draw up the battle plans for the following day. Mathematics was needed to calculate shell trajectory and crack enemy code. You needed some knowledge of electrics, mechanics and medicine, in order to operate wireless sets, drive around tanks and take care of your fellow, wounded soldiers. When you finally left the army, you still had to serve the nation, but this time as office workers, teachers, or engineers, building a modern economy and paying extorted taxes.

---

[3] (Shackleton 1993, 353-366)

The same went for the health system. Towards the end of the nineteenth century, the same countries, and more, began providing *free* healthcare for the masses. They paid for the vaccinations of infants. They paid for children's balanced diets. They paid for the physical education of the youth. They had festering swamps drained. They exterminated mosquitos and built centralised sewage systems. Amazing right? Not really. The aim wasn't to make people happy, but to make the nation stronger. Countries needed strong soldiers and workers (both physically and mentally), healthy women who would go on to give birth to more soldiers and workers, and public servants who'd arrive at the office at 8.30 a.m. prompt, five days a week.

The welfare system too, was originally planned in the interest of the nation first. You fought for your country at eighteen, and paid taxes when you were forty, so that you could rely on your government to take care of you when you were seventy.[4]

In 1776, the Founding Fathers of the United States established the right to the pursuit of Happiness as one of the fundamental human rights, alongside the right to Life and the right to Liberty. I want to point out, however, that the American Declaration of Independence guaranteed the right to the *pursuit of* happiness, not the right to happiness itself. Basically, if I think I will be happier marrying Priya instead of Pooja, living in Mumbai rather than London, and working as a writer as opposed to an engineer, then it is my right to pursue happiness in my own way, and the state should not interfere, even if I make a bad choice. Today, the right to the pursuit of happiness is misunderstood as the right to happiness itself. Human beings think that they have a natural right to be happy, and if something makes us feel dissatisfied, then it is a violation of our basic human rights, and our state is responsible to change things for us.

In the twentieth century, per capita GDP was one of the primary ways that nations evaluated national success. Take Singapore as an example. Each of whose citizens produces an average of £45,000 worth of goods and services a year. It is a more successful country than say, Costa Rica, who produce £11,000 a year. But in today's society,

---

[4] (Scheubel 2013)

thinkers, politicians, and even economists are calling to either replace, or at least supplement GDP with GDH (gross domestic happiness). Bhutan already uses this system. After all, what do people want? No one wants to *produce*; they want to be happy. In numerous surveys, Costa Ricans report far higher levels of life satisfaction than Singaporeans. So, would you rather be a highly productive but dissatisfied Singaporean, or a less productive but more satisfied Costa Rican? Something worth thinking about.

Today, if famine, plague and war are slowly, but surely, beginning to disappear, if mankind experiences unparalleled peace and prosperity, and if life expectancy is increasing quite dramatically, surely all of this will make humans happy, right?

Nope. When Epicurus defined happiness to be the supreme good, he warned his followers that it isn't easy to be happy. He told them that material achievements alone will not satisfy us for long. The blind pursuit of wealth, fame, and pleasure only makes us miserable. You know this, I know this too, but by the time you finish reading this book, you will hopefully be able accept it and seek the alternatives. Epicurus was clearly onto something. Happiness is not easy to achieve. Despite our unprecedented achievements in the last thirty to fifty years, we cannot say for sure whether we, today, are significantly more satisfied than our ancestors. But even so, despite higher prosperity, comfort, and security, why is it that the rate of suicide in the developed world is much higher than in traditional societies?

Even if we are somewhat happier than our ancestors, the increase in our well-being is far less than what we might expect. In the Stone Age, an average human had at his or her disposal, about 4,000 calories of energy per day. This included not only food, but also the energy invested in preparing tools, clothing, art, and campfires. Today, Americans use on average 228,000 calories of energy, per person, per day, to feed not only their stomachs but also their cars, laptops, tablets and televisions.[5] And so, the average American uses sixty times more energy than the average Stone Age hunter. But, is the average American sixty times happier?

---

[5] (Morris 2010)

The second half of the twentieth century was the golden age for the USA. Winning World War Two, followed by a decisive victory in the Cold War, made it into the leading global superpower. In a span of just fifty years, between 1950 and 2000, the GDP of USA grew from $2 trillion to $12 trillion. Real per capita income doubled. Cars, refrigerators, air conditioners, vacuum cleaners, dishwashers, washing machines, mobile phones, computers, and the like all changed our day-to-day lives almost beyond recognition. Yet, studies show that American subjective well-being levels in the 1990s remained roughly the same as they were in the 1950s.[6] Even compared to 2006 in the USA, self reported life satisfaction ten years later, in 2016, was roughly the same.[7]

In Japan, average real income rose by a factor of five between 1958 and 1987, in one of the fastest economic booms of history. This avalanche of wealth, coupled with the myriad positive and negative changes in Japanese lifestyles and social relations, had surprisingly little impact on Japanese subjective well-being levels. In the 1990s, the Japanese were as satisfied (or dissatisfied) as they were in the 1950s.[8] Life satisfaction in Japan in 2018 was the same as that in 2008. Do you see what I am getting at?

It is almost as though happiness is locked within a glass box, banging against the walls, screaming to get out, but it cannot. Even if we provide free food to every living human, cure all diseases and ensure world peace, it still may not be able to break and escape from the glass box.

---

[6] (Myers 2000, 56)

[7] Ortiz-Ospina, E., & Roser, M. (2013)

[8] (Suzuki 2009, 81-89)

PSYCHOLOGICAL VS. BIOLOGICAL HAPPINESS

On the psychological level, happiness depends on our expectations rather than objective conditions. It's like saying we don't become satisfied by leading a peaceful and prosperous existence. Instead, we become satisfied when reality matches our expectations. The sad news is that as conditions are met, expectations balloon. Dramatic improvements in conditions, as humankind has experienced in recent decades, translate into greater expectations, rather than greater contentment. On the biological level, both expectations and happiness are determined by our biochemistry, rather than by economic, social, or political situations. According to Epicurus, we are happy when we feel pleasant sensations and are free from unpleasant ones. John Stuart Mill says, "Happiness is nothing but pleasure and freedom from pain, and beyond pleasure and pain there is no good and no evil."

Unfortunately, as we all know, pleasant sensations quickly subside, and sooner or later turn into unpleasant ones. This is not our fault, it is a natural fault of evolution. For generations upon generations, our biochemical system has adapted to increase our chances of survival and reproduction, but never levels of happiness.

Imagine if a rare mutation created a squirrel, who, after eating just a single nut, enjoyed an everlasting sensation of pleasure. Technically, this is achievable by rewiring the squirrel's brain. But even so, that squirrel enjoyed an extremely happy and short life, and that was the end. The blissful squirrel would not have bothered searching for more nuts, let alone mates. On the other hand, rival squirrels, who felt hungry again after five or ten minutes of eating a nut, would have higher chances of surviving and passing their genes to the next generation. For this exact same reason, the nuts we humans seek to gather—well-paid jobs, big houses, fancy cars, or good-looking partners—none of these satisfy us for long. Of course, you can argue what's the harm? It isn't the goal that makes us happy, but the journey. Like, climbing Mount Everest would be more satisfying than standing at the top. Yet, this hardly changes the picture, but instead indicates that evolution controls us with a broad range of pleasures.

MANIPULATING HAPPINESS

In a famous experiment, scientists connected electrodes to the brains of several rats. This enabled the animals to create sensations of excitement simply by pressing on a pedal. When the rats were given a choice between tasty food and pressing the pedal, they preferred the pedal (just like the hit we get whilst we continue to play video games, despite being shouted down for dinner). The rats pressed the pedal repeatedly, until they couldn't take anymore, and collapsed from hunger and exhaustion.[9] Humans too, may prefer the excitement of the race to resting. But what makes the race so attractive is the exhilarating sensations that we feel along with it. Nobody would have wanted to climb mountains, play video games, or travel to unseen territory, if such activities were accompanied simply by unpleasant sensations of stress, despair, or boredom.[10]

They basically altered the biochemistry of the rats. Fifty years ago, psychiatric drugs carried a major stigma. Today, that very stigma is being broken. Arguably, for better or worse, a growing number of the global population is taking some form of psychiatric medicine on a regular basis, not only to cure debilitating mental illnesses, but also to face the more tedious depressions and occasional blues.

Let me give you an example of this. An increasing number of schoolchildren take stimulants such as Ritalin. In 2011, 3.5 million American children were taking medication for ADHD (attention deficit hyperactivity disorder). In the UK, the number rose from 92,000 in 1997 to 786,000 in 2012.[11] The original aim had been to treat these attention disorders, but today, completely healthy kids are also taking these types of medications to improve their academic and physical performance, as well as to live up to the growing expectations of teachers and parents.

Armies are following course too. 12 percent of American soldiers in Iraq and 17 percent in Afghanistan, took either sleeping pills or

---

[9] (Berridge and Kringelbach 2008, 457-480)
[10] (Csikszentmihalyi 1998)
[11] (Centers for Disease Control and Prevention 2014)

antidepressants to help them deal with the pressure and distress of war. Fear, depression, and trauma are not caused by machine guns or car bombs. They are caused by hormones, neurotransmitters and neural networks. Two soldiers may find themselves back-to-back in the same ambush, mindlessly firing away at enemies. One will freeze in terror, lose his senses, and suffer from nightmares for years after the event; the other will charge forward courageously and win a medal of honour. The difference is in the soldiers' biochemistry—it is within, and if we find ways to control it, we will at one stroke produce both happier soldiers and more efficient armies.[12]

The biochemical pursuit of happiness is also the number one cause of crime in the world. In 2009, half of the inmates in US federal prisons got there because of drugs; 38 percent of Italian prisoners were convicted of drug-related offences; 55 percent of inmates in the UK reported that they committed their crimes in connection with either the consumption of drugs, or the trading of them. A 2001 report found that 62 percent of Australian convicts were under the influence of drugs when committing the crime for which they were incarcerated. People drink alcohol to forget daily stress, smoke pot to feel peaceful, take cocaine or meth to be sharp and confident, and ecstasy to experience ecstatic sensations. What some people hope to get by working or raising a family, others try to get through the right dosage of chemicals.

But, is it worth investing this much in the biochemical pursuit of happiness of humankind? Some of you might argue that it is wrong to regard individual satisfaction as the highest aim of human society. Others may agree with Epicurus that individual happiness *is* the supreme good. Around two-thousand years ago, Epicurus warned his followers that the immoderate pursuit of individual pleasure is likely to make us more miserable, rather than happy.

A couple of centuries earlier, Buddha had made an even more radical claim, teaching his followers that *the pursuit of pleasant sensations is in fact the very root of suffering*. Such sensations are just passing and meaningless vibrations. Even when we experience them, we do not react to them with contentment; rather, we just crave for

---

[12] (US Army Office of the Chief of Public Affairs 2010), (Thompson 2010)

more. So, no matter how many blissful or exciting sensations I may experience, they will never satisfy me. The more I crave these pleasant sensations, the more stressed and dissatisfied I become. To attain real happiness, humans need to slow down the pursuit of pleasant sensations, not accelerate them.

This view of happiness that Buddha derived from the Vedic teachings, has a lot in common with the biochemical view, even though he later rejected the Vedas as part of his philosophy. Both agree that pleasant sensations disappear as fast as they arise, and that as long as people crave pleasant sensations without actually experiencing them, they remain dissatisfied. However, this problem has two very different solutions. The biochemical solution is to develop products and treatments that will provide humans with an unending stream of pleasant sensations, so we will never be without them. Buddha's suggestion, similar to Vedic teachings, was to reduce our craving for pleasant sensations, and not allow them to control our lives. According to this type of thinking, *we can train our minds to observe carefully how all sensations constantly arise and pass*. When the mind learns to see our sensations for what they are (fleeting and meaningless vibrations) we lose interest in pursuing them. What is the point of running after something that disappears as fast as it arises?

MEASURING HAPPINESS

In the last 500 years alone, we have seen a series of breathtaking revolutions. The earth has been united into a single ecological and historical sphere. Economy has grown exponentially, and today, humankind enjoys the kind of wealth once dreamt of in fairytale fantasies. Social order has completely transformed, as have politics, daily life, and human psychology. But are we happier? Has the wealth accumulated by humankind over the last five centuries translated into contentment? Can we say that Neil Armstrong, whose footprint apparently still remains intact on the windless moon, was happier than the anonymous hunter caveman 30,000 years ago, who left their handprint on a wall in a cave? Despite these questions probably being the most important questions of history, no one asks them. Then, how can we evaluate global happiness?

Many have concluded that social, ethical, and spiritual factors have a great impact on our happiness, just like material conditions. Perhaps, people in modern affluent societies suffer greatly from alienation and meaninglessness despite individual prosperity.

In recent years, psychologists and biologists have taken up the challenge to scientifically study what really makes humans happy. The generally accepted definition of happiness is *subjective well-being*. Happiness is a feeling that we experience within ourselves, a sense of either immediate pleasure, or long-term contentment, with the way that our lives are going. Now you may argue, if it is something that we feel inside, how can it be measured from outside?

To do this, psychologists and biologists have been trying to understand how people feel with the use of typical subjective well-being questionnaires. They are used in order to correlate happiness with various objective factors. This then provides a grounding for historians, who can examine wealth, political freedom, and divorce rates in the past. If people are happier living in democracies, and married people are happier than divorcees, a historian will have a basis to argue that democratisation in the last few decades contributed to the happiness of mankind, whereas the growing rate of divorce could indicate the opposite. Of course, this thinking is flawed, and isn't perfect, but some of the findings are interesting to see.

One such conclusion is that money does indeed bring happiness. But only up to a point, and beyond that point it has little significance (more on this shortly). For people stuck at the bottom of the economic ladder, more money means greater happiness. For example, if you are a single parent, earning £14,000 a year by cleaning houses, and you suddenly win £500,000 on the lottery, you will probably experience a significant and long-term surge in your subjective well-being (note that I don't use the word happiness). You will be able to feed and clothe your child without sinking further into debt. But, if you are a top executive, earning £250,000 a year, and you win £1 million on the lottery, or if the board of your company decides to double your salary, your surge is likely to last only a few weeks. Numerous empirical findings show that, it is almost certainly not going to make a huge difference to the way you feel in the long run. You may buy a fancy car, move into a five-bed home, own the latest mobile device, but it will soon all seem routine and unexceptional. And let's not deny it, we have all experienced this.

Another interesting finding is that illness decreases happiness in the short-term, but is only a source of long-term distress if a person's condition is constantly deteriorating, or if the disease involves ongoing and debilitating pain. People who are diagnosed with chronic illness, such as diabetes, are usually depressed for a while, but, if the illness does not get worse, they adjust to their new condition, and rate their happiness on a similar level to the healthy people.

Family and community seem to have more impact on our happiness than money and health. People with strong families, who live in tight-knit and supportive communities, are significantly happier than people whose families are dysfunctional, and who have never found (or sought for) a community to be a part of. Marriage is also particularly important. Repeated studies show that there is a very close correlation between good marriages and high levels of subjective well-being, as well as between bad marriages and misery. This stands true irrespective of economic or even physical conditions.

If these studies are to be relied upon, it may well be that, the average person might be no happier today than in the 1800s. Even the thing we call *freedom*, that we value so highly, may be working against us. We can choose our partners, friends, and neighbours, but they can choose to leave us. With every individual human having their own power to decide their own path in life, commitments are becoming more and more difficult. And so, we live in an increasingly lonely world of unravelling communities and families.

The most important finding of all is that happiness does not really depend on objective conditions of either wealth, health, or even community. Instead, it depends on the correlation between objective conditions and subjective expectations. When things improve, expectations balloon, and consequently even dramatic improvements in objective conditions can leave us dissatisfied. When things deteriorate, expectations shrink, and consequently even a severe illness might leave you pretty much as happy as you were before.

Summing up, prophets, poets, and philosophers realised thousands of years ago that being satisfied with what you already have, is far more important than getting more of what you want. Still, isn't it wonderful when modern research and studies reach the same conclusions that the ancients did millennia ago? Today, we have an arsenal of tranquillisers and painkillers at our disposal, but our expectations of ease and pleasure, and our intolerance of inconvenience and discomfort, have increased to such a great extent that we probably suffer much more emotional, and probably later translating to physical pain than our ancestors ever did. I know, it is hard to accept this.

If happiness is truly determined by expectations, then two pillars of modern society—mass media and the advertising industry—may be reducing the world's reservoirs of contentment. If you were an eighteen-year-old in a small village 2,000 years ago, you would probably think you're good-looking because the village wouldn't have many people in it anyway. And today? The majority of teenagers feel inadequate about themselves, even if their friends are not good-looking. They don't compare themselves to them, but instead against Hollywood stars, athletes, and supermodels that they see online and on billboards. It could well be that Third World discontent is formed not merely by poverty, disease, corruption, and political oppression, but also by the mere exposure to the First World standards.

CHEMISTRY OF HAPPINESS

Biologists also use the same questionnaires, but correlate the answers people give them with biochemical and genetic factors. The findings here are also surprising. They claim that our mental and emotional world is governed by biochemical mechanisms that are shaped by millions of years of evolution. Similar to all other mental states, our subjective well-being is not determined by external parameters such as salary, social relations, or political rights. Rather, it is determined by a complex system of nerves, neurons, synapses, and various biochemical substances such as serotonin, dopamine and oxytocin. Nobody is ever made happy by buying a nice car, winning the lottery, getting a promotion at work, or even finding true love. People are made happy by one thing and one thing only, pleasant sensations in their bodies. Every experience is a reaction to various hormones racing through your bloodstream, and to the storm of electric signals flashing between different parts of your brain.

I am going to burst your bubble now. Your internal biochemical system is programmed to keep happiness levels relatively constant. There is no natural selection for happiness as such. Evolution has moulded us to be neither too miserable, nor too happy. It enables us to enjoy a momentary rush of pleasant sensations, but these never last forever. Sooner or later they subside and give place to unpleasant sensations. Some scholars compare human biochemistry to an air-conditioning system that keeps the temperature constant, come heatwave or snowstorm. Events might momentarily change the temperature, but the air-conditioned system always returns the temperature to the same set point. Human happiness conditioning systems also differ from person to person. On a scale from one to ten, some people are born with a cheerful biochemical system that allows their mood to swing between levels six and ten, stabilising, with time, at eight. Such a person is quite happy even if they live in an alienating big city, lose all their money in a stock-exchange crash and even if they are diagnosed with cancer. Other people are cursed with a gloomy biochemistry that swings between three and seven, and stabilises at five. Such an unhappy person remains depressed even if they enjoy the support of a tight-knit community, wins the lottery, and is as healthy as an Olympic athlete.

Just think of your family and friends for a moment. You certainly know some people who always remain relatively joyful, no matter what befalls them. And then there are those who are always disgruntled, no matter what gifts the world lays at their feet. We tend to believe that if we could just change our workplace, get married, go on a few holidays, buy a new car, or repay the mortgage, we would be on top of the world. Yet, when we get what we desire, we do not seem to be any happier. Buying cars and going on holidays does not change our biochemistry. Yes, they can startle it for a few moments, but it soon springs back to its set point.

So, how can this be squared with the previously mentioned psychological and sociological findings that, for example, on average married people are happier than single people? First, these findings are correlations—the direction of causation may be the opposite of what some researchers have assumed. It is true that married people are happier than single people and divorcees, but that does not necessarily mean that marriage produces happiness. It could be that happiness causes marriage. Or putting it clearer, that serotonin, dopamine, and oxytocin, bring about and maintain a marriage.

If we wish to accept the biological approach to happiness, then history turns out to be of little importance, since most historical events have had no impact on our biochemistry. History can change the external stimuli that cause serotonin to be secreted, yet it does not change the resulting serotonin levels, and hence it cannot make people happier. I call this concept, *Level Z*.

For example, hundreds of years ago, when a peasant would complete the construction of his mud hut, his brain neurons would secrete serotonin, bringing it up to Level Z. In 2017, when a middle-class man made his final mortgage payment to the bank, brain neurons secreted a similar amount of serotonin, bringing it up to a similar Level Z. It makes no difference to your brain that the five-bed home is far more comfortable than the mud hut. The only thing that matters is that at present, the level of serotonin is Z.

Now, if we accept that the keys to happiness are in the hands of our biochemical system, we can stop wasting our time on politics, social reforms, and ideologies, and instead focus on the only thing that can make us truly happy—manipulating our own biochemistry. Prozac, for example, does not change regimes, but by raising serotonin levels it lifts people out of their depression. Money, social status, plastic surgery, beautiful homes, powerful positions, and the like—none of these will bring you happiness. Shri Vāsudev Krishna says in the Bhagavad Gitā, "Happiness is a state of mind. Dualities of all kinds—honour and dishonour, success and failure, pain and pleasure—come and go like the winter and summer seasons. One whose happiness is within is actually a perfect yogi. Such a person ultimately attains the Supreme."[13] Lasting happiness comes only from within.

---

[13] Bhagavad Gita 2.14, 5.24

ENDING THE LESSON

In a famous study, Daniel Kahneman—the writer of one of my most favourite books, *Thinking, Fast and Slow*, and winner of the Nobel Prize in economics—asked people to recount a typical work day, going through it episode by episode, and evaluating how much they enjoyed or disliked each moment. He came to find what seems to be a paradox in most people's view of their own lives. Let's take the work involved in raising a child. Kahneman found that when counting moments of joy, and moments of hard and menial work, bringing up a child turns out to be a rather unpleasant affair. It consists mostly of changing nappies, washing dishes, and dealing with tantrums, which nobody likes to do. Yet, most parents declare that their child is the main source of happiness. Does it mean that people actually have no idea what is actually good for them?

Another way to look at this is to understand that the findings show that happiness is not the surplus of pleasant over unpleasant moments. Instead, happiness consists of seeing one's life in its entirety as meaningful and worthwhile. There is an important cognitive and ethical component to happiness. Our values make all the difference. A meaningful life can be extremely satisfying even in the midst of hardship, whereas a meaningless life is a terrible ordeal, no matter how comfortable it is.

Imagine a psychologist sets out on a study of happiness amongst drug users. He polls them and finds that they declare, every one of them, that they are only happy when they inject themselves with drugs. Would the psychologist publish a paper declaring that heroin is the key to happiness? Many religions and philosophies already knew about this a long time ago. Hinduism has systematically studied the essence and causes of happiness for millennia. Vedic teachings (used synonymously to Hinduism throughout this book) share the basic insight of the biological approach to happiness, namely that happiness results from processes occurring within one's own body and mind, as opposed to coming from events in the outside world.

Most people identify happiness with pleasant feelings, whilst identifying suffering with unpleasant feelings. Consequently, people ascribe immense importance to what they feel, craving to experience more and more pleasures, whilst avoiding pain. Whatever we strive to do throughout our lives, whether scratching our leg, fidgeting slightly in the chair, buying that Porsche, or fighting a world war, we are all just trying to get pleasant feelings.

The problem is that our feelings are no more than momentary vibrations, changing every moment, like the waves of the ocean. If five minutes ago I felt joyful and full of purpose, now these feelings are gone, and I might well feel sad and dejected. So, if I want to experience pleasant feelings, I have to constantly chase them, whilst driving out the unpleasant feelings. And even then, if I succeed, I immediately have to start the cycle again, without ever getting any lasting reward for my previous troubles. So what is the point? Why struggle so hard to achieve something that disappears almost as soon as it arises?

The Vedic teachings have shed light on this, saying that the root of suffering is neither the feeling of pain, sadness, or meaninglessness. Rather, the real root of suffering is this never-ending and pointless pursuit of passing feelings, which causes us to be in a constant state of tension, stress, restlessness, and dissatisfaction. Due to this pursuit, the mind, our monkey friend, is never satisfied. Even when experiencing pleasure, it is not content, because it fears this feeling is short-lived, and craves that this feeling should stay and intensify. This is the happiness paradox. Today, more and more people are beginning to realise this, and accept that happiness does not depend on external conditions. Many of you reading this book will also know this. Happiness truly depends only on what we feel inside. We need to stop pursuing external achievements such as wealth and status, and instead, connect with our true, inner self. Put simply, happiness *does* begin within.

THE BIG ISSUE

Around 600 BC, in and around the Himalayas of present-day Nepal, a young child by the name of Gautama was born. He grew up in a grand palace with a lavish lifestyle. His dad was responsible for this; he wanted the perfect life for his child. No suffering, no pain, and every desire and need fulfilled.

The palace was surrounded by high boundaries to prevent the young prince from discovering that there was a world beyond these four walls. As set out by the king, his child grew up ignorant of the cruel existence in the world outside. Obviously, the young prince became annoyed, and got tired of the lifestyle he had. Nothing seemed to satisfy him anymore. One night, he snuck out to see what was on the other side of the walls. He took a servant with him, to show him around the unfamiliar local village. What he saw, shook him. He saw people coughing; he saw old people unable to walk; he saw people sleeping on the streets; he saw people without arms or legs; he even saw someone's dead body being carried to the crematorium.

He returned to the palace, a little shaken, unable to process what he had just witnessed. Blaming his father for not showing him the true nature of the world, he ran away, giving up everything to live on the streets and experience the suffering himself. Time passed and he noticed that he wasn't learning anything worthwhile from this type of life. He began to think that there had to be a deeper meaning and purpose to life. After bathing and sitting underneath a tree for about two months, he came to a number of realisations about life. The key realisation being that life itself was a form of suffering. Regardless of where you go, or what you do, suffering is going to stay. The wealthy suffer because of their wealth. The poor suffer because of their poverty. Those without any loved ones suffer because they are lonely. Those with a family suffer because of their family. Those who pursue pleasures and temptations suffer because of the very same indulgences.

Many years later, this prince traversed from the Vedic philosophy he grew up with, to start his own philosophy and share this knowledge with the world. And this became the primary tenet of the philosophy: *pain and loss are inevitable parts of life and we should not try to resist them.* As his teachings and following grew, the prince became popularly known as Buddha.

In today's society, there is a problem with the majority of beliefs, particularly in regards to happiness. The belief that happiness is algorithmic is one such problem. Many also claim in their speeches and writing that happiness is our birthright, and we all *deserve* happiness. Now, truthfully think, do you think Hitler deserved happiness? What about Bin Laden? We are brought up to believe that happiness can be worked for, earned, or achieved. If you get A, then you can be happy. If you look like B, you will be happy. If you marry C, you will be happy. If you visit D, you will be happy. If you follow in the footsteps of E, you will be happy. This belief is the big issue.

Happiness is not a directly solvable equation. Nor is it a directly achievable product, but instead it is a byproduct of a particular mindset and lifestyle. It is definitely a byproduct of living *The Keshav Way*. Problems, dissatisfaction, and suffering are mandatory in human life, and as we will explore together, a necessity to create your own happiness. Suffering is a natural part of life. Humans are programmed to become dissatisfied with what they have, and satisfied by what they don't have. It is what has kept humans on top of the evolutionary cycle, constantly surviving and conquering this planet. Likewise, pain is required too. It is what gives us a 'wake-up call' when we are doing something we shouldn't be. Put your hand on the hob, and pain will make you pull your hand away. So, we won't even be talking about eliminating pain from our lives, because as you can see from this scenario, that would probably kill you. Pain is not just physical, it is psychological as well; it messes with your mind. Scientific studies show that your brain cannot differentiate between physical and psychological pain. Similar to physical pain, psychological pain also indicates that something is going wrong. And so, sometimes experiencing this psychological pain is also necessary. You probably picked up this book thinking that you will find a solution for everlasting happiness, but you live on Planet Earth, and here problems and suffering are a part of life; we learn how to manage them, and work towards a more blissful life. Life is an endless series of problems. Some problems are just easier to handle than others. Whether you're Jeff Bezos or a homeless guy—everyone has problems. When you solve one problem, another problem crops up. We must learn to deal with our problems, instead of avoiding them. We will venture into the topic of problems in a short while.

THE HAPPY DRUG

The happy drug is found in many forms. For some it will be alcohol, for others it will be the task of blaming others, or going to the beach for a holiday. The happy drug's effects are only temporary. The majority of the self-help industry teaches us to take the happy drug now and again, rather than try to solve the root issues. They teach you ways of denial, embed the victim mentality within you, or give you exercises to make you feel good for a fleeting period of time. Though, the root issue is ignored. The truth is that, no one who is actually happy, has to stand in front of the world and tell everyone that they are happy. Read that again. This drug is also addictive. The more you rely on it to feel better about your issues, the more you seek it. We all have our own ways to deal with pain, and there is nothing wrong with this at all. But unless you get to the root issue, the problems will only escalate, making them more difficult to deal with at a later point in time.

During the 1960s, having positive thoughts and feelings about yourself, and developing individual self-esteem, became the pinnacle of psychology. Research began to show that people who *thought* highly about themselves usually performed better and caused fewer problems. And so, many researchers and policymakers began to believe that if they raised the self-esteem of the population, it could lead to a number of social benefits: crime rates would decrease, academic records would improve, employment would increase, and there would be lower budget deficits. Consequently, at the start of the 1970s, self-esteem exercises began to be taught to parents, emphasised by therapists, politicians, teachers, and instituted into educational policy. As an example, grades were inflated to make children who achieved low marks feel better about their lack of achievement. Kids were given random trophies for simple activities. They were given assignments to write down reasons why they thought they were special, or five things they loved about themselves. This was when the first seed of the business and motivational seminars were planted, reiterating constantly: every one of us is exceptional and can be successful.

Thankfully this research has been analysed recently, and it has been found that not everyone is exceptional. Just feeling good about yourself doesn't do anything unless you have a valid reason to feel good about yourself. It was found that by teaching people to believe that they are exceptional or successful, and to feel good about themselves, doesn't create a nation of Mark Zuckerbergs or Malala Yousafzais. Measuring self-esteem by how positive people feel about themselves is a problem. Instead, self-worth should be measured by how people feel about the *negative* parts of themselves.

Some people feel they are entitled; that they deserve the good things without actually earning them. Believing that they should have this amazing lifestyle without actually sacrificing anything. It comes from a certain level of self-confidence, which can be alluring for a while, but damaging in the long run. The problem with entitlement is that it makes people *need* to feel good about themselves all the time. Entitlement fails. It's just another happy drug. It *isn't* happiness. Someone who actually has a high self-worth can look at the negative aspects of their character honestly and then act to improve on them. Entitled people, incapable of acknowledging the problems openly and honestly, cannot improve their lives in any meaningful way. They continue to take the happy drug.

WHAT'S WRONG?

The problem is that we tend to look for happiness in the wrong places. What we *think* makes a huge difference in our happiness and our lives, really only makes a very small difference, and this is proven time and time again by various studies. So why are we acting oblivious to all these facts? Statistic samples of US adults have indicated that slightly more than 50 percent are 'moderately mentally healthy', yet not *flourishing*.[14]

We lack enthusiasm and zeal in the things we engage with in this world. Maybe you feel like this too; you have everything around you, you are financially comfortable, yet, something seems missing. This could be one of the very reasons you have picked up this book. The desire to be happier is not just felt by those who are clinically depressed, but the majority of the global population have this desire too.

Everyone wants to bring more joy and meaning to their life, people want more stimulating relationships and jobs. The idea that happiness must be *found* is wrong too. The very concept that happiness can be pursued implies that it is an object that we have to discover and chase. This is why I prefer to use the notion of *ānanda*. We already have an innate ability to attain the state of joy and equilibrium that is inherent to the *ātmā*. All we need to do is mould ourselves back into it. I will repeat this again, happiness truly is a state of mind and it comes from within.

For those diagnosed with depression, this book should not replace any traditional and modern treatments, such as medical advice, cognitive-behavioural therapy, and anti-depressant medication. Please continue to seek appropriate consultation for this. But I hope that this book can go hand-in-hand for you all, in order to help you feel better quicker, stronger, and for longer.

---

[14] Keyes, C. L. (2005)

THE 'SOLUTIONS'

Most of history has shown us the futility of the rat race and basically told us to quit. The truth is that *happiness comes from within, and it cannot be found by making the world conform to your desires.* Both Vedic teachings and the Stoics taught that to find peace and happiness we should understand that striving to obtain goods and goals in the external world cannot bring more than a moment of happiness. You must work on your internal world. If this is true, it would have major implications on how we should be living our lives.

The second biggest finding in happiness research, after the influence of genes—our biochemistry—is that most environmental and demographic factors have very little effect on our happiness. Though marriage is one of the life factors most strongly correlated with happiness, the correlation is the reverse, happiness leads to lasting marriages. Happy people marry sooner and stay married for longer, as opposed to the people with a lower 'base level' of happiness.[15] Religion also plays a key role, showing that on average, religious people are happier than non-religious people.[16] Men have more freedom and power than women, yet they are not, on average, any happier (women experience more depression, but also more intense joy).[17] It may surprise you that older people are happier than younger people, because despite their probable health issues, they quickly

[15] Harker and Keltner (2001); Lyubomirsky, King, and Diener, in press.
[16] Diener et al., 1999; Myers (2000)
[17] Fujita, F., Diener, E., & Sandvik, E. (1991)

adapt to problems. And as for money, well, let's just hold onto that thought for a few more pages. But, what if there really is a set point fixed into every brain—a set level of happiness? This would mean that the only way to find true happiness is to change our internal setting, instead of changing the environmental factors around us.

In the late 1990s, the founders of positive psychology introduced what they called the *happiness formula*[18]:

> **H = S + C + V**
> The level of happiness experienced (H) is determined by your base level of happiness—a biological set point (S), plus the conditions of your life (C), plus the voluntary activities (V) you undertake.

The goal of positive psychology is to work out what kinds of C and V push our level of H to the top of its potential range. Sonja Lyubomirsky, psychologist professor and author of *The How of Happiness*, has also given a similar idea in understanding happiness with *the happiness pie-chart*:

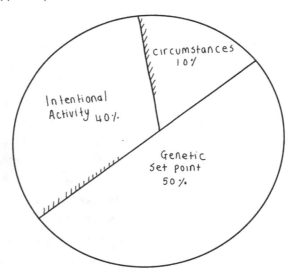

---

[18] See Lyubomirsky et al., in press, and Seligman (2002)

The chart explains that 50 percent of our happiness is set by our genetic set point. You may be wondering where such an assumption comes from, so let me tell you. Growing research done on identical and fraternal twins suggests that each of us is born with a particular set point of happiness that is inherited from our biological mother or father, or even both. This is the baseline, or potential for happiness, that we return to even after major setbacks or wins. This links very closely to what we call the *adaption principle*, which we will discuss shortly. This set point governs the extent of how happy we will be throughout our lives.

The most counterintuitive fact is that, on the chart, we see that only 10 percent of our happiness is determined by circumstances and situations. This means, whether you are rich or poor, healthy or unhealthy, beautiful or plain, married or divorced, all of this only has a 10 percent effect on our levels of happiness.[19] A number of other studies have also backed this up. For example, one study showed that the richest Americans (those earning more than $10 million annually) reported levels of personal happiness only slightly greater than the office staff and blue-collar workers that they employ. Moreover, although married people are deemed happier than single people, the effect of marriage on personal happiness is minute.[20] If you accept that circumstances *do not* define your happiness, you will feel more empowered, believe me.

The remaining 40 percent is the most important. This is our behaviour, mindset, and voluntary activities. The key to happiness isn't in changing our circumstances, but in our reaction to the circumstances, along with our mindset and activities. To understand that you control 40 percent of your happiness is huge. In this book, we focus on the intentional activities and actions that we can take to improve that 40 percent. Only *you* are in control of, and can influence, that 40 percent. As cliché as it may sound, happiness begins with you. Making changes requires dedication, commitment, and a drive from within. The fruits of which will be rewarding.

---

[19] Diener, E., Sah, E. M., Lucas, R. E., and Smith, H. L. (1999)
[20] Diener, E., Horwitz, J. And Emmons, R. A. (1985)

WHAT'S THE POINT?

I really hope that if you are still reading this book, you won't be asking this question. But, in case you need to be convinced, the evidence and studies are conclusive.

Happier people are more sociable and energetic. They are more charitable and cooperative. They are also liked *more* by others. Happier people are more likely to get married and stay married. They are also more likely to have a better network and more social support. They are better leaders and negotiators, and earn more money. They are more resilient in the face of hardship. Their health is better both physically and mentally. Happy people live longer. A study found that those who were happy as college freshmen earned more sixteen years later (in their mid-thirties) and no other factors gave them an advantage.[21]

Another study following undergraduates over years found that women who expressed joy in their yearbook photos were relatively more likely to be married by the age of twenty-seven, and had more satisfying marriages at the age of fifty-two.[22] Of course, being happy doesn't just benefit you. If you are happier, this will positively impact all those around you—your partner, your family, the community, and even society at large.

---

[21] Diener, E., Nickerson, C., Lucas, R. E., and Sandvik, E. (2002).
[22] Harker, L., and Keltner, D. (2001)

THE HAPPINESS MYTHS

The majority of animals learn by trial and error. They have to try things, and sometimes they get what they want, and at other times they don't. The mouse has to try and run away from the cat, sometimes it works, at other times it doesn't. Humans were like this two million years ago. They had to survive and hunt, they had to *try* and *test* to see how things would go; they had to make mistakes to learn from them.

But, what if we were able to learn without making the mistake in the first place? What if we could learn things without making the mistake ourselves? Over the last two million years, the human brain has evolved a number of times. One of the most important evolutions of the human brain was the development of the frontal lobe (refer to Appendix A). This is the part that makes you human—the part that allows you to project yourself into the future. A study was carried out on an individual with a damaged frontal lobe. He was asked a series of questions, including "What will you be doing tomorrow?"

The man replied, "I don't know."

He was living only in the moment, he had no concept of the past, nor the future. No concept of yesterday or tomorrow. It is like being in a plain white room, with no door or windows; like swimming in the middle of the ocean, with water stretching thousands of miles with nothing in sight. This study showed how important the development of the frontal lobe is for our thinking. We know not to put our fingers in a plug socket, even though we have never done it. Our imagination feels the future, it can project into it without experiencing the good or bad itself. The frontal lobe is your simulator—the monkey simulator.

Unfortunately, not every simulation that the monkey gives to you is right. Someone buys the lottery thinking that if they win, they will be happier in the *future*, but statistics show that those who have won the lottery are hardly as happy as they had predicted.

The same thought applies with the majority of good and bad that occurs in our lives. Couples plan to have a baby, their happiness knows no bounds, and then after a few years when they finally have a baby, they aren't as happy as they predicted. If you were told that tomorrow you will go blind, you would probably feel distraught, you'd say "I will never be happy again!" But, those who have lost their eyesight end up to normality after a while! What is going on here? Simple: the monkey simulator causes us to make mistakes—not only physically, but mentally too. The monkey is consistently focussing on the present moment, it doesn't care about where it has already been, or where it is going; it is trapped in the moment, a prisoner of the present. If you're confused, let me show you where you, yourself, have experienced this:

At some point you will have eaten a lot. You will have felt so full that you probably even said, "I will never eat again!" But unsurprisingly, you will. Maybe within the next few hours itself, you will be hungry again. But in the moment, we all kind of believe it, right? We all feel that we won't be able to eat again, let alone imagine in a few hours. This type of hunger may seem to be limited to the digestive system, or to our bodies, but it actually applies in the broader sense, to you as a whole.

Psychologists who studied trauma in individuals found that in the first few years, the individuals are generally very unhappy. A few years after that, some go downhill, whilst others recover. Some are resilient, and they are happy even in the moments of difficulties, and years later too. It has been found that 20 percent will be completely devastated, about 25 percent will recover within a couple of years, 5 percent will go completely downhill, and 50 percent will be resilient.[23] Yes, the largest group will be resilient; they will be fine at all times. You see, humans are not fragile, they are tough, but the monkey makes us feel fragile. It feeds us myths and takes us to wrong destinations.

---

[23] Bonanno, G. A., & Kaltman, S. (1999)

WRONG DESTINATIONS

Many think that happiness must be *found*; that it's somewhere out there, a place to be reached, but it isn't. We search for happiness in the wrong places. Happiness isn't out there for us to find, it is *inside* us. Happiness is a state of mind, a way of perceiving and approaching ourselves. It is in our way of perceiving and approaching the world around us. You know it and so do I. As much as your monkey is to blame for stopping us from accepting these truths, so is the passenger. For some strange reason, the passenger fails to inform the monkey that it is heading in the wrong direction. The monkey, projecting you into the future, gives you the wrong ideas. With all of these ideas there are always two sides, so don't think I am being biased, I am just stating the facts. Let us explore the key myths that the monkey feeds us.

Marriage

Let's start with marriage. It *does* make people happier. Research has shown that amongst all groups of people, married people are happier overall. They have better health and they earn more money. Below you can see what we call the *u-curve of happiness*.

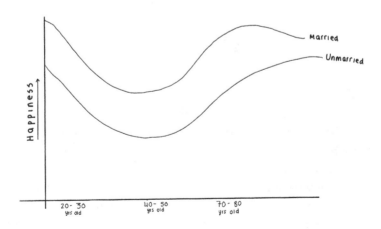

It shows that over the course of an average person's lifetime, married people are happier than unmarried people. This graph also shows us that younger, or older people, are generally happier than those in between. But, at every stage, married people are happier. Still, marriage seems to only have a temporary effect on happiness. The boost lasts a couple of years and then returns to the baseline—the happiness set point. Does this mean that marriage makes people happier? It could be. Or, it could also be that happiness causes marriage.

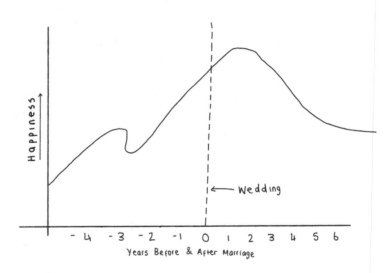

Years Before & After Marriage

The above chart illustrates even more interesting findings. The peak that you see after the wedding is known as the *honeymoon period*. After that, around six years later, happiness levels off to where it began. Surprisingly, divorces also make people happier. Now you may think, "Does this mean I should follow the marry-divorce cycle, similar to what movie stars do?" Of course it doesn't. This is where we need to be clear that it isn't marriage that make us happy, it's good marriage. We will venture into this a little later, but an important question to ask yourself at this point is, "Is my partner my best friend? This question is often used to show if marriages are good. Married people—now would be a good point to pause and think.

Money

The Greek philosopher Epictetus says, "Wealth consists not in having great possessions, but in having few wants." When we talk about becoming richer, this *does* make you happier, but only to the point of financial comfort. Yes, money does make you happier, I won't deny it. Try going to a homeless person and tell them that it doesn't matter, and that they can still be happy without money. Record their reaction and send it to me if you do. By assuming that you are able to afford this book, and have the time to read it, your household income is likely to stand above the UK national median.[24] Research shows that the potential peak for financial happiness is around $75k (around £57k). So, if you earn around this, you are basically at the epitome of happiness that can be derived from money.

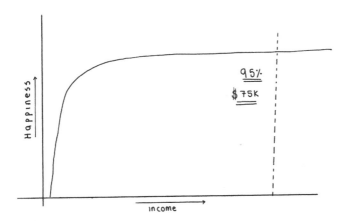

This yearly figure is up to which people report themselves as incrementally happier. Obviously, this amount is relative, and greatly depends on the cost of living, but more importantly, when people earn higher than a 'comfortable' amount, they don't *continue* to become happier. Happiness is found indirectly in the absence of a stressor, such

---

[24] In 2019, the median household income in the UK was £ 29,400.

as money troubles, as opposed to not *having* it. This is what we want to try and do; to switch our focus from directly chasing happiness, to removing needless frustrations.

Since 1967, a study has been taking place every year called the *American Freshman Survey*. It looks at the attitude and plans of freshmen across the US. In 2019, around 127,000 students at 178 colleges and universities took part in the study. 84 percent of them said it is very important to be 'very well off financially', compared with 42 percent in 1967.[25] Interestingly, only 50 percent admitted that it was very important, or essential, to 'develop a meaningful philosophy in life', compared with 86 percent in 1967.

In another study of 792 *well-off* adults, more than 50 percent reported that wealth did not bring them more happiness, and a third of those with assets greater than $10 million said that money bought *more* problems than it solved.[26] Understandably, those with higher incomes report being somewhat more satisfied with their lives. Studies of how they actually spend their days find that they don't spend more time in any enjoyable activities than their less prosperous peers and, in fact, they are more likely to experience daily anxiety and anger.[27]

It is more appropriate for us to treat wealth as a satisfying side effect. If we get it, it's great; if we don't, oh well. Nice to have, but not always in our control. Any object that you chase directly will never prove gratification. Simply having more money is not good enough, and money won't make your worries go away. Another problem seems to be that the majority of people today are not spending their money in the right way. Money is spent on objects as opposed to experiences. Doing *nothing* is also not a source of happiness. You may think that if you have a million pounds in your bank account, just like the beach scenario earlier, then you will be able to rest and be happy. But, we will explore this myth in detail later.

---

[25] Stolzenberg, E. B., Eagan, M. K., Aragon, M. C., Cesar-Davis, N. M., Jacobo, S., Couch, V., & Rios-Aguilar, C. (2019)

[26] Kristof, K. M. (2005, January 14)

[27] Kahneman, D., Krueger, A. B., Schkade, D., Shwarz, N., and Stone, A. A. (2006)

Beauty

The American Society for Aesthetic Plastic Surgery reports that more and more of us are remaking our appearances every year. In 2004, there was an increase of 44 percent in the number of cosmetic procedures than in 2003. This included 2.8 million Botox injections, 1.1 million chemical peels, and hundreds of thousands of breast augmentations, eyelid surgeries, nose reshaping, and liposuctions.[28] Those who have surgery to improve their physical experience do report being satisfied, but only for short periods of time.[29] Beauty is not associated with happiness. Instead, coming to believe that you are already beautiful is even more powerful.

Children

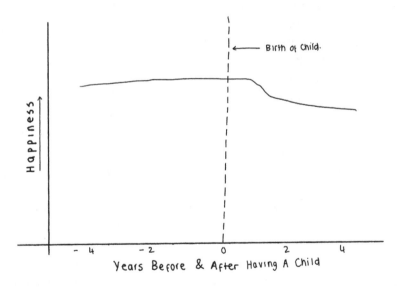

I don't want to come across in the wrong way here, and this will be hard to digest for many, but, people without children are happier than those with children. Research has shown that the general happiness of parents decreases after the birth of their first child, and unfortunately it

---

[28] American Society for Aesthetic Plastic Surgery (2004)
[29] Wengle, H. (1986)

never returns to any previous level. It is understandable that this may not be true for you, but it doesn't mean it isn't for the rest of the world. On average, children have a small but negative impact on their parents. Two-thirds of the world's nations have this negative impact, and one-third positive. Again, there are many factors in play here, including marriage which plays an obvious role too.

THE PROBLEM WITH 'WANT'

Our ancestors had a struggle *living*. They woke up everyday for the sole purpose of *surviving*. If they managed it through till the evening, that was success. Happiness to them was a dreamy state that could be attained, if they got everything they wanted. But that didn't happen, and it doesn't happen. Two-hundred thousand years later, we have been through the Agricultural Revolution (8000 BC), the Industrial Revolution (1800s), and the Technological Revolution (1960s), and for the first time in history, we have everything we could possibly want (well, almost), yet, we are still not happy. The five richest men on this planet have a combined net worth of $500 billion (the gross national product of India). They have all the money in the world, but as we will explore, they are not *always* happy. Surely, if happiness is what we acquire, when we get what we want, these people should be billions of times happier than us right? Happiness can't be the only thing we gain, when we get what we want. Honestly, it seems like we really don't know what makes us happy.

Every single person has taught us a different meaning of happiness: our parents, teachers, family, friends, motivational speakers, talk-show hosts—everyone has their own theory about what you must do if you want to be happy in life. We are the recipients of this wisdom. Most of the time, this wisdom that has been fed to us isn't really wise, nor helpful in the long run.

I want to briefly touch upon the ideas of 'entitlement' and 'getting what we want'. In no way am I against any self-help books or the industry. Even parts of this book can be considered self-help, but I disagree with the idea often given in the self-help industry, with the mantra that some give of '*get what you want*'. This idea makes it seem as though each of us have an inherent birthright to accumulate whatever we think will make us happy. This thought relating to having more and more desires, is actually one of the key causes of misery and unhappiness. Of course, we can say that our desires increase at different levels. Right now, I only desire to complete writing this page and hopefully you decide to read it. We carry out almost all of our actions in order to fulfil some future goal that we desire. For example, you may choose to quickly skim this page so that you can get up, go to the kitchen, and grab yourself some cookies. In one form or another, we are slaves to our desires. Desires are just part of an endless chain: we will eat the cookies, and then, after an hour or so, we will desire again to eat. But why?

After the First World War, there was a mass production of products like washing machines, stoves, and canned food that advertised convenience. Why wouldn't you get one? It drove the economy forward. In the 1927 issue of *Harvard Business Review*, Paul Mazur wrote, "We must shift America from a needs to a desires culture. People must be *trained* to desire, to want things, even before the old have been entirely consumed. We must shape a new mentality in America. Man's desires must overshadow his needs."

FAME

In a 2010 Telegraph survey, young people were asked the question: "What would you like to do for your career?" 54 percent answered, 'Become a celebrity'. More than a fifth said they aimed to achieve this by appearing on a TV reality show, another 5 percent through dating someone famous. But nearly 70 percent of those who said they prioritised fame, when asked how they might achieve this goal, had no idea how to go about it. The consequence is that today children know nothing about hard work and progressing their way to reach their own successes. Other than a few rare cases, *fame does not make you happy*. Some aspects will make you happy; others are very unpleasant. Fame is also fleeting, and if you feel a need to achieve fame in the first place, that desire will only grow more as you struggle to hold onto it.

What attaches us to celebrities is this false sense of *desire*. Not just the desire to get a following or boost our ego. We want to be like them, eat like them, to *hold* them in some way. Why? Because when they are rich, good-looking and glamorous, they give out the message of 'you too can succeed and have these things in life'. And so they continue to point you, and the rest of the population, in the direction of pursuing material aspirations. Celebrities serve as a distraction from the material inequalities of modern society. Have you seen how they are used to promote products? The desire attached to them is then passed to the objects, that we begin to attach over, and the wheel keeps spinning at higher speeds.

THE ADAPTION PRINCIPLE

Take a minute to think about the best and worst things that *could* happen to you. Some of you may say wining the lottery, and losing your arms and legs. Obviously, winning the lottery would give you some sort of freedom from certain limitations; enabling you to pursue your dreams, maybe become a philanthropist helping others. You can live a life filled with comfort, bringing you prolonged levels of happiness, as opposed to a shot of dopamine. Losing your arms and legs on the other hand, would limit you from mainly everything, you will become dependent on others, and many would probably think they would be better off dead. But they are wrong. Clearly, it is better to win the lottery than to lose your body parts, but not by as much as you might think. Whatever happens, we are likely to adapt to it, but we don't realise this beforehand. We greatly overestimate the intensity and duration of our emotional reactions. Within less than 12 months, lottery winners returned mostly to their base level of happiness.[30] They might buy a new house, a new car, quit their job, and eat better food, but within a few months the pleasure fades. The mind is programmed to changes in condition, not to absolute levels.

In contrast, the one without arms and legs takes a huge loss upfront. They probably think their life is over, and may give up all hope. But similar to the lottery winner, their mind is also sensitive to changes, and so, after a few months they also adapt to the new situation. Maybe physical therapy can expand their abilities, they can set themselves new goals. In his early twenties, when physicist

---

[30] Brickman, Coates, and Janoff-Bulman, 1978; Schulz and Decker, 1985

Stephen Hawking was diagnosed with motor neurone disease, he too felt the same. Yet, he went on to carry out groundbreaking work in cosmology, win numerous prizes, and write a bestselling science book.

Our judgements about our present state are based on whether it is better or worse than the state to which we have become accustomed.[31] This type of adaption is simply a part of our biology; it is a property of our neurons. Nerve cells respond vigorously to new stimuli, and then gradually *habituate*, firing less information to the stimuli they have become accustomed to. But, humans don't just habituate, they recalibrate. We create a never-ending stream of targets for ourselves, and every time we hit one, we replace it with another. We aim higher after a success, lower after a failure. Instead of surrendering our attachments and allowing events to happen as they do, we surround ourselves with hopes, goals, and expectations, and feel pleasure and pain accordingly.

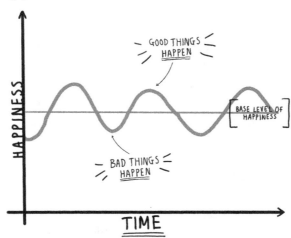

This continuous cycle of desire fulfilment is known as *hedonism*, meaning 'the pursuit of pleasure'. We spend our entire lives chasing one pleasure after another, but truthfully we are never satisfied for long. Wealth, power, fame, and sex are all fleeting. They may temporarily satisfy the monkey, but never the passenger. We all are

---

[31] Helson, 1964

continuously running on a *hedonic treadmill*. On a treadmill, we can increase the speed as we want, but we always stay in the same place. Similarly in life, we can work as hard as we want, accumulate however much we want, but it doesn't necessarily mean we will always get ahead. When we want something (and perhaps we get it) we feel good for a while, but then return to whatever default level of happiness or sadness that we enjoyed before. Nothing really changes. Everyone has a base level of happiness that they are born with and it cannot be changed. Sometimes some good things happen, other times something bad happens. These are short-term sensations of pleasure or distress, and then we return to our individual 'base level'. This is how humans are programmed. In the long run, it doesn't even matter what happens to you—good or bad—you will always return to your base level of happiness. This is the default level of happiness in your brain and as we have already seen, it is largely determined by your genes.

I had laser eye surgery aged twenty, after being almost blind all my life, and tired of continuously wearing glasses. The result felt amazing, I could see street signs clearly and I could read at night without discomfort. It made me *happy*. However, about six months later, I adapted to my new vision. It no longer provided me with the happiness boost that I felt on the first day. You will also have stories like this: moving to a new home, getting a new job, securing a promotion, or flying first class. Every person who is thoughtful, rational, and reasonable, will have considered this truth at some point whilst considering a purchase, or an upgrade of their phone or laptop. This level of desire is when we see the treadmill in full action. I *desire* at the time of writing for the brand-new iMac instead of my current one. I know it won't really make me any happier, but I just want it. After some time (roughly equivalent to the time it takes me to buy it, explore its new features, and get used to the feel of using it) I will feel exactly the same about it as I do about my current device. Obviously Apple know this and keep developing newer models at such a speed that will make me desire the latest model, adding more negativity to the process. There is the pleasure of the new model *and* the displeasure of knowing mine does not have certain features that are being enjoyed by everyone else. I can't stand that. So why not just buy it?

My favourite example of this thought is the one given by Professor Irvine, in his book, *On Desire*. Please read this carefully.

> Suppose you woke up one morning to discover that you were the last person on Earth: during the night, aliens had spirited away everyone but you. Suppose that despite the absence of other people, the worlds buildings, houses, stores and roads remained as they had been the night before. Cars were where their now-vanished owners had parked them, and the gas for these cars was plentiful at now-unattended gas stations. The electricity still worked. It would be a world like this world, except that everyone but you was gone. You would, of course, be very lonely, but let us ignore the emotional aspects of being the last person, and instead focus our attention on the material aspects.
>
> In the situation described, you could satisfy many material desires that you can't satisfy in our actual world. You could have a car of your dreams. You could even have a showroom full of expensive cars. You could have the house of your dreams (or live in a palace). You could wear expensive clothes. You could acquire not just a big diamond ring but the Hope Diamond itself. The interesting question is this: without people around, would you still want these things? Would the material desires you have had when the world was full of people still be present in you if other people vanished? Probably not. Without anyone else to impress, why own an expensive car, a palace, fancy clothes, or jewellery?

What Irvine suggests here is that, alone in this imagined world, you might try certain luxuries for some time but would soon, for example, find a place that was easier to maintain and live in, rather than choosing to live in a palace; get clothes that are comfortable as opposed to being expensive, and you probably wouldn't care at all about how you look. This thought experiment shows that we choose our entire lifestyle (our home, clothes, cars, etc.) with other people in mind. In essence, we project a style that is designed to make others look up at us, or envy us. Irvine's thought exercise teaches that our desires would gradually diminish if we didn't need to impress other people. We spend so much time and energy in seeking approval from our peers. Additionally, the things we desire actually do very little than fuel other desires and teach us what greed is. Whilst accumulating material objects, we find no deep satisfaction, other than fleeting pleasures and short-lived gratification of impressing others, before we return to our base level of happiness. Ultimately, we allow ourselves to be controlled by other people and objects.

Robert Frank talks about this in his book, *Luxury Fever*, where he endeavours to understand why people are so devoted to spending money on luxuries and other goods, to which they adapt completely, rather than on things that would make them happier in the long run. For example, people would be happier and healthier if they took more time off and spent it with family and friends, yet every first-world country has long been heading in the opposite direction. People would be happier if they reduced their commuting time, even if it meant living in smaller houses, yet trends are towards even larger houses and even longer commutes. People would be happier and healthier if they took longer holidays, even if that meant earning less, yet holiday times are shrinking globally. In the long run they would be wealthier, if they bought basic, functional appliances, vehicles, and watches, and invested the money they saved for the future; yet, we spend almost everything we have—and sometimes more—on goods for present consumption, often paying a large premium for designer names and features.

His explanation is simple, conspicuous and inconspicuous consumption follow different psychological rules. Conspicuous consumption refers to things that are visible to others and that are taken as markers of a person's relative success. People see the value of these items not from the objective properties, but from the statement that they make about their owner. See it this way, when no one had a mobile phone, the first person to buy one stood out. When everyone started to buy one, the one to get a smartphone stood out. A few years later, when someone bought an iPhone, they made the statement—they had an iPhone, wow! What Frank tries to explain is that conspicuous consumption is a zero-sum game: each person's move up devalues the possessions of others. On the other hand, inconspicuous consumption, refers to goods and activities that are valued for themselves, that are usually consumed more privately, and are not bought for the purpose of achieving status. These thoughts have also been supported by recent research on the benefits of "doing versus having."

Psychologists Leaf van Boven and Tom Gilovich asked people to think back to a time when they spent more than $100 with the intention of increasing their level of happiness and enjoyment. One group of participants was asked to pick up a material possession, and the other was asked to pick an experience or activity. After describing their purchases, participants were asked to fill out a questionnaire. Those who described buying an experience (like a ski trip or a great meal) were happier when thinking about their purchase, and thought that that money was better spent, than those who described the material object. They conducted different variations of this experiment but found similar findings every time. They concluded that experiences give more happiness in part because they have greater social value; most activities that cost more than $100 are those that enable interaction with other people, but expensive material objects are often purchased, for the most part, to *impress* other people. Whilst activities connect us to others, objects separate us from others.

Envy also plays a huge role here. Envy is different to jealousy. It is a dangerous wheel that keeps on turning. We desire some object in order to impress *others*; we obtain, or sometimes fail to obtain, that object; the *others* are also likely to feel a similar envy; and so, they too will seek out a similar status object for themselves; and we continue this pattern of acquiring more objects and status symbols to keep the wheel turning. What makes it worse is that we often feel this envious of those that are closest to us. Our closest ones suffer most from this. Envy is fuelled by our sense of entitlement and the comparison of ourselves to our close ones. Sociologists refer to the *reference group theory*. The idea that in the process of forming our self-identity, we compare ourselves to those close to us. Furthermore, this process is magnified by our cultural assumption that we all have the same right to become rich and famous if we desire to. Basically, the belief that we are all inherently equal. It may surprise you, but this concept is quite modern.

Before the 1800s, across the globe, the differences in wealth and status that existed between various levels of society were rarely questioned. People managed to get on with their lives, and the aspirations that we have today were almost non-existent. And we must know that wealth is like seawater—the more you drink, the thirstier you become. The same is true of fame and recognition. Epicurus explained that human needs can be divided into three categories, which Schopenhauer clarified.

- Natural and necessary needs, which cause pain if they are not satisfied. (food and clothing, which are easily attainable for the majority of people);
- Natural but unnecessary needs, difficult to satisfy and not a necessity. (sexual satisfaction and partnership);
- Neither natural nor necessary needs, they are without an end and difficult to satisfy. (getting the largest gadget or car).

Unnecessary desires are 'without end', and naturally we will always desire more and more, pushing us towards further dissatisfaction. This is why we are often surprised when we see people who live with simplicity, but seem happier than ourselves. We search for happiness in distractions. One such distraction is travel. You may have had the experience of looking forward to a holiday; viewing the photographs on a booking website in order to choose a destination, imagining yourself there, swimming in the sea, or lying on that beach. The prospect of course, is amazing, and often making that trip will be a means of dealing with our stress or discontent. The reality of the holiday, though, is often very different and disappointing in the end. Socrates explained why, *when you travel, you always take yourself with you.* When you are on that sandy strip of paradise, you realise that you have brought all of those disappointing and stressful parts of yourself along with you. The rest is just a fancy backdrop we paint. Happiness, and the desires we associate with it, are a delusion. Happiness derived from desires are imaginary and deceiving in many and most forms. Yet we are always wanting more than we have, we keep running like hamsters on a wheel. These are the happiness myths.

IS POSITIVITY A PROBLEM?

I don't want to challenge the belief of positive thinking, but there is the possibility of it being just as destructive, as it is good. The universe does *not* rearrange itself to give you what you want. This is just you being more focussed on your ambitions and thinking more positively about them.

There is also a major problem in the way we goal-set. Just think of the average life. When we are young, we choose *certain* subjects for GCSEs, in order to study *certain* subjects at A-level, to then go to *this* university, to get *this* job, to get *this* promotion and work our way up *this* ladder, and then? I am not saying to make money is bad, but you should never confuse it with happiness. We've already seen this when we discussed that once you begin earning a comfortable amount, more money will not make you happier. You may get richer, but you won't be more content.

Happiness levels are largely defined by the balance of your character and personality. Changes to our happiness levels do not come from external circumstances, however much we may admire this idea. Of course, some external conditions, like having an accessible network, are statistically shown to make a difference in the levels of happiness that people report. But you should never depend on things like this to make you feel truly happy. When our friend, Alexander, saw the breadth of his domain, he cried for there were no more worlds to conquer. Positivity is all good, but the self-help industry often tells us that we shouldn't pay attention to people that criticise us, or what we do. This is dangerous. By ignoring or removing sources of honest feedback, you are fuelling your self-deception. Most of what happens in life is entirely out of your control, and as much as blind self-belief or self-help might disguise this fact for short splutters of time, you will eventually have to face this hard fact.

Schopenhauer uses the game of chess to help us picture how the idea of goal-setting might be unrealistic. When playing chess, we start out with a plan, but our plan is affected by the inclinations of the other player. Our plan must be modified constantly, to the point that, as we carry it out, several of its fundamental features are unrecognisable. To stick blindly to the same goals would be to deny that a second, independent player was at the board. Similarly, we are told that we should live our lives focusing on the future and by believing in ourselves, no matter what. This results in frustration and anxiety. By projecting yourself too far into the future, you lose out on the present, current moments. By trying to control what you can't, you only guarantee yourself frustration and disappointment. Is this the kind of life you really wish to have?

PART THREE

FIVE PRINCIPLES

PRINCIPLE ONE

FOCUS ON YOURSELF

The first important principle that will play a huge role towards your happiness (from now on happiness becomes synonymous to *ānanda*, bliss, or joy; not material happiness), is your focus on yourself. This may seem like an obnoxious statement to make, but, no one really cares about you as much as they make out to, or as much as you think they do. You have to accept this. Take a minute to walk yourself through your average day, and try to think about it from your own perspective. Every minute of every day, you are trying to please someone directly or indirectly.

There is a bird called the crane that has white feathers, a long beak, and stands on one leg in a stream of water. It spends its day looking down into the water for food. It sees hundreds and thousands of little fish swimming by, and the crane observes and lets them pass. As soon as it sees a big fish, it snaps and devours it. What is the crane doing? It is keeping its attention focussed on what is actually significant, and lets the little things go. Unless you are focussed on the higher principles in your life (like focussing on yourself), the most valuable things that form part of your life, then you will easily be distracted by every little fish that comes your way. And in this distraction, you will never be able to set your eyes on the big one. You must have the patience and willingness to let the small stuff pass; especially if you want to experience *ānanda*.

Imagine that you have to go to your friend's home in the next hour for their birthday. You haven't been told that there is any particular dress attire, so you rummage through your wardrobe to find something to wear. You struggle to choose something. It can't be too formal, because that would be odd; you don't want to be 'too much' either. You finally end up choosing something in between. At the time, you recall when, at last year's birthday party, someone came dressed in a suit, even though it was just a casual get together—everyone laughed and made comments about them. You rush to make your way to your friend's home, constantly recalling this memory in your head as you try to map out what the plan is for tonight. You arrive at their home, ring the doorbell, and your friend opens the door. As soon as they see you, their face drops; mouth wide open, they eye you up and down.

Now, what thought comes straight to your head at this moment? If we're being honest, we aren't even entirely sure what they will say. We don't know if they will comment on our clothes being amazing or terrible; judging us for wearing something we shouldn't be. For all you know, it could simply have been pouring it down with rain. You could be soaked and they are shocked at your state, more so than about what you are wearing. But what did you think about? We instantly become unhappy the more we think about other people's opinions and perspectives of us. Expectations are premeditated resentments. This is just one example, but this is a continuous cycle for us day-in and day-out. Face the fact that it doesn't even matter to anyone how we are as an individual. Why should it even matter? Why do we let the opinions of others shape our personality, and who we are to such a great extent? Sometimes to the point that we end up living our lives in different costumes for different people. Isn't it high time we stop living to satisfy others in the world? No one will ever be fully satisfied. See it this way, are you wholeheartedly satisfied with any one person alive today? I mean—wholeheartedly, one-hundred percent—where you wouldn't change a single thing about that person.

I don't think so. But, don't blame yourself either for this thinking. It is how we have been programmed since we were children. Our parents would have expectations that my child should get high marks in class, or that we should top our class with best marks. Then, we would try our best to bring good grades home to our parents. Still, were our parents satisfied enough to say, "Okay kid, you're all good. You got ninety-five marks, well done! You don't need to do anything in life anymore." Of course they weren't! Next, further expectations stemmed for us to pursue a degree and study further. Whether that be to become a doctor, an engineer, a pharmacist, a lawyer, or whatever it may be—the expectations were still there. Were they satisfied once we got our degree? No, because then came marriage, grandchildren, and the list goes on. Expectations never stop. Likewise, nor does our desire to meet those expectations. We fear that, not only will we displease our parents, but others too. This frustrates us further, making us fearful and anxious. Our mind begins to ruminate and fall into a deep and dangerous trap.

I am not saying that you shouldn't fulfil the expectations of your parents; that is a personal choice for you to make. But, you must have the constant reminder in your head that, even after trying your best, not everyone will be happy with what you do. Expectations only increase, like desires. Expectations actually stem from desires, and so, you must work on pleasing yourself first. Expecting life to always turn out the way you want it to does nothing but open the floodgates to disappointment.

Self-awareness also plays an important role on your self-focus. Most self-help professionals ignore this deeper level. They take sad people who want to be rich, and give them various types of advice on how to make more money, but ignore the underlying question: *Why* do you want to be rich in the first place? *How* do you measure your own success or failure? This type of self-questioning is extremely hard. You need to ask yourself these basic questions which are often difficult to answer.

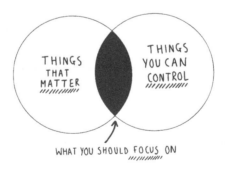

WHAT YOU SHOULD FOCUS ON

Life will not always turn out the way we want it to, nor will events that occur in our life. There will always be certain things out of our control. Some things will matter, but won't be in our control; other things will be in our control, but they won't really matter. You need to focus on what falls in both categories. Don't waste your time on anything that fits outside.

* * *

Stop *Always* Caring

Most of us spend our life worrying about what other people think. What can we do to stop always caring about what people think of us?

1. Why do I care?

The first step is to understand what it is that makes you care so much about what others think of you. If you worry too much about what opinions others have of you, it is usually because you seek external approval and validation. You want everybody to love you and accept you. You do this by controlling your self-image. You believe that if you avoid making any noise by being extra careful, people will love you. But this is not normally the case. You cannot control what other people think of you because you cannot remove the freedom that they have to think what they want. We normally give ourselves two choices: do nothing and hide to avoid being criticised, or try to be this ideal person that everybody will love. In either scenario, you are sabotaging your own freedom to express who you really are, and you are halting your own potential and happiness.

2. It isn't me

Be aware of this self-image that you claim of yourself, realising it isn't you. It is illusory, and constrains you, leaving you with unfulfilled potential and useless worries that serve no purpose.

3. Your uncontrollable image

Realising that you cannot control the image of yourself that you are projecting onto others is powerful. You do have some control over this through your thoughts, actions, words and behaviours. However, in the end, people will always judge you based on *their* own perception. They will want to project *their* beliefs and values onto you, and when you don't live as they think you should live, they will judge you for this.

The main point I am trying to get across here is that you can't, and shouldn't, change yourself to meet with other people's expectations. If you do this, you will end up living a life either so 'perfect', or so 'poor', that you might end up not having lived your life at all.

4. No one cares

People do not care about you as much as you think they do. Everyone has their own lives to live—they are too busy dealing with their own personal issues than worry about you. They don't check your every Instagram post, remember all of your mistakes, or keep tabs on your life. You are not the centre of the preoccupations of others. A famous saying goes:

> When you are twenty, you care what everyone thinks.
> When you are forty, you stop caring what everyone thinks.
> When you are sixty, you realise that no one was ever thinking about you in the first place.

Caring too much about what people think of you often results from your own inability to think about yourself accurately. Spending every moment of every day with yourself, seeing things from your point of view, everything you do automatically matters to you. You are the one that keeps track of your successes and failures, and you take everything personally. You try to give meaning to words, actions and events that mean nothing. When people are rude to you, you wrongly assume something is wrong with you. Most of the time, people are just in a bad mood. The bottom line is: not everything is about you.

5. None of your business

Remember, what people think of you is none of your business. It isn't your responsibility to be loved by everybody. Your responsibility lies in becoming the best person you can possibly be, while having the purest intent you can possibly have. This encompasses not caring too much about what others think of you, and not trying to please everyone. The way people judge you or react to you is their own business, not yours. Let them make their own assumptions; give them the freedom to create their own image of you in their mind. You may think they will be mistaken and look at you in the wrong way, but they will never truly know you—no one will. Stop fighting against the 'wrong' image that they hold of you; stop justifying yourself to others; stop being defensive. Instead, purify your intent, actions, and behaviours. Maybe one day they may see you for who you really are. Nothing else is in your control. Other people fall in that circle of 'out of your control', likewise what they think of you. Some people will love you even before knowing you, others will never love you or accept you, no matter how hard you try. You could be the humblest, most beautiful person ever, with the purest intent, and millions in your bank account, yet some people would still not like you. Caring what people think of you is like playing at the casino. You trade yourself with a fictional approval of people who do not know who you are. You exchange your true personality for a short-lived boost of your ego, for artificial approval. Who wins? The casino always does. What do you end up with? Being bankrupt. Not of your money, but of your dreams, personalities, values and beliefs—ultimately yourself. The choice is yours.

A LETTER TO GOD

There was once a poor, frail, elderly lady. She used to be happy in her younger years, but her life changed as she got older. She was all alone and her financial situation was on the brink. One day, she decided to write a letter to God and explain how she was struggling financially, more so than anything else that bothered her. She wrote a letter addressed to God, asking for help with a thousand pounds. She wrote that if she got this, she would be over the moon. Asking for the money to be sent to her address, she sealed the letter. She posted it into the postbox, eagerly expecting a response from God. A few days later, the letter reached the post office. The mail sorter going through the post saw the letter and was curious when he saw the words 'To God' on the envelope. He wondered what to do. Out of curiosity, he opened the letter. After reading the story that the lady had detailed in her letter, and coming to know of her financial situation, he thought something should be done out of goodwill to help her. He didn't want her to lose faith in God. He explained the letter to all of his colleagues, who agreed that something should be done. He urged everyone to contribute money towards a pot for the lady. Everybody in the office contributed. Some contributed fifty pounds, others contributed a hundred. After all the workers had contributed, the total came to nine-hundred and fifty pounds. This was just fifty pounds short of the lady's request. So, putting the money gathered into an envelope, he wrote, 'From God' and sent it back to the address of the lady.

In a matter of two days, the envelope reached the lady. With great joy and shock, she opened the letter and found the money in it. She was overjoyed seeing this money and tears rolled down her face. I mean, God had replied to her! He had answered her prayer! She counted the money and found that it was fifty pounds short of a thousand. She was utterly shocked and disappointed. After some days, the same mail sorter received another letter, addressed 'To God'. He opened it, it was from the same lady:

> *Dear God,*
> *Thank you so much for listening to my prayers in the form of my letter and thank you for sending me this money. I almost lost faith in you, but you restored it. I can never pay you back for this!*

After reading this opening paragraph, the mail sorter's face lit up with joy. He felt happy that he had helped this lady and restored her firm faith in God. He continued to read…

> *God, I have just one more thing I must tell you personally. The employees at the post office in my area are selfish thieves! I am sure that you had sent me the thousand pounds I had asked for, but the cheating dishonest workers at the post office have taken fifty pounds for themselves! Please punish them!*

After reading these lines, the mail sorter was shocked and disappointed. All his efforts had gone to waste. This is the reality. No one is actually pleased all the time. And, even if they are pleased, it is only for a short amount of time. Just wait until you make your next 'mistake' to see if people are really pleased with you or not. We wouldn't get upset when a cup of tea doesn't make itself right? But we would easily get upset if someone doesn't pour us a cup of tea when making some for themselves. Where does this notion of powerful thinking, that simply expecting others to behave the way we want them to will make them change to behave that way, come from? What entitles us to get angry with those around us when they cannot meet our expectations?

Sometimes, we feel that the world should revolve around us, but it isn't always about us and our expectations either. People are at different levels of awareness and the most 'Keshav' thing to do is to allow people to be who they are. Remember, life is a journey, and every individual is on their own path; with different thoughts, feelings, experiences, spirituality, etc. It is not for anyone, me or you, to judge another, but to accept them, encourage them and love them as much as possible. This is 'The Keshav Way'. It's quite simple—don't expect things from *others* all the time; don't let others expect things from *you* all the time. Learn to let go of your expectations and find things to be grateful about. Even when things don't turn out the way you hoped for them to. This will help you experience serenity rather than resentment.

PRINCIPLE TWO

A HIGHER POWER

There are only two ways to live your life.
One is as though nothing is a miracle.
The other is as though everything is a miracle.
Albert Einstein

Once a man boarded a flight, and the flight attendant said to him, "Welcome aboard. Please kindly take your seat, we guarantee take off."

The man replied, "What about landing, madam?"

She said, "You have to pray to God for a safe landing."

We all know that when we board a flight, even the takeoff is beyond us. It isn't in our hands. It is in the hands of the pilot. Likewise, with landing, even that is beyond our control. It is in the hands of the pilot. Have you ever experienced a flight that had been so smooth, you did not even realise when the aircraft had landed? How relieved did you feel despite knowing that the landing was beyond your control? How can we forget about the turbulence during the journey? That too was completely above our control. The speed of wind is beyond our control. When the aircraft flies through the clouds and shakes, that too is beyond our control. But, what is in our control during the journey is our choice. Some people doze off for the entire journey, while others eat and drink happily. Some watch movies, make friends, and build relationships. What you do during the journey is totally up to you.

This applies to us in the journey of life as well. The takeoff is the day we were born, that is completely out of our control. We didn't choose our parents. We didn't choose the country we were born in. We didn't choose our skin colour, height, socio-economic class, nor the genes that were passed down to us. Many people say they wish to leave this world quickly, such as through the likes of a heart attack or dropping dead. This way there is no trouble for them, no need to lie in the hospital suffering, have drips attached to them, and no trouble caused to others around them. No matter how much we may wish for that, it is beyond our control. How we will go, the landing of this journey, is beyond us too.

What about the turbulence, disturbances, and the problems during this journey of life? Some of them are within our control—solvable. But most problems, issues, and turbulences that we face are above us. They are caused by situations that are mightier than the power we hold. They are caused by individuals who are beyond us. In this journey of life, the takeoff, the landing, and the turbulence in between are not in our control. But what is in our control is the choices that we can make. It is about learning how to make those right choices in our journey. When we learn to make those right choices, we learn to live a transformed, happy, and fulfilled life, *The Keshav Way*, despite any hurdles. Wherever you happen to stand on this issue, I would just like to say that the process will be a lot easier if you keep an open mind about the idea of a higher power in control.

THE STORY OF NEWTON

Most of the time, we take things around us for granted. With our glasses of ego, we think it was all meant for us, but we never think to wonder who made it for us. To live The Keshav Way, you must accept a certain level of spirituality in your life. You have to surrender to a higher power. Again, for the acceptance and ease of addressing this truth, I will use the word 'Keshav' to describe the higher power. Faith gives us the strength and power to develop a positive mindset and face the challenges of life.

"It is our faith in God which provides the greatest strength of society."
Swami Vivekananda

Faith requires great moral strength; an invisible force that we have to tap into and experience. Some say faith is for the fainthearted and that it is a sign giving up. In fact, they are correct. We *are* 'giving up' to a higher power. We are 'giving up' to Keshav. Keshav is something much more than what we can see with our eyes. It is invisible. Surrendering to Keshav isn't giving up, it is a form of connecting to something much greater than us.

When we give tests in our first year of school and then in our tenth year, the exams are different. Why is that? It is because if we want to progress, we need to make sure we are eligible for the next academic year. As we grow, our exams will only get tougher. Similarly, the problems of our life will not necessarily get easier as the years go on. Instead, we will have the knowledge and mindset to pass through every problem that this tough world throws at us.

Don't think for a second that you control everything in your life. To a certain degree you do, but, Keshav controls your life more. We need to tap into that Keshav to understand true bliss. After a long and tiresome day, when we head to bed, we don't always fall asleep immediately. But when we do, we struggle to wake up. If a thief broke into your home in the middle of the night and you were sound asleep, would you know? I know of so many people that have literally woke up to their house broken into, and their wardrobes trashed. When there are times where we cannot even control the state of our own body, how can we expect to control that which surrounds us? This doesn't mean we should just sit back and do nothing. Draw a very fine line between believing in a higher power and your own hard work. We still need to put our own efforts into the likes of our studies, our career, our businesses and our relationships.

Isaac Newton, the original apple man, had a friend who did not believe in any higher power. One day, this friend visited Newton, who was just completing his model solar system machine. When his friend saw this machine, he started cranking the handle, and the planets moved around. He asked in amazement, "Who made this?"

Newton said, "Nobody did!" Then carried on with his work.

The friend confused, thinking Newton didn't hear him, said, "Did you hear me, Isaac? Who made the machine?"

Newton replied, "I told you. Nobody made it."

"Okay, now listen Isaac. Someone has made this marvellous machine. Don't keep saying nobody made it. That's just impossible!"

Newton stopped his writing, put his pen down and got up. He looked at his friend and then spoke, "Isn't it amazing? When I tell you that nobody made a simple toy like this, you don't believe me. Yet, you gaze out into the solar system, the real intricate marvellous machine that is around you, and you dare say to me that no one made that? I don't believe it!"

His friend quickly understood how foolish he had been, trying to be logical against a scientist of this calibre. He realised that there had to be a some sort of Master Designer or Creator of everything. A Higher Power. Regardless of our beliefs and thinking, let's just call him God.

There is only one God. Everything that exists, or did exist, sources from him. He is known by many names, in many languages, in many different parts of the world. The Riga Veda (the oldest volume of the Vedas) echoes this by saying, "The truth is one, but the wise call it by different names."[32]

Like Newton saw, when we look around at the wonders and precision of the universe, or even this world alone, it is natural to wonder who created it and why. When we see majestic mountains, flowing rivers, the DNA of organisms, we begin to realise that there is surely a divine intelligence behind this creation. In Vedic belief this supreme entity is known as *Parabrahman* (the supreme being) or *Paramātmā* (the supreme soul). The Bhagavad Gītā says, "Those who conquer the mind realise *Paramātmā*. To one who realises *Paramātmā*, joy and sorrow, heat and cold, honour and dishonour—all are the same."[33]

---

[32] Riga Veda 1.164.46
[33] Bhagavad Gita 6.7

PRINCIPLE THREE

KESHAV RESIDES

The desire to know your own soul
will end all other desires.
Rumi

This is a principle close to my heart, and everyone is entitled to their own belief, but, it is a very detailed concept which will take time and faith to understand, should you choose to do so. It details a deep spiritual concept of the Self being distinct from the body and more inclined with the soul—the *ātmā*, an eternal entity as described by a number of world religions and belief systems.

For me, this is the most important principle, taught by my gurus, and one which I wish to share with you all. My prayers that I will have succeeded in helping you understand this principle as you continue to read through this section. Hear me out. You are lucky. You are important. Your existence matters. Every human life is important.

For thousands of years, lions lived in caves. Today, they continue to live in the caves. They haven't progressed much. A thousand years ago, birds made nests and lived amongst trees. Today, it is the same for them. It is us humans that have progressed so drastically. From the time cavemen used to hit themselves in the head (I don't think this is true, but let's say it is for arguments sake) and made their own tools whilst repeating 'Ugg' in their terminology, and take a look at us today! We live in top-end, high-tech, luxurious homes.

Hundreds of years ago, cheetahs ran at the average speed of 93 km/hr and today, they run at the same average speed. Humans used to run at the speed of 32 km/hr and today, we can travel at the speed of sound, and even beyond that. It is the power of thoughts, and personifying our thoughts, that differentiates us from any other form of life. We do not understand the rarity of the life and so, here we are, taking it for granted. I am not trying to make you feel bad about yourself, but most of us are not even sure why we are born, and what we should really aim to achieve before we leave this world. The sad thing is, we have become so engrossed in tiresome routines that we often forget to 'live', to do what we are supposed to do as a human being. This is our life: we are born; we go to school; we get a degree; we work; we get married; we travel to a few countries—get some momentary happiness; have some kids, retire and die. But, is that all that there is to life?

I hope you are not one of those who waste away and spoil their precious life with addictions of smoking, drinking and drugs; ignoring the beautiful life that you have been given in the form of your body. It is sad to see, especially when some go to the extent of complete conformity, and end up taking their own lives. The waves of problems and miseries in life drown some people, leading them to decide that life is no longer worth living. More people die from suicide than any form of fight, terrorism and accidents globally. From the time you started reading this paragraph, at least one or two people have taken their lives. One person, every forty seconds. We won't discuss this in detail, as it is addressed in Principle Five. But, before anyone thinks about giving up their lives, or getting addicted to vices, let's talk about why we struggle to find a reason for meaning. Why do we struggle to find purpose in life? Some of you reading this will have a purpose, and that is great! We all must discover our own purpose.

As per Alexander's example, life is not merely about getting a better job, creating a vast business, getting a pay rise at work, marrying a beautiful person and definitely not to live forever. If we can put all of this aside, then what is the aim of our life? There is one important purpose of our human life, which is the basis for me writing this book. Pramukh Swami taught that the purpose of our life is to elevate our *ātmā*—to liberate it from the cycle of birth and death—this is only achievable by humans who can think intelligently and rationally. To each and every one of us this will mean something different. Let me throw something at you. See how you take this example.

Take any animal. It could be a dog, a horse, a lion, anything. Most animals live for three primary purposes; they build homes, get food and reproduce. The funny thing is that even though they don't have any form of education, career, a bank account, or significant knowledge behind procreation, they still do a better job than us. If we spend our lives just to attain the above three fulfillments, what makes us any different than these animals? Perhaps you could argue that the difference is in the size of our homes, or the quality of food. But in the eyes of nature, what can be measured as greater? The power of thought helps us to understand life and the soul. If we chase after other goals, like Alexander, we will never be satisfied. Humans have the power to think ahead and work towards their ambitions.

- We used to wear leaves to protect our bodies, today we wear top quality clothes made from various materials.
- We used to eat food raw, today we eat cooked cuisines.
- We used to live in caves today we live in smart homes.
- We used to cross small rivers by swimming, today we cruise across the oceans using ships.

This list could go on, but the most important thing is that the ideas and thoughts that we humans get, can easily be converted into reality. No other being on this Earth has the intelligence to do this. We are the only ones able to discuss and contemplate on life and what is beyond death. Humans spend time introspecting, questioning, debating, and deeply contemplating on their actions. Animals never question why they do what they do, they simply act and react.

Animals sing. So do we, but we make it into music.
Animals breed. So do we, but we make it into love.
Animals kill. So do we, but we try to feel remorse.

The Soul

There are over 7 billion people on this planet, and around 115 billion people that have ever lived in the history of the world. That means that a 108 billion people are already dead. They've lived their lives and passed away. Put simply, fourteen out of every fifteen people who have *ever lived* will never see another sunset again, never finish that Netflix series, or kiss their kids good night. Fourteen out of every fifteen people will never drive to work again, never go on a holiday again, never cuddle their partner again, and never cut another birthday back again. You are the lucky one in fifteen.

A Vedic text called the Padma Purana states that there are 8.4 million forms of life in the world. These include aquatics, plants, insects, reptiles, birds, animals, and of course, human beings. It is believed that after going through this cycle, we have now attained the human birth. Mahant Swami emphasises this in Satsang Dikshā, "Rare and perishable, this body is not repeatedly attained."[34] Humans have the ability to reason, allowing them to question their place in the universe and seek something greater than themselves. We have the opportunity to transcend *samsāra*. Only us, humans.

Samsāra is Sanskrit for 'wandering', or, 'world'. Put simply, it refers to the repeated cycle of birth and death, and is compared to a constantly revolving wheel. The *ātmā* is trapped in this cycle due to the attachments it harbours, but it can rise above it too. This is a fundamental part in the belief of karma and reincarnation. The *ātmā* is eternal, it never dies.

Whilst we talk about how lucky we are, let's also touch upon financial comfort, because we all really do want to hear it. In fact, if you are holding this book, you are probably amongst the richest people in the whole world. Let me tell you how. The average global income is five thousand dollars. If you earn more than that, you are already in the top 50 percent. If you earn more than fifty thousand dollars, you are in the top 0.5 percent. You have it good. You already have more than almost anybody else on the planet. You sitting here, reading this today, is in itself a miracle. Waking up everyday is a miracle that we should be truly grateful for.

The solution to most of our life's problems lies in the belief that we are the *ātmā*. When you realise yourself to be the *ātmā* and not the body, it gives you relief from the troubles of physical illnesses, financial issues, and relationship issues. We know that one day this body will vanish, it will be nothing but dust. Yet, we attach ourselves with people, objects, and places so often that we're left with no choice but to experience misery.

---

[34] Satsang Diksha 2

The science of the soul helps give a broader perspective to life and all surroundings. An experiment performed in 1979 by neuroscientists Benjamin Libet and Bertram Feinstein unearthed impressive and pretty compelling evidence for the independent existence of the soul. Measurements of the time taken for patients to react to an electrical stimulus given at various points on their skin, nerves and brain (using electrodes) have shown that their consciousness of the stimulus is actually delayed between 1 to 1.5 seconds after the stimulus has been registered in their brain. One of the clear implications of this phenomenon, pointed out by Professor Roger Penrose, of the University of Oxford, in his bestselling book, *Emperor's New Mind*, is that our consciousness is some sort of independent spectator residing within the human body, witnessing a type of 'action replay' of everything. *Problems are mandatory, to suffer is optional.*

There was once a senior monk whose wisdom revealed itself at every moment and situation that occurred in his life. One day, some of his disciples saw that their teacher was bleeding from his small finger. The disciples ran around to find some aid and get a bandage. On seeing their teacher suffer, several disciples felt uneasy and posed a question to him, "Why don't you let us know that you are hurt?"

The monk replied, "My body felt the pain, but I didn't! I was more engrossed and focussed on my soul whilst preaching to you all. Not just now, this state remains always and thus, suffering becomes optional!"

One disciple asked, "But you should at least take care of your own body too, right?"

The monk said, "When we take care of the body, that's when we suffer! It's God who takes care of us, and he likes us to live believing ourselves to be the *ātmā*. So don't you think he will take care of us? He took care of me, in the form of you all!"

The entity of the *ātmā* is hard to understand by logic alone. You need faith. Logic and faith are not opposing thoughts, they are two sides of the same coin. Behind logic there is faith, and behind faith, there is logic. To begin to understand the *ātmā*, we first need to know what our body is made up of.

* * *

Three Bodies: The Vedic Belief

The *ātmā* is distinct from the three types of bodies.

1. **Physical (Gross) Body:**
    It is visible. It is what others see. It is what we see in the mirror every morning. It is composed of the five basic elements: earth, water, light, air and space. According to Vedic philosophy, the *ātmā* attains a different physical body at each birth. This is made up of mechanical materials such as blood, flesh, bones, veins, and proteins.

2. **Subtle Body:**
    It is invisible, unlike the physical body. It is made up of nineteen elements. Namely, the five sense organs, the five-action senses, the five vital airs, and the four inner abilities. We will look at the four inner abilities, and how they function shortly, but before then, let's experience our subtle body.
    After reading this line, close your eyes and imagine the moon for a second. You should be able to see at least a rough image of the moon in your head. But your eyes were closed, right? Surely we should only see when light waves enter the retina of the eyes? That's your subtle body at work there.
    Let's try another. Say your name in your head. Done? You said it and probably heard it too. You spoke your name without using your mouth, and you heard your name without using your ears. That is the work of the subtle body. This proves that apart from just our physical five sense organs, we can do more inside, using the subtle body. I'm a computer scientist, so I would put it this way—the physical body is our hardware, and the subtle body is the software.

3.   **Fundamental (Causal) Body:**
The fundamental body holds all the *ātmā's* desires and is the reason for attachment. It is what causes the *ātmā* to take constant rebirths. The fundamental body itself is the attachment that has been fused with the *ātmā*. It retains the karma done and is also is the root cause of the physical and subtle bodies; just as a seed is the root cause of a tree.
The fundamental body is the engineer who creates the hardware and develops the software.

The ātmā is distinct from the 'three mental states':
1. Awaken State: When we are awake, the *ātmā* is there.
2. Sleeping State: When we are asleep, the *ātmā* is there.
3. Unconscious State: When unconscious, the *ātmā* is there.

The ātmā is distinct from the 'five sense organs':
1. Eyes: To see. Behind our actual eyes, the *ātmā* watches.
2. Nose: To smell. Who smells scents and stores them in our memory? We instantly know what an orange smells, or what the trash smells like without having to think about it.
3. Ears: To hear. But who hears? If you placed some earphones into the ears of a dead body, and played their favourite music, would they hear it?
4. Tongue: To taste. The tongue is made up of muscles and has taste buds. I don't think I need to give an example here.
5. Skin: To sense touch. To feel hot and cold. Let's take a simple example. We all have touchscreen phones. When the phone is off, powered down with no software working, does the touchscreen functionality work? No, it just remains as a blank device. In the same way, our *ātmā* activates the sense of touch.

The ātmā is distinct from the 'four inner abilities':

1. Mind *(manas)*
2. Intelligence *(buddhi)*
3. Consciousness *(chitta)*
4. Ego *(ahamkāra)*

Suppose that you are watching a series on TV one evening, and in between, during the adverts, a movie trailer comes on. The **mind** generates a thought, 'I want to see this movie'. **Intelligence** helps the mind decide if you should watch the movie. It helps to analyse and weigh out the pros and cons of the thought. Then, based on the data provided by the intelligence, the mind makes a decision.

If the mind decides 'yes', intelligence once again takes over to find a cinema, timings and then finally buy the tickets. Once the entire plan has been set out by the mind and intelligence, it brings the **consciousness** to the forefront, to experience and accomplish the goal. Now imagine, when you are just about to head out for the movie, your family tells you they have made plans and want you to stay home? That's when the sleeping ego wakes and takes reign. You would become angry at your loved ones. Why? Because the plan to watch the movie was set by your mind, intelligence and consciousness, and now a disturbance has been caused. This is an example of how the four inner abilities carry out their work continuously.

But again, your soul remains distinct from these four inner abilities. The soul is ultimately eternal and imperishable. The body is the Tesla, the passenger changes vehicles from time to time. Just as we wear fresh clothes every day, similarly, the soul leaves behind this body at the time of death, and takes up a new one. This is the Vedic concept of reincarnation, also known as *punarjanma*.

The concept of soul realisation isn't easy to grasp. But, when we try to live by this concept (as detailed in the later parts of this book), it helps with many problems in life such as physical illnesses, controlling your ego and greed, differentiating between individuals, success or failure, and the likes of it.

The Body Meeting

Once, all the body parts had gathered for a meeting. The brain chaired it. The petition was to discuss who played the most important role for the body. The nose said, "If I wasn't present, how would the body be able to smell and breathe?"

The mouth interrupted and said, "Wait, sometimes I play the role for breathing, don't I? It's not you that is important. I am important."

The brain said it was important too, for it did all the thinking and decision-making. The heart gave its opinion, "Nope, even if you were all not there, the body would still live and be alive. But if I am not there, the body would perish and die."

The intelligent brain who had chaired the meeting took the opportunity, "Hold on! There are many artificial hearts available to keep the body going. Don't big yourself up unnecessarily."

The hands and legs sat silently. No conclusive solution was reached, so they all approached God for an answer. They went to God and asked, "You tell us, who is the most important for the body."

God listened to each one of their arguments with patience. He laughed and said, "A body can survive without you all, in fact, the most important role is not played by any of you; it's played by the *ātmā*. It's what keeps you all going. The day that the *ātmā* leaves, all of you become useless, even if you are carrying out your work properly. Without the *ātmā*, what are you all? In fact, the *ātmā* is so great that it didn't even turn up to your meeting. It is continuing to do its work behind the scenes, without wanting any praise, or without wanting to be in the forefront. That is its greatness."

When the body parts heard this from God, they were all convinced, except for the eyes and the brain. They questioned, "God, if it is the most important, then why can we not see it?"

God smirked and said, "You cannot see it because it is the *ātmā* who sees everything, not you. When a person dies, if you hold their eyelids open and hold them up in front of the mirror, will they see themselves?"

The eyes and brain both replied, "No, because there is no *ātmā*."

God smiled, and in that smile, they too were convinced that the *ātmā* is the one who truly keeps the body going.

SUMMARISING THE SOUL

The soul cannot be measured by any instrument, but science has spoken about it. I would like to touch upon the work of Dr. Ian Stevenson, a Canadian psychiatrist who spent his entire life studying deaths and rebirths. He found some interesting data that appears to provide scientific proof that reincarnation (or rebirth) is a reality. He didn't just get it out of thin air, or just one simple case. He collected and studied thousands of cases of children who spontaneously, without any previous hypnosis, recall their past lives quite vividly. He used this approach because in a young child, whose mind is still developing, the memories can be investigated using strict scientific protocols. He could have easily used hypnosis, but, as useful as it is in researching into past lives, it is much less reliable as you would assume from a scientific perspective. He had over 3000 documented cases in his files. Many scholars and sceptics have agreed that these cases offer the best scientific evidence for reincarnation till date.

I will not detail any of the cases or stories in this book, but I will leave this to you if you wish to look into it. However, the message I do wish to get through this book is that we really are the *ātmā* which never dies. It is actually the *ātmā* that is, in its natural state, the source of all joy and peace, and through it, we are all enjoying the temporary happiness we experience in life.

If we really tap into the full potential of the *ātmā* (the Keshav within), we can develop and experience true *ānanda*. Life will always have difficulties, but it is how you handle yourself in these situations that brings you a sense of happiness and peace.

This is the principle behind the Keshav in you. Within that *ātmā*, the higher power resides. We do not know what the *ātmā* exactly comprises of, but it is surely divine. And so let's say that in each and every *ātmā*, Keshav resides. The *ātmā* has no good or bad, it has no yours or mine; it has no false ego, no attachments, no jealousy, nothing. That is all attached to the body, whereas the *ātmā* is pure. In essence, each and every one of us is pure. You are not the body you inhabit. You are not the mind. You live in the body and in the mind. You are the eternal *ātmā*.

PRINCIPLE FOUR
KESHAV IN OTHERS

Who sees all beings in his own Self,
and his own Self in all beings, loses all fear.
When a sage sees this great Unity and his Self has become all beings,
what delusion and what sorrow can ever be near him?
Isha Upanishad 6-7

Just as Keshav resides in your soul, he resides in others too. If you understand this principle, the world truly becomes a beautiful and amazing place to live in. If we keep this thought constantly in our minds, how can we get mad at another person? How can we hurt someone with our words? Simple, when you wrong others, you are wronging Keshav. This thought is to be applied for yourself only. Don't put it on others. If someone insults us, or hurts us, it is not the person trying to wrong us; it is the higher power testing us, to make us better. Always take a positive perspective on this. If you want to continue to take things negatively and play the victim, I'm sorry to say, but, you may as well put this book down now.

STONE AND SAND

Two friends, Tom and Harry, were walking along the shore of a beach, talking about their own lives with one another. Suddenly, the talk got heated and turned into a fight. Tom slapped Harry, yet Harry said nothing, nor did he retaliate. Instead, he kneeled down and using his finger he wrote into the sand, "Today, my friend Tom, hurt me."

They let it go, kept the conversation to a minimum, and continued their journey. When they saw pristine blue water of the ocean, they both decided to take a dip in the waters. Harry didn't know how to tread deep water and so he struggled to stay afloat. Seeing this, Tom rushed in and saved him. After getting safely to the shore, Harry picked up a stone and engraved in it, "Today, my friend Tom, saved me."

Tom was really confused, and he asked Harry, "When I slapped you, you wrote into the sand, but when I saved you, you wrote onto a stone, why?"

Harry replied, "When someone hurts you, consider it a lesson from God; he wants you to learn something and write it into the sand. This way, the winds of forgiveness can erase it; but when someone does good to you, engrave it onto stone, so that way it stays forever, and the message of positiveness from a form of God remains in you."

Situations can arise where you begin to see people in a negative light, through certain incidents or behaviours, even with those closest to us. At that time, taking a step back and affirming that the higher power resides in that person too, accepting them for who they are, is the answer. No one is perfect, so who are we to judge anyone?

When a robot is made, there are several electrical motors, hydraulic systems, and microprocessors that are used, all which enable the movement of just one arm. The robot needs to be recharged for it to work for a few days. It requires an original source of energy. See it this way: we, too are 'robots' made up of flesh, bones, and blood. How do we move our arms with no motors fixed at our shoulders? How do we move our head up or down, left or right, with no type of hydraulic system used? The energy that is taken in by us in the form of food is digested. So then, how does it reach the parts of our body to control movements? It is all due to the *ātmā*, and in that *ātmā* forever resides *paramātma* (the supreme soul), which transfers the energy, and maintains coordination within the entire body.

CREATION OF EMOTION

I pose a question to you. We know that the kidney purifies the blood; the heart pumps the blood; the lungs aid us in breathing; and the digestive system digests the food. Every part of our body is there for a purpose, to keep us going. But which physical part of our body creates emotion? What makes us independent of our emotions? The truth is, nothing drives our emotions—not one physical part of our body. We ourselves *create* them. Let's take love for example, we can all *feel* love, but we do not see it. Similarly, it isn't always that we need to *see* in order to believe. The ultimate source of all forms of energy is the higher power, Keshav, who resides in all of us equally; in our parents, partner, siblings, children, friends, our manager and co-workers, animals, everyone.

Imagine that you work for a company. In this company, you are just an ordinary, everyday employee, working a standard nine-to-five job. In all seriousness, only you know how much effort you are, or aren't, putting in daily. One day, you get the thought that you should be paid based only on the actual efforts that you are putting into your work. So one day, you approach your manager and say, "Hey, when you are not observing my work for the full time I am here, how can you determine if I am working well? Surely, that means I don't deserve to paid so much." To be honest, none of us will have the guts to say this, but it is just another scenario, so go along with it.

Your manager agrees and replies, "That is true, but I look at the results and that is how I come to know if you have worked well or not."

On the following day, your manager comes and sits next to you, to watch you closely. He makes note of the time you have come into the office, the number of breaks you take, the time you 'waste'. The manager comes to realise something: since he has to see all appraisal, promotion or demotion, he would need to sit next to all his employees, all the time. This is impossible, but only then logically and ideally, could he judge his employees fairly, 100 percent of the time. Though, there could be loopholes for sure, and many employees would take advantage of this. The only way he can monitor all the employees would be to multiply himself to the same number of employees working under him. Now, this is impossible for your manager, but it would be the only accurate way to judge people, right?

Although it is impossible for your manager, it isn't for the higher power. The higher power independently decides to reside within each and every one of us, to keep seeing us and our actions—always. You will ask, why? What is the point? Well, for the same reason as your manager. To give every person what they deserve. You may know of it as the law of karma. When someone does harm to others, the bad comes to that person, maybe not today, maybe in ten years; but one day it surely will. Likewise, if you do good, it is only returned to you. If not today, then one day for sure. This is an eternal law of life, and the fourth principle of Keshav residing in one and all.

PRINCIPLE FIVE

INNER FULFILMENT

Be content with what you have;
Rejoice in the way things are.
When you realise there is nothing lacking;
The whole world belongs to you.
Lao Tzu

I will say something which you probably won't like. At first, I didn't like to tell myself this either, and it isn't a principle that can be mastered straight away, but it is possible. The more I contemplated, and heard about it from my gurus, I came to realise that it has its merits. They not only live by it, but also prove it to be true. It is that, to remain truly fulfilled means having no desires, no expectations and no attachments. We will call this notion 'Zero'. Sounds hard, right?

Desires, expectations, our internal enemies like ego, greed, jealousy, lust, and anger—as well as the attachments towards worldly objects—are the root cause of misery. When we have none of these, only then can we remain fulfilled in the genuine sense. Although, this has to go hand-in-hand with the belief that there is an all-doer—a higher power. But how is it possible to practice Zero? We live in a world surrounded by such things that bind us—work, family, and other mounting responsibilities—and isn't that the way of life? In understanding this, we draw a fine line: desire, but do not get compelled; expect, but be ready for the unexpected; attach, but do not be bound. We all need to reaffirm in our minds, "I have already achieved everything that I need to."

When we are all going to face the same fate as Alexander and leave everything behind when we die, why do we become unhappy if we do not get what we want? What if you earned £10,000 a month? The average body only needs about 1.8kg of food in a day. If you are getting food twice a day, clean water, and you have a roof over your head, then technically, you are already fulfilled.

Let me give you another example that may seem weird. It works. I've tried it and maybe you should too. Say that you want to buy a Ferrari, but you don't have the money to afford it, and you don't think you will ever have the financial capacity to get one. Then whenever you see a Ferrari on the road, imagine it as yours. Imagine you've just handed the keys to someone to drive it. Actually, every one of your favourite cars out there is owned by you. Others are just driving them. Be happy for them. It works. You will feel content and a sense of fulfilment. Apply this logic to any desire, and with time you will see how you can overcome your mind. In the end, remember, the passenger is in control. Keshav is in control.

DESIRES, EXPECTATIONS & ATTACHMENTS

We all have desires. Maybe the desire to get with someone, to see or taste something, or to make lots of money. As we have already seen, desires never end. Try to think of a few things you desire and note them on the back pages.

Similarly, we all have expectations, even from our partner, children, or family. Expectations from parents to give us what we want, maybe some nice food on our plates? From friends to support us in our times of need, or when we reach out to them. Expectations from our sons and daughters to do their best, and tread a righteous path. Or even from your company, to one day give you a pay raise or promotion. Again, expectations too are never ending. Note yours.

There is a very thin line that we need to draw for this understanding. We must play our role within our families, society, and in all our relationships. But, we shouldn't be blindly attaching ourselves to someone as though we can't live without them. This applies to every person and object. We came alone into this world and will go alone as well. Be constantly aware of this fact. You must be able to rely on yourself, not merely on others. Make a note of the things you are attached to.

Reality check: if all these were really the source of happiness, then why is it that the people who have these things in their lives, sometimes resort to taking their own lives?

THE SAD TRUTH

In earlier principles, we have highlighted the sad truth of suicide. It is astonishing to see that most suicide cases are of the educated and higher class in society. Those that have everything, are the ones who think life is no longer good enough to live. So, does happiness really lie in gaining more wealth?

On 17 November 2010, Paul Castle—a self-styled businessman and property developer, who owned a private plane, several Ferrari and Bentley cars, and his own properties in Switzerland, France, London and Berkshire—threw himself in front of a London underground train, at the Bond Street tube station. The reason? Castle had several property deals fail over the last year of his life; he had also lost capital in a gas and oil surveying company. He also suffered from a chronic heart condition and tumours. He was married three times and was due to be married for the fourth time to his girlfriend, Natalie Theo. What was he lacking?

Peter Smedley was an English millionaire, hotelier and businessman in Australia, who owned a tinned food empire that provided him with a huge income. He and his wife Christine had been married for 33 years and enjoyed a luxurious lifestyle. Sadly, he was also suffering from motor neurone disease. He ended his life through assisted suicide, from the Dignitas clinic in Switzerland. What was interesting though, is that the BBC filmed his death, with segments televised as part of a documentary about assisted suicides. Then, what use is wealth if we aren't physically able to make use of it?

A study showing reasons behind why successful people are ending their lives states, "Under more pressure than ordinary people, patients suffer from a range of mental disorders." In the nicest way I might put this, be grateful that you are an ordinary person, and be content as you are. It is for the best that we are simple, and that we stay this way. But it isn't just about successful people. It is also the successful countries, the developed countries, that have heightened reports of suicide cases.

EPIDEMIOLOGY OF SUICIDE

0.5 percent to 1.5 percent of all people die by suicide. In 2009, suicide was the eighth global leading cause of death for those between the age of 15 and 44. Today it stands as the third leading cause. Rates of suicide increased by over 60 percent from the 1960s to 2012, with the highest increase seen primarily in the developing world. For every one completed suicide, there are 20 attempted. Suicide rates differ significantly between countries and over time. In the USA, over 40,000 people die by suicide every year.

WHO (World Health Organisation) figures show that a suicide takes place, somewhere in the world, roughly every 40 seconds. Another report states that nearly a million people take their own lives every year. That is more than those murdered or killed in war.

In the United States, it is greatest in men above the age of 80 years of age, even though younger people attempt suicide more frequently. What is more alarming is that, on average, 80 percent of suicide victims are literate. In another global study, sociologist Phil Zuckerman noted that countries with higher levels of atheism had the highest rates of suicide.

In Peru, Guatemala, the Philippines and Albania— all developing countries suffering from poverty and political instability—about one in every 100,000 people commits suicide each year. In rich and peaceful countries such as Switzerland, France, Japan and New Zealand, twenty-five people per 100,000 take their own lives annually. In 1985 most South Koreans were poor, uneducated and tradition-bound, living under an authoritarian dictatorship. Today, South Korea is a leading economic power, its citizens are among the best educated in the world, and it enjoys a stable and comparatively liberal democratic regime. Yet, in 1985, about nine South Koreans per 100,000 killed themselves, whereas today the annual rate of suicide has more than tripled to thirty per 100,000. Now think, if the fulfilment of all needs, wants, desires, and attachments are leading people to end their lives, why are we also running behind these same things?

THE CROW & THE PEACOCK

There once lived a crow in a forest, who was absolutely satisfied in life. One day he met a swan, and upon seeing it he said, "Look at how dark I am. You must be the happiest bird in the world."

"Actually," replied the swan, "I too felt that I was the happiest bird in the world. That was until I saw the parrot. He has two colours, and now I think the parrot is the happiest and luckiest bird."

The crow approached the parrot who explained, "I lived a merry life until I saw the peacock. I only have two colours, but the peacock has an array of colours."

The crow visited the peacock in a zoo, and it saw how hundreds had gathered to see the peacock. Once the people left, the crow approached the peacock and said, "You are so beautiful! Every day, thousands come to see you. Look at me! When people see me, they shoo me away. You are the luckiest bird in this world."

The peacock replied, "I always thought I was the most beautiful and happiest bird on the planet. But, because of my beauty, I am trapped in this zoo. I examined the zoo carefully, and I realised that the crow is the only bird not kept in a cage. So now I wish that if I were a crow, at least I could happily roam anywhere and everywhere."

We face this same problem. We make useless comparisons with others. We don't value what the higher power has given us, and so the vicious cycle of unhappiness continues in our life. If we value and appreciate the things we have been given, we begin discarding the comparisons that lead us down the road of pain and unhappiness.

Socrates believed that the wise person would instinctively lead a frugal life. He himself didn't wear shoes, yet, he constantly fell under the spell of the marketplace and would go there often to look at all the shoes on display. When one of his friends asked why he did this, Socrates said, "I love to go there and discover how many things I am living perfectly fine without!"

A king had great fascination and love for paintings. Once, he offered a chest of gold to whichever artist in the kingdom could paint a beautiful picture depicting peace. On the ultimate day of judgements, many painters brought their work, hoping to win the gold. The king observed all the paintings, selecting two in particular. Now, he had to choose one. The first painting was of a beautiful, calm lake with clear, transparent waters. The lake mirrored the towering mountains surrounding it. Above the lake was the bright blue sky with white, fluffy clouds. Everybody who saw this painting thought it was the masterpiece depicting peace. The second painting had mountains too, but they were rugged, bare, and dry. Above the mountains was an angry sky, overcast with gloomy clouds, lightening here and there, a huge downpour of rain, a rumbling, ferocious waterfall cascaded down the side of one mountain. As the king observed closer, he saw behind the rumbling waterfall, a branch of a bush was growing out of a crack from the face of the mountain. On the branch was a female bird who had made a nest in which it peacefully, and with great affection, was feeding its little ones. The king instantly chose the second painting. He explained, "Peace doesn't mean to be in a place where there is no noise, trouble, struggles, hard work, or difficulties. Peace means to be in the middle of all the mayhem and chaos, and yet, stay calm and focussed."

This principle helps to maintain stability within our lives. The Keshav Way is the art of bringing us to that same inner calm and peace, in our actual life with all the different difficulties, troubles, and problems surrounding us. That is the true definition of peace.

LIVING LONG

In the Okinawa islands of Japan (no, it's not a fairy tale), people live on average of seven years longer than Americans. They also have the longest disability-free lives on Earth. In Ancient China, the island was known as 'the land of the immortals'. More people over the age of a hundred years live there, compared to anywhere else in the world. Researchers from *National Geographic* studied the Okinawans to discover what enabled them to live long lives. They found that they eat from smaller plates, and they stop eating when they feel 80 percent full. They also have a social setup where they are put into groups from when they are babies, so that they can slowly grow old together.

The most astonishing difference from the West, that gives them prolonged life, is that they have no concept of retirement. No one retires. In fact, they have no word for retirement! Instead, they use the word *ikigai,* which translates to 'reason for being'. Think of it as what drives you the most. Researchers from the Tohoku University Graduate School of Medicine put ikigai to the test. Spending seven years in Sendai, Japan, they studied the longevity of over forty thousand Japanese adults, taking into account age, gender, education, BMI, smoking and alcohol habits, exercise, employment, perceived stress, medical history, and even self-rated health scores. What did they do? They asked every individual one question: "What is your ikigai?"

Participants reporting an ikigai at the start of the study were more likely to be married, educated, and employed. They had higher levels of self-rated health and lower levels of stress overall. But what happened after seven years? 95 percent of those who had an ikigai were alive. Want to find your ikigai? Scan below.

THE TRUTH ABOUT RETIREMENT

Retirement is a fairly new concept invented by the Germans in 1889. It was created to free up jobs for the younger generation, by paying those aged sixty-five and over, to do nothing until the day they died. But there is one major difference between 1889 Germany and 2020 World. The average life span back then was sixty-seven years old.

Otto von Bismarck, chancellor of Germany in 1889, said, "Those who are disabled from work by age and invalidity have a well-grounded claim to care from the state." It was easy to say back then, given that retirement age and average life span were only a couple of years apart. Otto was the one who set the world standard for the retirement age at sixty-five. The only significance in 1889 was the fact that it had close proximity to the age that people died. But still, other developed countries followed in the footsteps of Germany. In his book, *Purpose and Power in Retirement*, Harold Koenig shows the percentage of men *over* the age of sixty-five working by year. There is a massive decrease between 1880 with 75 percent still working after sixty-five, and in the year 2000, where only 16 percent are working.

On 3 August, 1962, *Time* magazine featured a cover story on the rapid ageing of American people, who had lots of time and money but no place in society. The article talked about how Del Webb's Sun City and similar age-segregated housing developments focussing on leisure in Arizona and other places were transforming the image that American's had of retirement into a time of self-absorption, relaxation, and fun. The results were jaw-dropping. In 1951, among men receiving Social Security benefits, 3 percent retired from work to pursue leisure; in 1963, 17 percent indicated that leisure was the primary reason for retiring from work; and by 1982, almost 50 percent of men said they retired to pursue leisure. As many positive results there are for older people retiring, we cannot put off the fact that it has led many into self-absorption and prejudice, tensions with younger generations, boredom, depression, and lack of a sense that they were able to contribute to society and to the lives of others.

Retirement is broken. It is based on the assumptions that we enjoy doing nothing instead of being productive, that we can afford to live well, and pay others, while earning no money for decades to come.

James Watson, one of the discoverers of the DNA structure said: "Never retire. Your brain needs exercise or it will atrophy." So what can we do? I mean, the choice is up to you, do you want to retire or not? Maybe you could change your career to keep your synapses lit. I first-hand saw this idea in action in the life of Pramukh Swami, who continuously served till his last breath at the age of 94. In his footsteps, at the tender age of 87, Mahant Swami continues to travel across the world, inspiring and serving his followers. In the last hundred years, life expectancy for Americans has risen from 47 to 77. We are all living longer. With the cures for diseases like cancer, heart disease, and stroke around the corner, organ transplants and regeneration certain, it seems that the goal of the next century will be to prolong life.

Work gives you much more than you think. Work helps us live truly rich lives, and gives us a sense of purpose and contribution towards society. Keep learning, keep changing, and keep growing.

PART FOUR

KESHAV

THE KESHAV WAY

By now, it should be clear to you that happiness doesn't lie in changing your genetically determined set point, or by trying to alter your circumstances, which will only have a limited impact. Of course, you may achieve temporary boosts in well-being if you move somewhere else, get a promotion, or the like, but they won't last long. This again is all about adaptation; humans adapt quickly.

Happiness can be found in the way we behave, think, and set out to achieve in everyday life. There is no happiness without action, and this brings us to the next part of the book—understanding how this can be achieved using The Keshav Way. Through various habits and *ways*, we explore how we can build upon our *ānanda*. Happiness comes and goes, whereas *ānanda* is to be built upon. We aren't striving for happiness. Instead, we are actually looking for *ānanda;* the natural state of bliss, joy and contentment in everyday life. I am sure that there are many more *ways* that can be practiced to achieve this, but these are a stepping stone for us. Your character is formed by your habits. Habits are formed by discipline, or the lack of discipline. Discipline becomes habits, those habits then become our character.

We all have habits, both good and bad. The majority of us probably associate the word with annoying behaviours and tendencies like chewing fingernails, fiddling with our hair, and continuously interrupting conversations. How can we forget smoking and drinking too? So what really are habits? These behaviours are labelled *habitual* because they come about to us naturally; we don't need to decide to do them, they aren't intentional, they just happen. Habits form from repetition and practice. They are a redundant set of automatic thoughts, behaviours, and emotions, that are acquired through repetition.

Researchers believe that every time you repeat a behaviour, associations develop within your brain and memory, between the behaviours and the context in which they occur. They take time to form and endure, but the first step must be taken.

With the *ways* that are presented in this book, I would say that the best way to approach all of them is by using the 1 percent rule. This is shared by James Clear in his book *Atomic Habits*. He states that if you improve yourself by 1 percent everyday, then in a year you are 37.78 percent better. This again all depends on how exposed you are to unfamiliar situations and if you remember what you need to do. Slowly, it'll form part of your day-to-day life and you will notice these minor changes making a difference, to help you experience *ānanda* in your everyday life. Start small, but start somewhere. Have patience and faith in yourself, and with yourself. It is The Keshav Way, the keyword being 'way'. It isn't necessarily about the destination, it is about the journey.

The next part of the book breaks down my acronym "Keshav" into six key areas. Each area will discuss various thoughts, ideas, and of course, ways. And so, just to remind you:

K is Know Thyself.

E is Engagement.

S is Social Living.

H is Health & Well-being.

A is Ambition, Purpose & Meaning.

V is Voluntary Actions.

K

KNOW THYSELF

Have you ever asked yourself the question, "Who am I?" Charles Horton Clooney, the American sociologist that came up with the idea of the *Looking Glass Self* wrote: I am not what I think I am. I am not what you think I am. I am what I think you think I am.[35] Read that again. We mould our identity to what others think of us, or to be more accurate, what we believe others think of us. Our life has become a movie, and we are the actors. We play different roles online, at work, when we are with our friends, and at home with family. Throughout our lives, we switch between so many *acting roles* that we lose track of who we truly are. I don't blame you for this, nor should you blame yourself. You and I, have been brought up in a world where different images and voices have been telling us what we should *be*. Our parents, our relatives, our friends, teachers, society, and even the media. Everyone has been flooding us with ideas of what we should be and what we should do. I'm honestly glad that you're holding this book right now, because it is high time we filter out all that noise and truly start to *know thyself*.

WHO AM I?

It is unfortunate, but the truth, that the majority of us have lost sight of who we truly are, and what identifies us as *us*. If I asked you what your values were, how would you respond in the moment? We are all born in different countries, in different economic status, to look different, to speak different languages, but what defines us all as a collective is our values. These values are different for all of us, but they are defined by our experiences on this planet. For years, the monkey has been absorbing whatever it has been fed, and has shaped your values based on that. But we are not our minds, the monkey is the mind, and it has been choosing which route is 'best' for the passenger.

---

[35] Cooley (1992)

It has been deciding what is important and what is not. Numerous studies have shown that the way in which we expose ourselves, and absorb media, gossip, drama, celebrities, violent video games and shows, and troubling news affects our cognition and behaviour.[36] This has a direct impact on our values which are then showered with envy, jealousy, judgement, competition, and discontent.

The problem is that most of us don't spend time with ourselves to even think about what our values are in the first place. As Viktor Frankl put it, "We are all prisoners of our own thoughts." We are scared to be alone with our own thoughts. We are inclined to avoid silence, throwing information constantly at the monkey to keep it occupied, moving, and distracted.

The morning rituals had concluded, as swamis began to rush off to breakfast and their independent morning studies. Peacocks, perched on top of the domes and pinnacles of the mandir, looked up at the glorified sun. I swiftly made my way to the the gardens of the monastery, to meet the fellow swami I spoke to earlier. As I was making my way to the gardens, I saw and then began to think, how that despite hundreds of training swamis living together, having a packed and tiring schedule, they all seemed at peace and relaxed. I came to know that they make a proactive decision to limit their exposure to external influences. They even avoid obsessing over how they look; I mean, they practically shave their heads and carry two sets of clothes. They have a simple, staple diet. They sleep on thin mats on the floor, sometimes with none, and they take part in prolonged periods of meditations, rituals, and studies. Of course, they are not oblivious to the events of the world, as they will soon end up living amongst us in society. But, apart from this, I noticed that there were literally no distractions. When the guru—Mahant Swami—wasn't in Sarangpur, there was a unique and serene silence. You could hear the sounds of the peacocks, the singing of mantras and devotional songs, and even the wind brushing against the trees. It is within this type of silence that the swamis are able to look within, clearing the voices in their heads, and aligning their values with their true identity as the eternal ātmā.

---

[36] Dominick, J. R. (1984)

THE POWER OF THOUGHTS

Researchers from the University of Virginia and Harvard conducted a series of studies asking participants to spend around 15 minutes alone in a room with no electronic devices, no writing instruments, and nothing to read. After some time, the researchers let them listen to music or use their phones. Can you guess what they found? Participants not only preferred to use their phones and listen to music, many of them even chose to have an electric shock rather than be alone with their thoughts.[37]

We fill our lives up with unimportant activities and thoughts, leaving no room for us to reflect on our true values. We start work on a Friday morning, and we are already planning on how to keep ourselves occupied over the weekend, as though we *have* to be occupied. We can't be free, can we? These distractions that we feed the monkey, become our values and identity by default. Your thoughts shape your values, your values shape your character, your character forms your identity. When we are preoccupied, we cannot address our thoughts, to truly explore and learn how to manage the monkey. How you make use of that 'free time', especially on that weekend at home, really shows you what you value.

Studies show that by the end of our lives, each of us will have spent, on average, 33 years in bed (seven years of which will be spent *trying* to sleep), a year and four months exercising, and more than three years on holidays. If you are a woman, you will spend 136 days of your life getting ready. If you are a man, this number drops to just 46 days.[38] Of course, these are just estimates, but what you do day-to-day does say a lot. On average, each of us will spend more than 11 years of our lives looking at TV and social media.[39] Now, some of you may argue and say, "I only go on Instagram for fifteen minutes a day!" Well, fine. But again, choices add up, and time reflects values. If you have an iPhone, head to the settings and just check your screen time for the last

---

[37] Wilson et al. (2014)

[38] Curtis, Your Life In Numbers. (dreams.co.uk)

[39] Ibid

week. You will see how much time you spend on various apps like social media, games, email, and even browsing the web. Don't like what you see? Set yourself limits. Similar features are also available on Android devices too.

I cannot stress how important it is for you to decide what your values are, and whether or not your choices are aligned with them. You won't know until you truly spend time thinking about them. The aim is to let go of the false values that the monkey has, and fill them with true values which will help the passenger on its journey. Humans like to cling—to close ones, ideas, material possessions—thinking that it's wrong to purge and let go. But, letting go is the easiest path to stillness and space—literally space. You can spend time with yourself, separating yourself emotionally and probably physically from the people, ideas, and things that continuously fill your life. Learn to spend time on yourself and with yourself.

CREATORS OF OUR OWN BELIEFS

A famous experiment took a set of random people, and put them in separate rooms with some buttons to push. They were told that if they do something specific (but they weren't given the details of what to do) then a light would blink, indicating that they have won a point. The aim was to see how many points they could earn in thirty minutes, after figuring out what to do.

This experiment has been repeated time and time again by psychologists, and the results are as expected. People randomly smash at the buttons until the light eventually blinks, telling them they have earned a point. Naturally, they try to repeat exactly what they did before, to get more points, but the light doesn't blink. So they start testing more complicated sequences, pressing this button three times, then that button, then this button, and *beep!* They get another point. But soon, that stops working too. They begin to think that it might not be to do with the buttons, but the way they are sitting, or touching, or the way they are blinking. *Beep!* Yet another point. It must be to do with the blinking. *Beep!*

Normally, in ten to fifteen minutes, each person figures out their own specific sequence of behaviours, to try and get as many points as possible. Whether that be standing on one foot, blinking twenty times within ten seconds, or memorising a long sequence of buttons whilst looking away. The funny part is that the light just comes and beeps randomly, and at random times. There is no sequence, and there is no pattern. It's cruel, I know, but the point of the experiment is to show how quickly the human mind is capable of architecting and believing stuff that isn't real. We're really good at it though. Every individual in this experiment, leaves their respective room convinced they are geniuses, who have nailed and won the experiment. But they don't know that every one of them did something different. This is how our brains work; through the association of two or more objects or experiences. We see a table. We see it's made of glass. Our brain then associates glass with the table and forms a meaning, 'the table is made from glass'. Our minds constantly generate numerous associations to help us understand and control the world around us. Every thought and impulse we have, our perceptions are all composed of thousands and thousands of neural connections, firing away together. We, as humans, shape our own beliefs. There is a direct link between our mind and body. The monkey has full authority to override the Tesla.

Some of the most famous sets of experiments were done by Pavlov. In one of his experiments, dogs were given food, and at the same time a bell was rung. Upon seeing the food, the dogs would salivate. After a couple of days, Pavlov found that even when no food was brought, just the ringing of the bell alone would cause the dogs to salivate. The dogs had begun associating the sounds of the bell with the serving of food.

A similar set of studies have been carried out in the dental field too. Normally, when the lower wisdom teeth are extracted, your gums swell up post-surgery. To ease and control this swelling, dentists prescribe massaging with a dental instrument attached to an ultrasound machine. Using this, the swelling disappears in 30 percent of the cases. A few decades ago, researchers at Kings College, London, conducted an experiment in which they used an ultrasound machine with zero frequency waves on the patients (like a placebo) and it appeared to work, despite emitting no rays at all. To begin with, it was placed at a particular spot on the patient's swollen gums. The swelling reduced to 35 percent. Then, the instruments with zero emissions was moved around on the patients' jaws. The swelling was found to reduce in 30 percent of the cases. Finally, the machine was given to the patients. They were told to hold it on their jaws themselves. This time, the swelling reduced by only 15 percent, but it still worked. The results revealed that just the mere thought of being cured, this is sufficient enough for affecting the healing in the patient. The patient's belief affected the cure.

The complete opposite can occur too. You might have heard of the phrase 'white-collar hypertension'. Many people have normal BP at home, but when they visit the doctor, they find that their BP has increased. The reason behind this is that their mind thinks, "I am at the doctor's and I am surrounded by patients, so I must be ill." These types of thoughts raise our blood pressure. This is a case of 'remembered illness' where the mind makes the body sick. Numerous studies have revealed that psoriasis, eczema, stomach ulcers, high blood pressure, and heart disease, all have high correlations with the mind.

The confirmed medical link between stress and diabetes emphasises this further. When you feel stressed the hypothalamus in the brain signals the adrenal cortex to produce cortisol. It also uses the adrenal medulla to produce epinephrine. The release of these hormones causes the liver to produce more glucose. If that isn't used up, it makes you susceptible to diabetes. Thus, the link between stress and diabetes is a confirmed medical fact.

The power to make these choices lies with you. And it is fundamental that we understand this first. William James says that the greatest discovery of any generation is that a human being can alter his life by altering his attitude. One of my favourite authors, Shawn Achor, says in his book *The Happiness Advantage*, "It's not necessary the reality that shape size but the lens through which your brain views the world that shapes your reality." We know it isn't that easy, because sometimes our brain focuses on the negatives more. Each and every single one of us will face this at some point, maybe even now.

How you think not only about yourself, but the world and other people too, is single-handedly more influential to your happiness than any other circumstance in your life. John Milton says in *Paradise Lost*, "The mind is its own place. In itself it can make a heaven of hell, or a hell of heaven."

I was amazed when I found out about the research carried out by the University of Kentucky on nuns. Basically, they accidentally found boxes full of autobiographies of US convent nuns in the 1930s and 1940s. They began to look at them and categorise them based on how positive the attitude and emotion of each nun was. I think it's important for me to point out now that all of the difficult control variables would have been clearly managed; nuns do not smoke, drink, or get married. They remain celibate, and so don't have any children either. So, their positivity seventy years ago would be the prime indicator of how long they lived. Here is what they found.

Firstly, the happiest nuns lived ten years longer than the least happy nuns. By eighty years of age, the most happy group had lost only 25 percent of its population, as opposed to the least happy group that had lost 60 percent. 54 percent of the most happy nuns reached the age of ninety-four, compared to 15 percent of the least happy nuns.

This study shows a very strong link between how a positive attitude, and relative happiness, influences how long you live. Happy people don't have the best of everything; they make the best of everything. Not just ourselves, but the people that we surround ourselves with, shape our thoughts and values too. Multiple studies have shown how the way in which we relate to the world around us is contagious.

A 20 year study, of thousands of people living in a Massachusetts town, showed that both happiness and depression can spread within social circles.[40] The people that we surround ourselves with help us to stick to our values, and inevitably achieve our goals. If you are unsure about where others fit in relation to your values, ask yourself: When I am with this person, or these people, am I getting closer to who I want to be, or further away?

---

[40] Fowler, J. H., & Christakis, N. A. (2008)

You will experience that you feel good around people who are good for us, and this comes about naturally. Then there are other people who it doesn't feel good to be around; those who don't support us, or those that promote the bad habits in us.

Who you eat with, who you talk to, who you hang out with, what you watch, what you listen to, what you do with your time—all of it shapes your thoughts, beliefs and values. Identifying your true values early on helps to guide you in filtering out the influences that are slapping the monkey right in the face.

THE FIGHTING DOGS

I am who I am today
because of the choices I made yesterday.
Eleanor Roosevelt

Let's shift from the monkey to another animal for a while. A Cherokee legend shares the analogy of two dogs. It states that within the heart of every person there are two dogs, a good dog and a bad dog. The bad dog represents all the habits we want to improve on—envy, anger, greed, lust, and arrogance. The good dog represents positive habits of being generous, grateful, compassionate, helpful, and above all, remaining humble. These two dogs are constantly fighting each other. The question is, which one will win?

The answer remains, the one you choose to feed shall be

victorious. We feed the dogs through the choices we make everyday. If we make the right choices, to express our compassion and live with integrity, it nourishes the good dog and starves the bad dog. Unfortunately, for some of us, the bad dog has become so strong that its ear-piecing howls become the driving force of all our actions. Meanwhile, the good dog, weak and undernourished, is only a whimper in the corner of our heart. This is how habits and addictions develop.

Bad habits are like soft beds; they are easy to get into, but hard to get out of. Now that we have fed the bad dog for so many years, the good dog doesn't have the strength, nor the will, to keep fighting. Many of us will surely experience this in our lives. There will be habits we want to break, or that we have tried again and again to overcome, but somehow we can't find the strength and courage to conquer them. What do we do now? Start feeding the good dog, giving him the courage and confidence to stand up and fight again. This happens through the small decisions and choices that we make.

In 2012, a fourteen-year-old girl was shot in the face as she took the bus home from school one day, simply because she chose to speak out against the injustice going on in her country. She would have died; they wanted her dead; and she slipped into a coma and almost did die. The attackers publicly stated that if she somehow survived, they would not only kill her, but her father too. Fortunately, that girl is still alive today, speaking out against the violence and oppression towards women in Islamic countries. She is a best-selling author, and she won the 2014 Nobel Peace Prize for her efforts. Her name is Malala Yosafzai. She could have simply stayed quiet and carried on living her life as dictated, but she made a choice. The choices that we make define us.

At every point in our life, we too are given a choice. Do we choose to be kind or cruel, truthful or dishonest, generous or greedy, forgiving or vengeful, hopeful or hopeless, to be with an enlightened individual who brings our spirits up or to be around those who pull us down? Studies have shown that habits and addictions form well early in our childhood, where a certain mindset has already formed. Despite this, we always retain the freedom to create new impressions and new habits, and even break past our unwelcomed habits and addictions.

Our past decisions have shaped our current lives, but our present decisions will shape our future. All our choices are driven by our values, whether they be good or bad. Surrounding yourself with people who fit your values also helps you to understand what you truly appreciate. We alone are responsible for the choices that we make. Whatever reactions we are experiencing because of our past choices, we have the choice to respond in a way that will be beneficial for us, and also for those around us. The tendency to stagnate due to a feeling of guilt, frustration, or depression can be overcome by simply making positive choices that are encouraged in the company of positive people. It is important that we establish the goals, values, and priorities of our life. Just like a captain at sea keeps his attention on his compass to guide him, we too must also keep our attention on our inner compass in order to help us through the storms of life.

The choice of words may make or break our relationships.

The choice of timing affect the outcome of our pursuits.

The choice of diet and exercise determines our health.

The choice of Keshav can change our experience of life.

Choices create impressions in our mind that allow us to act beneficially even in challenging times. If we sweat at the time of peace, it will protect us from bleeding at the time of conflict. If we make the right choices when things are going positively, it will give us the inner strength to make the right choices when things are not going so well.

THE GREAT ACT

It is better to live your own life imperfectly than
to live an imitation of someone else's life with perfection.
Bhagavad Gita 3.35

Pretending that you are happy by smiling, engaging, showing energy and enthusiasm, not only shows reciprocation of happiness from others, but it can actually *make* you happier. Decades of research support the view that expressions shown outwardly intensifies those within. Those studying psychology may have learnt about a study in which participants were asked to hold a felt-tip marker in their mouths, either gripping it directly between their teeth (to form a smile) or between their lips (to form a frown).[41] None of the participants were aware of the impact this would have, they just did what they were told. They were then told to examine a set of cartoons and judge how funny they thought they were. Those simulating a smile found the cartoons more funny than those who were simulating a frown. This study could suggest that by simply mimicking facial expressions your actual experiences can be influenced.

Look at the aged people that you know, and the facial lines that they have. They usually match their personality. A very old and happy person will have a sort of happy face, compared to a sad or angry person. This has been scientifically supported. Repeated contractions of the orbiculares oculi muscle, which constricts both sides of the eyes, raising the cheeks, and gathering the skin in towards the bridge of one's nose, causes eye wrinkles, the crinkly eye lines that give an impression of a smile.

Have you ever heard of a contagious smile? Pramukh Swami had a contagious smile. Not only was he content from within, it shone through his smile, which in turn brought a smile to the faces of millions of people around the world. Agreed, it may seem difficult to just put on a smile when we are voyaging through the problems in our life, but I want to share some of the following thoughts with you.

---

[41] Strack, F., Martin, L. L., and Stepper, S. (1988)

If you smile, the world smiles with you. People respond positively, initiate conversation, and engage with you. Studies have shown that every time you smile, your brain feels *happy*. Smiles are infectious and they can even help you live longer. It also activates the release of feel-good-messengers that aid in fighting stress. Every time you smile, dopamine, endorphins and serotonin are all released into your bloodstream, making your entire body relaxed, lowering your heart rate and blood pressure. Endorphins are natural painkillers, produced naturally by your body. No medications, no negative side effects. You may notice that when you smile, people will also look at you differently. You'll be seen as reliable, relaxed and sincere. Scientific studies have shown that seeing someone else's smile activates your orbitofrontal cortex, the part of your brain that processes sensory rewards. This suggests that when you see a person smiling, you feel that you're being rewarded. It is a cycle, and it begins with us.

This doesn't end with just your smile, but your entire body is like this too. The way we act can affect our thoughts and feelings. By altering the outside, we mould the inside. Some may argue that this is unhealthy, but that is not necessarily true. It is in fact a proven concept, which you can also experience when you see other people's smiles. Pramukh Swami proved this concept through his contagious smile and positive body language. This does not mean you get the wrong idea and begin to fake your skills and talents just to get people's attention. It doesn't mean that to make yourself feel good, you need to fake your assets. Do it to enhance your confidence and feel good about your journey, to mould your Self. Imagined confidence slowly turns into true confidence and eventually becomes genuine. By focussing on the good, the good only becomes better. Smile, laugh, act lively, be energetic, be confident and optimistic. Begin to experience *ānanda* today.

> *Keep smiling, because life is a beautiful thing,*
> *and there is so much to smile about.*
> **Marilyn Monroe**

EMOTIONS

A man is but the product of his thoughts.
What he thinks, he becomes.
Mahatma Gandhi

Emotions are part of the evolutionary process of humankind. They serve little purpose other than simply helping us to live and reproduce. I don't want to go into detail here, but if you just ponder upon it, you might understand what I mean. Emotions simply tell us what is right and what is wrong. They are biological signals in your mind designed to direct you on a beneficial path. Feelings of negative emotions should prompt you to act. Feelings of positive emotions come from your mind giving you a pat on the back for doing the right thing. Emotions are suggestions from the monkey, not commands. That is why you should never trust your emotions, nor your mind. Instead, you should be continuously contemplating and questioning them.

Though, you should never suppress your emotions either. Whether that be for personal, social, or cultural reasons, especially negative emotions. Remember, pain serves a purpose. If you don't deal with your negative emotions, you will struggle to deal with other issues throughout your life. Some people over-identify with their emotions, justifying everything for no reason other than *feeling like it*. "I moved to London because I felt like this", or, "I didn't go to his house because I didn't feel like it". Making decisions based on your emotional intuition is bad. It's what animals do. Obsessing or investing too much in your emotions will lead to failure, because emotions never last. Something that makes you happy today won't make you happy tomorrow, because humans always need more. It's a never-ending pursuit of something new—a new car, a new house, a new partner, another kid, another promotion, and then how do we feel again—the same. Remember the hedonic treadmill? Whatever you strive for or achieve, positive or negative, will actually make very little difference. It is because we run away from this fact, that our problems occur again and again, and then become unavoidable. The person you choose to spend your life with is the person you argue with. The car you buy is the car you repair. The job you get is the job you stress over. The home you buy is the home you maintain. Whatever makes you feel good will also make you feel bad someday. What we gain is what we lose. What gives us positive experiences also gives us negative experiences.

Our thoughts greatly affect our emotions too. They play one of the most important roles towards discovering our happiness. These can be both positive and negative. An important note to remember is that, there will always be situations where there are people and circumstances beyond your control. In cricket, there is a practice known as 'sledging'. In this players seek to gain an advantage by insulting or verbally intimidating opposing players. The motive is to weaken the opponent's concentration, causing them to make a mistake, or to underperform. Sachin Tendulkar, widely regarded as one of the greatest batsman in the history of cricket, was known for keeping his cool in these situations. Opposing players have sworn at him and abused him amidst games, yet he remained stable and relaxed.

Can we remain stable in situations that occur in our life? When people sledge us in this game of life, are we able to keep our cool, or do we lose control? Let's lighten the mood with a story for my many Gujarati friends.

One Gujarati lady, whose birthday was approaching, asked her husband, "It's almost my birthday! What will you be gifting me?"

The husband, on the other side of the room, shouted, "Kutri!" (meaning dog in Gujarati)

The wife got so mad on hearing this and she retaliated, "Your mum is a kutri, your dad is as well, your brother is one too! In fact, your whole family are!"

The husband—shocked—spat out the tobacco from his mouth, walked over to his wife and said gently,, "Honey, I said Q3. I am going to get you an Audi Q3!"

There will always be people who are out of control. Can you stop anyone from judging you? No, you can't. Someone, somewhere, will always want to judge you. It may be to make you feel low and inferior, or to make themselves seem superior to you. It's all part of what is out of your control. A batsman batting expects an in-swing ball, and that is exactly what the bowler balls. But, a single breeze of wind changes that in-swing to an out-swing. The batsman is caught out. What went wrong? The wind came in the way. Is that in control of either of the players? Many times in your life, people and situations are totally out of your control. Don't consume your mind about people or situations that you can do nothing about.

In 2005, the National Science Foundation published an article that summarised research of human thoughts on a day-to-day basis. It found that an average person has between 12,000 to 60,000 thoughts per day. Of those, 80 percent are negative thoughts and 95 percent are repeated thoughts. Now, if those repetitive thoughts are the negative thoughts, then how can we expect to have positive thoughts at all?

We tend to remember the bad things more than the good things. The bad moments of our lives stick around much longer than the good moments. We give more emotion to these bad moments and let them hang around. The good things we tend to only remember for a day, before we forget about them. Negative emotions consume us. When we live through a negative experience, we feel it through all of our senses. The reason we don't feel the same way about the positive moments in our life is largely due to the fact that we take them for granted. Another interesting study in the field of thoughts found that 85 percent of the stuff that we worry about, never actually happens. Secondly, with the 15 percent of the worries that do actually happen, 79 percent of the subjects discovered that either they could handle the situation better than they expected, or that the difficulty taught them a valuable lesson for life. So, what is it that we should do? We should learn to respond, instead of just reacting. I know that it is easier said than done, but so is everything. In every situation that occurs in our life there is a stimulus and response, the time in between is where you make a choice. The abuse that Tendulkar got was the stimulus, and he responded by keeping his cool, without majorly reacting. He wasn't born like this, he made the choice to develop such a mindset over time to respond, instead of just reacting. Likewise, when there are all kinds of stimuli around us, we have to learn to respond. If we are not strong from within, it is impossible. Don't ask *why* there are factors beyond us, as you will never get an answer. Look back at Principle Two to further understand this. Instead, ask *how*? *How* can I deal with this situation? I don't want to react. I want to respond. *How* will I do that?

We often think we know what others are going through, but we are never completely sure. Truthfully, if someone is making you feel bad, only you are allowing them to make you feel that way. I know how tempting it is to just run away from your emotions, or to avoid them and bury them deep down, but it takes courage to face and address them. This is long-term growth, and this is how we begin to experience *ānanda* in everyday life. How should we deal with the uncontrollable stream of thoughts crossing our minds? How do we overcome the tendencies of the mind to cling onto negative thoughts and prevent them from lowering our physical energy?

RESPONSE ABILITY

The word responsibility itself implies the freedom of choice. It is made up of two words 'response' and 'ability', meaning the ability to choose one's emotions regardless of the circumstances. No matter what the situation, you are free to choose your response. You will be aware of the gap between the stimulus (the circumstances) and the response (your projection of emotion). To think that the steering wheel of your emotions is in the hands of others is foolish. Repeatedly suffering emotional ups and downs based on others' behaviours is also foolish. You are the passenger and the monkey is your driver. You alone are responsible for your emotions. Let me tell you about Viktor Frankl, a holocaust survivor of the Second World War. He presents his memoir in his book, *Man's Search for Meaning.*

Frankl, an Austrian Jew, was a practicing neurologist and psychiatrist with a deep interest in psychology. His expertise in this field can be seen in the fact that he submitted his papers on psychology to Sigmund Freud, the father of psychoanalysis, which impressed Freud so much that he later got them published.

Unfortunately, when Hitler went on his rampage against Jews in Europe, Viktor Frankl was rounded up along with his family, and thrown into Auschwitz—the worst of the concentration camps. It is known mostly for its inhumane treatment of its prisoners. He was separated from his wife and daughter; and later came to know that they had died. Describing the barbaric treatment in the camp, he mentions that, at times, he would be forced to walk naked through the camp at night, not knowing if he would be alive the next morning. However, even through this, he discovered one freedom that he possessed that nobody could snatch from him. It was the ability to choose his emotional attitude and responses. He *chose* to be cheerful, no matter what. Often, he would smile and even laugh. When others asked him how he could remain so happy, he responded that he did not have control over the external situation, but he did have control over his mind, and he *chose* not to let others disturb that. He realised that a person who has nothing left in the world can still experience peace by harbouring the right thoughts. Not only did he become an inspiration to his fellow prisoners and guards, but he decided to live through the ordeal to later announce his discovery to others. When WWII ended, and Frankl was released, he returned to Vienna. He began practising his profession once again, forming a new school of psychology called *Logotherapy,* also known as *Third Viennese School of Psychotherapy.* It is based upon the attitude we have towards unavoidable suffering, and how meaning can be found in it. Frankl travelled throughout the world, speaking in over 200 universities and receiving twenty-nine honorary doctorates. There are over a 100 books in fifteen languages published about him and his life. The message I want to get across to you is that whether we like it or not, undesirable things will happen to all of us. Life will not always give us chocolates, it will send lemons our way too. But it's up to us if we leave the lemons to turn sour, or choose to make lemonade out of them. You alone are responsible for the reactions to your emotions.

MANAGE EMOTIONS

Let's now look at another practical way of managing our emotions. Cognitive Behavioural Therapists have a term for the negative thoughts that bounce around in our minds. They call them ANTs (Automatic Negative Thoughts). It is vital that you understand that not all negative thoughts are bad, but, most negative thoughts are useless. They just create unnecessary drama within our mind. It doesn't mean you should suppress your negative thoughts, in fact, never do this. One way that you can understand the thoughts going through your head is by writing them down. We are basically writing down our needless worries, fears, regrets, and complaints about our own selves and others. Once you have listed every negative thought, make another column or list, and for every negative thought, you will write one positive thought. For example, if you fear that you are insecure about a failure in your life, write how you learnt from that failure. If you have failed a relationship in the past, write about the joyful time you spent with one another. If you are stressed about work, write a thought about how your work is helping others. And as my guru teaches, if your mind begins thinking negatively about another person, think about the positive qualities they possess.

I know it sounds easy, but it isn't, I'm with you on this. It will take practice. Once you make it a habit to practice this, it'll eventually become part of your permanent thinking process. Then, you will have no need to use a pen and paper, and instead, you will be able to counter a positive thought for every negative thought that comes to mind. As per the principles we have looked at in the earlier part of the book, we know that the inner state of our mind is the key influencing factor on why we do what we do, the way we live our lives, and what we can achieve in our lives. Put simply, the condition in which the state of our mind exists, has a direct impact on the quality of our lives. Another way to practice the control of your emotions is through meditation and self-introspection, which we will explore later.

PROBLEMS

We cannot solve our problems with the
same thinking we used to create them.
Albert Einstein

Murphy's Law states that, "Anything that can go wrong, will go wrong." When issues inevitably crop up (which they will) how do we face them? What mindset do we adopt towards them? Do we break down, cry, and give up? Or do we make the most of the opportunity to grow and progress?

This is what distinguishes successful and *happier* people. It isn't that they don't experience problems at all. Instead, they have the right mindset enabling them to remain positive, even in the face of adversity, utilising the negative situation for the benefit—to see the silver lining. Problems are unavoidable. That is the reality of life. Problems come from all directions, and nobody is exempt. Even after you become successful, or reach the ultimate state of *ānanda*, problems will still remain. This is just how the monkey plays. The true state of *ānanda* can actually be defined as your ability to face and solve problems, and yet remain in a state of equilibrium. Those who are able to do so, are the most valued in every area of life. Think about this, without problems, there would be no jobs or businesses.

The first step in handling problems is, of course, to expect them. I've heard people say things like, "I didn't expect that to happen," or, "I thought it would've been fine!" Usually, it isn't the problem that causes us to feel disturbed, but misunderstood expectations of the problem. Be realistic and expect problems. If you were to climb a mountain, you naturally expect it to be uphill for the majority of the way. Similarly, if you wish to progress upwards in life, expect adversities and hardships.

One of the best ways to prepare for problems is simply to anticipate them in advance. That way you will be ready to tackle them, or at least, try to prevent them before they even happen. Of course, you can only predict to an extent, and some problems will catch you off-guard. But, anticipating problems is always helpful, just make sure it doesn't cause you to fall into a deep trap, where you worry about them all the time. When, and if, a problem arises, what should you do? First, accept that you have a problem. Some people shrug it off and deny the reality of the situation, trying to run away from the issue.

You might have heard of the phrase, 'the elephant in the room'. It refers to an obvious problem in front of you, that you are choosing to ignore. An old TV commercial depicted it well. It showed an average family's home. In their living room there was an elephant; but all the family members went about their day normally, as if they hadn't seen it. They refused to see the problem at hand. If we refuse to face an issue, it doesn't make the problem go away. Instead, it is counter-productive, it is like the ostrich sticking its head in the sand, and the issue could grow bigger. Alternatively, acknowledging the problem and then taking small actions to remediate yourself can save you from immense difficulties in the future.

There is a vast difference in having a big problem and in making a problem big. The monkey tries to make mountains out of molehills, because it loves to keep you, and itself, occupied. This attitude is evident in marriage counselling. All couples have compatibility issues. Some brush aside their differences and see them as insignificant, whilst others make tiny issues seem big. You've probably heard people say, "There are people who have it harder out there," or, "It could be worse." When you feel down, because you have a terrible problem, you can console yourself by thinking of those who have bigger problems. Another way is to reflect on how much worse the problem could have been. Then ask yourself whether the problem is really as immense as you are making it out to be. Inner strength is your biggest asset in the face of adversity. The passenger *must* remain in control; not the monkey. Every problem has a positive side to it. It is through facing them that we grow from within. It is how the passenger learns to take control. The more hardships you face, the stronger you become. This doesn't mean that you invite hardships into your life, but if and when, they do come, see them as opportunities to grow. Franklin Roosevelt said, "A smooth sea never made a skilled sailor." Adversities have inherent opportunities in them, and opportunities don't come without problems. Both go hand-in-hand.

NEGATIVITY

Refuse to entertain negativity.
Life is too big and time is too short
to get caught up in empty drama.

After scurrying my way through the maze-like monastery, I eventually found the fellow swami I conversed with earlier. Again, he called out to me, as I turned to see him sat on a bench with a scripture in his hand. Upon approaching him, I smiled and sat on the floor (as a sign of respect).

There was silence for a minute, before he put the scripture aside and asked, "Vinay, is everything okay?"

With a deep sigh I opened up, "Swami, I try to remain positive in everything that I do, but it's so difficult. I always seem to have a negative view about everything. Even when I am working with other people, or just simply being around others, my mind is drawn to focus on their faults, and then I keep on thinking about them. I really don't know what to do."

*This is where I learnt a life-changing exercise in which I had to keep a tally of every criticism that I spoke or thought about in regards to another person, at any point in the day. For each criticism, I had to write down five good things about that person. I called it the **guna-diary** (diary of qualities), based upon a practical teaching taught not only at the ashram, but continuously emphasised by my guru too, called **gun-grāhak drashthi** (recalibrating focus to see the good in others). It is a difficult exercise, especially when you observing people close to you, and then, having to write about their good qualities. But the point of the exercise was simple, it helps us to see that everyone has more good in them than bad. This not only helps us to see others in positive light, but it also allows us to be critical of our own behaviour.*

The swami continued, "You see Vinay, when you set out to find faults in others, you notice the faults in yourself. This will do more harm than good, unless you are critically evaluating yourself. On the other hand, if you begin to look for the good in others, you will start to see the good in yourself too."

NEGATIVITY IS EVERYWHERE

Everywhere, everyday, we are surrounded by negativity. It's probably the reason why the majority of us do everything with a sense of negativity, and feel that others are negative towards us as well. Rather than focussing on the good things, we talk about the troubles, aches and pains of the day. Most of the time negativity comes from within, springing from fears linked to thoughts of bad things happening, not being loved, or the thought of being disrespected. We manifest these negative feelings through behaviours like complaining, comparing, and criticising.

Okay, we can all agree that bad things *do* happen, and at some point we are all victims. But if we constantly adopt a victim mentality, we are more prone to behaving selfishly, arrogantly, fearfully, and sometimes even with a sense of entitlement.

Psychologists at Stanford took 104 subjects and split them into two groups; one was told to write a short essay about a time they were bored, and the other to write about a time when they felt life seemed unfair or when they were 'wronged by someone'.

After the experiment, the participants were asked if they wanted to help the researchers with a simple task. Those who had written about the time they had been wronged were 26 percent less likely to help the researchers. In a similar study, participants who identified with a victim mindset were not only more likely to express selfish attitudes afterwards, but were also more likely to leave behind rubbish and even steal the pens belonging to the researchers.[42]

NEGATIVITY IS A VIRUS

The monkey is able to adjust to any positivity or negativity. It is up to us what we feed to it. Unconsciously, in everything we do, we try to please others again and again. We also want others to be pleased with (and agree with) us. Repeated studies have confirmed that most humans value social conformity so much that they will change their own responses, behaviours, and even perceptions to align with a

---

[42] Zitek, E. M., Jordan, A. H., Monin, B., & Leach, F. R. (2010)

group, even if the group is wrong. Humans are programmed to conform. The monkey doesn't like to deal with conflict and debate—especially with other monkeys, and so it conforms. At times it prefers to sit back, relax, and allow the Tesla to run on autopilot. This may be a bit easier (or arguably harder) if we all had to stay among the swamis, in the serene village of Sarangpur, but we don't. We live in a constantly changing society, surrounded by gossip, drama, conflict, and negativity, so this is how we begin to perceive the world too.

The more that we are surrounded by negativity, the more negative we will become. Complaining and 'venting' anger is also not a solution to process our anger. Research confirms that even people who reported feeling better after venting are still more aggressive after venting than people who did not engage in venting at all.[43]

Studies also show that negativity increases our aggression towards random people who are, most of the time, not even involved. The more negative our attitude is now, the more likely we are to follow on with that negative attitude in the future. Chronic, long-term stress, like that stemming from compulsive complaining, has been shown to shrink your hippocampus—the part of your brain that affects memory and reasoning; through this the immune system is also impaired by cortisol (the stress hormone).[44] Think about it this way, remaining positive can actually keep you fighting off disease.

I noticed that this is where the swamis at Sarangpur stood out. Detaching from material life, leaving behind everything, they didn't see themselves as having relatively achieved something compared to the rest around them. Regardless of their background (socially or economically) they lived harmoniously with a collective purpose. Senior swamis often reiterate the example that in a hospital everyone is a patient, we don't judge anyone based on their symptoms, disease, or illness. Likewise, we shouldn't judge anyone based on their background, flaws, or good or bad differently. Don't expect that anyone is perfect. Don't think that you are perfect either. Everyone is on their own journey, and perfection is a lifelong journey.

---

[43] Bushman, B. J. (2002)
[44] Sapolsky, R. M. (1996)

TAKE IT OR LEAVE IT

One day, Buddha was touring a small village. He met a religious man (called a brāhmin), who was also travelling from village to village, sharing his message. But obviously, when people heard Buddha was coming, they would flock to listen to him. The brāhmin lost his audience. Furious at Buddha, he went to him at night and started shouting at him, "Who are you to teach things to others. You are dumb and fake! Stop cheating people!"

Buddha smiled as the brāhmin continued to shout and vent his anger. When he was done, Buddha remained seated and composed, this just got the brāhmin even more furious. "Why are you just sitting there and not saying anything?"

Then, Buddha began to speak.

"Tell me my friend, do you have relatives, friends, or village folk ever come to your house as guests?"

"Of course," replied the brāhmin.

"Then tell me," Buddha continued. "Do you serve them hot food and snacks when they come?"

"Yes, of course I do!"

Buddha said, "And if they don't accept them, who does the food then belong to?"

"Well... I guess it belongs to me," said the brāhmin.

"Exactly," spoke Buddha. "Likewise, I do not accept your anger and criticism, so it is all yours. That with which you have insulted me, who is not insulting, that with which you have taunted me, who is not taunting, that with which you have berated me, who is not berating, that I do not accept from you. It is all yours. If you become angry, that anger will only fall back on you. Only you will become unhappy, you will hurt yourself."

Buddha then closed his eyes. The brāhmin, perplexed and taken aback, bowed at the feet of Buddha and left without saying anything more.

Your brain contains about 100 billion neurons, with another billion in the spinal-cord. The total number of connections between neurons (the cells responsible for processing) has been estimated at 100 trillion synapses. Our powerful brains are constantly processing all sorts of experiences and analysing them in the form of thoughts. Thoughts form our perception of reality. We may be able to control and direct our thoughts, but it often feels like our thoughts have a mind of their own, and control our feelings and actions. Thinking is necessary for solving problems, analysing, making decisions, and planning.

You are constantly in a dialogue that is distracting you from what is happening around you, right here and right now. It causes you to miss valuable experiences and sabotages the joy of the present moment. Nearly every negative thought we have relates to the past or future. The more fearful or guilt-ridden the regrets we have are, the more stressed, anxious, depressed, and angry we feel. Sometimes our thoughts paralyse us with bad feelings, and it's those feelings that rob us of inner peace and contentment. There is not one individual on this planet who doesn't have, at least, one other person that has something against them. Put simply, everyone has at least one hater. I have experienced it, just as you will have too. Even if you do good, some people will have something bad to say about it. From childhood through to adulthood, everyone is affected by the negativity that blankets this world, or at least, we allow it to affect us.

We cannot blame anyone for this either, it is within base human nature to have our own perception of what 'normal' is. You will have your own idea of 'normal', and others will have their own idea of 'normal'. We must keep reminding ourselves that negativity from those around us will always stay. Being exposed to the world, and interacting with it, this is a given. Sometimes, we are faced with a situation where we cannot even distance ourselves from the negativity. So in such situations, how does one remain at peace?

OPPOSITION OF PROGRESSION

When you are progressing in life and people see you happy, some will oppose it. When you climb the ladder of success, people will try to knock you over. These negative people feel threatened, jealous, or hurt by your success. They feel inferior, and they dislike this idea of not being able to achieve a similar level of success. This is simply the person's ego at work here (more to come on this shortly). They want to damage your will and drive, so that their ego can win. On your path of

The Keshav Way, these people will turn up, and in fact, they have always been there, but as you begin to mould yourself for the better, your inner self will reveal these people to you. When this happens, do not react. A reaction is exactly what their ego is searching for.

GET DOWN HERE

People who are suffering feel comforted knowing that others are also unhappy. It gives them a sense of validation and justification as to why they are feeling the way they are. Being on social networks you will see a lot of 'grabbing the popcorn' or 'the beef has started'. When you see this, don't let it get to you, it is actually these people who are negative and want to make you feel that way.

HURT PEOPLE HURT

People project their inner world to the outer world. If someone makes you feel bad, it is most likely because they feel bad internally. When you understand this, you will be able to handle situations with care. You cannot blame them either. It is part of a domino effect of sadness. People who are not in a pleasant mood have most likely been hurt by someone else. They in turn, naturally hurt other people causing the dominos to continue toppling. Dalai Lama says, "If you can, help others. If you can't do that, at least do not harm them."

THE LAW OF KARMA

We've all heard of the world *karma*, and today it has become quite taboo. The word 'karma' is rooted in the theological concept of Hinduism, known as reincarnation. It is the belief that your actions now will have consequences either in this life, or your next. Today, more and more people around the world are accepting this fact. Even if you do not believe in reincarnation, many of us believe in the law that, 'what goes around, comes around'. Think back to your science lessons and the concept of 'cause and effect', or Isaac Newton's third law stating that, 'for every action, there is an equal and opposite reaction'. We all know this principle, but like many others, we often fail to practice it in our daily lives. When someone mistreats us, we don't think about karma catching up with them in the future, and simply moving on. Instead, our ego takes over, our emotions get the better of us, whilst our rational thinking seems to step away. Don't allow for the actions of others today, to shape your tomorrow.

Let's also clear some misconceptions about karma, as the word is used very lightly in today's society. In Vedic scriptures, God is described as the all-doer, and this is true, but also often misinterpreted. I'd like to share two terms from the ancient Vedic texts.

Prayojak Kartā is the one who bestows the power to perform actions. God is *prayojak kartā*, as he is the one who provides our senses, mind, and intellect with the power to act.

Prayojya Kartā is the one who uses the power. The individual *ātmā* (the passenger) is the *prayojya kartā*, for it is meant to utilise the power it has been gifted.

Based on these beliefs, there are three kinds of karma, namely *sanchit karma, prārabhda karma,* and *kriyamān karma.*

Sanchit karma form the stockpile of our karma from countless lifetimes. God keeps account of these. At the time of birth, when we arrive into the world, a portion of our *sanchit karma* comes with us, allowing us to enjoy and suffer accordingly. This becomes what we call *prārabhda karma.* The *prārabdha* is fixed for this life. But at every moment, we have the freedom to act as we choose. These form the *kriyamān* karma—the actions that we perform in the present life out of our free will. The *prārabdha* is predetermined, but *kriyamān* is not—we choose these. It is in our hands and can be changed as we wish. In modern society, the karma that most of us refer to us is *kriyamān.*

Compare it to a game of cards. The hand that is dealt to us is fixed; it cannot be changed. But how we choose to play the cards is down to us alone. Good players win even with bad cards, while bad players lose even with good hands.

ATTENTION-SEEKERS

Why do you think memes are popular? Simple because people like it when others laugh at their attempts of making fun of others. When your own life isn't interesting, you switch your attention to others. To seek excitement and attention from putting others down and provoking reactions. Whether someone is doing it for likes, comments or shares, it is all about the temporary happiness, to block off their true inner feelings, making them feel a sense of worth even for a short amount of time. Some will judge you and say stuff about you, but when they do, know that they are showing their true colours. Their insecurities and behaviours are painting a clear picture. By them judging us negatively, it shows that they may never achieve a peaceful and happy life.

EXTERNAL NEGATIVITY

The first thing you must do when you counter external negativity is **step away**. More so emotionally than physically. Look at the situation from the third-perspective. Understand without judging. If someone is negative, it is just a trait, not their entire identity. Would we want someone to judge us by our last action? We must be careful not to do the same with others. Again, hurt people hurt. When someone hurts you, it is most likely because they are hurt. They should be understood and helped.

Then it is time to **back away**. If you can't let go physically, then don't expect to do so emotionally either. Letting go opens the doors to freedom, and it is freedom that is the condition of happiness. If you cling to anything—anger, anxiety, or possessions—you won't be free. It's even harder though when it comes to family, friends, and colleagues. How can we just back away from them? That's not an option; we need other strategies.

If you can't do either of the above, then you need to try and surround yourself with people who are better than you in some way. Whether that be spiritually or positively. Being around better people enables you to grow. The people we spend time with affect us. The Sanskrit word for association, or community, is *sanga,* and it suggests seeking refuge where people serve and inspire one another.

If you can't remove negativity, manage your energy. How much of your time and energy are you allowing that person to consume? Allocate time to spend, don't overdo it. Sometimes all someone needs is a listener. If you can, do that, but don't try to be a problem-solver or genie. Tthis will only lead to frustration when someone doesn't take on your amazing advice. This desire to *save* people sprouts from the ego. A saying goes, "Don't count the teeth in someone else's mouth."[45] Don't try and be a saviour, attempting to fix someone's problems without the necessary skills. If you have the skills, time, and stability, then surely help. If not, refer them to someone who can.

INTERNAL NEGATIVITY

Once you recognise and begin to deal with the external negativity, you will be able to see your own negative tendencies, and begin to work on them. We so easily blame those around us for this culture of negativity, but don't think about purifying our own thoughts, to protect the passenger, and even the monkey, from the external influences. Envy stems from competition. Competition fuels envy. In the Mahābhārāta, one warrior envies another warrior and wants him to lose all he has. The evil warrior hides a burning block of coal under his robes, planning to launch them at the other, who he is envious of. Instead, it catches fire, and the evil warrior himself is burned. His envy makes him his own enemy.[46]

The German word *schadenfreude* means to 'take pleasure in the suffering of others'. This is the worst thing we can do; deriving joy from other people's failures, suffering, and bad luck. If you find yourself judging others, take note, mentally or written; don't let your monkey fool you. It will make you think that you are moving forward, when in reality you are just stuck in traffic. The more that you define yourself compared to those around you, the more lost you will be.

We often think that freedom means being able to say whatever we want, whenever we want. We think freedom is pursuing all our desires but, the truth is, real freedom is the complete opposite. Real freedom is letting go of the things that we don't need or want. Unchecked desires lead to unfulfilling ends. Letting go doesn't mean you totally eliminate negative thoughts and feelings. They will always arise. It is how you choose to deal with them that makes all the difference.

---

[45] Jeon, A. (2005)
[46] Buck, W. (1976)

THE SOLUTIONS

Listing negative thoughts and comments can help you work out where they have come from. Keep track of the negative thoughts that cross your mind over the course of a duration. Introspect and work towards minimising those negative thoughts. It is an ongoing practice.

Bhagwān Shri Swāminārāyan emphasised greatly on the austerity of speech. He said that we should only speak words that are truthful, beneficial to all, pleasing, and that don't agitate the minds of others. My guru's guru, Yogiji Maharaj also said that speech should be used like milk, not like water. Milk is richer than water.

Initially, we may be hesitant on limiting our negative speech, because we will speak less. This will help you realise how much of our talk is negative. The journey is worth it because you are freeing yourself. Judgements also play a part here. They create an illusion that if you judge someone, you must be better and greater than them; if someone else is failing or lower than us, then we are progressing more.

Researchers have found that happy people also complain. But, they do so mindfully. While thoughtlessly venting complaints make your day worse, it's been shown that writing in some form—like a journal about upsetting events, giving attention to your thoughts and emotions—can foster growth and healing, not only mentally, but physically too.[47]

CHOOSE POSITIVITY

Negativity will cause problems that will make you sad. We should try to solve them if we can, but regardless of the outcome we should remain happy and positive. There will also, always be, people with a negative mindset we encounter in life. Accept this fact, and accept them, because even they have a positive side. Don't try to change people and make others positive, that isn't going to work. Never keep hatred for anyone, as this will only affect you in the end. Just try and think of someone you got annoyed at five years ago. You will probably struggle to think of someone. The majority of negativity passes by, and

---

[47] Murray, B. (2002)

we don't even remember it, your brain is great at this. Remember, the monkey adapts to negativity or positivity equally, it simply doesn't care. Just focus your energy and work on yourself, not on others. Positive emotions really do make you happier. Depression itself has been described as a *deficit* of positive emotions; a lack of joy, curiosity, contentment, enthusiasm—the half-empty cup. Recovery from depression has been found to be jumpstarted from positive emotions and events. Researchers in the UK analysed 49 instances of women who improved or recovered from depressive episodes.[48] They found that the majority of changes came from positive experiences, largely from the feeling of having a 'fresh start'.

ACCEPTANCE

It is not your responsibility to correct others;
Just mend yourself.
Nishkulanand Swami

This thought isn't really a habit, it is more of an understanding based on the Principle One. It is the understanding that you cannot change people around you, but what you can change is how you perceive those around you. The example of the glass of water is very fitting to explain this.

---

[48] Kendler, K., Neale, M., Kessler, R., Heath, A., and Eaves, L. (1992)

An upset and frustrated employee, working at a small firm, went to his manager and complained, "I can't work here anymore! I want to quit this job!"

The manager asked, "Why is that? Tell me what happened?"

"The entire atmosphere is so toxic to my mind," replied the young man. "There are people here who are into a lot of politics. Then there are those who talk negative all the time. Some spend most of their time gossiping rather than working. I don't think I can handle this any longer!"

The manager said, "Okay, but I have one request for you before you leave."

The man asked, "Sir, please tell me, what can I do for you?"

"I want you to fulfil this one task sincerely," replied the manager, "Take this glass of water filled to the brim and walk around the entire office three times, without spilling a single drop of water. Once you've done that, you are free to leave."

Confused as to why he was told to do this, the man still carried on, setting out to complete the task to please his boss one last time. Taking the glass of water, he walked around the office floor three times. He then came back to the manager to tell him he had completed the task.

The manager asked, "When you were walking around the office floor, did you see any coworker speaking badly about any other employee? Any gossiping? Any disturbances?"

The man shook his head and replied, "No sir, I didn't."

"Did you see any of your coworkers looking at another employee in a wrong way?" asked the manager.

"No actually, I did not."

"Do you know why?" asked the manager, "Because you were focussed on the glass of water, to make sure you didn't trip or spill any of the water."

The same goes with our lives. When we focus on what is important (our *ānanda*), we don't have the time to see all the commotion going on around us. Accept the fact that wherever you go, there will always be toxicity. Whether it be a change of job, college, or even a situation, it doesn't necessarily promise your freedom from toxicity. I am not saying that you should just sit back and take negativity either. You should certainly do what you can to positively change the things around you, but when you know you have done the best that you can and there is still no change, shift your focus to the glass of water.

You may have noticed times in your life, where you approach someone, or they approach you, and you do not get a good feeling about them. This is negative vibes at play. If someone or something gives you this feeling, stay away. Instead, stay around people that give you a sense of positivity and make you smile. These types of people are more likely to have an optimistic mindset, and this will also conform your mindset to help you look at situations from a positive perspective. We automatically attract people based on how we are. If you feel those around you are negative, it is because you are negative or because you are becoming negative. Stop right there and do something about it. Bring positive people into your life to evoke your strength within, making you capable of avoiding all specks of negativity.

Focus on your priorities, growth, excellence, progress and inspirations. Focus on your Keshav, because only then will you realise that we need to focus on ourselves, and not allow for the toxicity around us to influence us. Let me remind you again that it is not selfish to focus on yourself. If you do not focus on yourself, who will? Only you can dedicate and give full attention to yourself.

The swami continued, "You must be able to accept life as it is. Negativity will always be here; suffering will always be here. Acceptance is the key to handle the in the various turbulences of life. The Bhagavata Purāna mentions, "It is said that great personalities almost always accept voluntary inconvenience because of the suffering of people in general. This is considered the highest method of worshiping the Supreme, who is present in everyone's heart."[49] We could see the highest level of acceptance in Pramukh Swami's life. He not only understood this, but embodied it. Joy or sorrow, fame or shame, to him it was all the same. He accepted everyone as they were; that is why he has a home in everyone's heart."

---

[49] Bhagavata Purana 8.7.44

THE MIND

When the five senses in the mind are still,
when the reasoning intellect rests in silence,
then begins the highest path.
Katha Upanishad

Through my analogy, we've already established the mind as the monkey, based upon analogies from ancient Eastern philosophies. In the Hitopadesha, the mind is compared to a drunken monkey that's been bitten by a scorpion and haunted by a ghost.[50]

The *ātmā* processes information it receives through the senses, using the faculty of the mind. The brain is the tangible, physical organ of the physical body, that links the physical body to the intangible mind. Western philosopher and mathematician, René Descartes gave the idea that is is thanks to the mind that we know we exist, *cogito ergo sum*, "I think, therefore I am." The Vedic teachings switch this around and give the idea of "I am, therefore I think." Without the *ātmā*, the mind is not able to think. It is the *ātmā* that gives life to the body. The passenger guides the monkey.

Humans have up to 60,000 separate thoughts each day. Ernst Pöppel, a German psychologist and neuroscientist, has shown through his research that, our minds are only in the present moment for about three seconds at a time. Other than that, our brains are jumping back and forth, filling in ideas about the present time based on what we have experienced in the past and anticipating what is to come.

Lisa Feldman Barret, author of *How Emotions Are Made*, says, "Your brain is not reacting to events in the world, it's predicting… constantly guessing what is going to happen next."[51]

The Samyutta Nikaya, a Buddhist scripture, describes each thought that we have as a branch, and there are monkeys, swinging from one branch to the next, often aimlessly. Usually these thoughts stem from fears, concerns, negativity, and stress. This is the jungle of

---

[50] Haksar, A. D. (1998)
[51] Barrett, L. F. (2017)

the untrained mind. Or as I like to call it, the real motorway jam. The Dhammapada is a collection of verses respected in the Buddhist faith. In it, Buddha says, "As irrigators leave water where they want, as arches make the Irish straight, as carpenters carve their wood, the wise shape their minds."[52] This battle in our mind is waged over the smallest daily choices (what will I have for lunch?) and the biggest (should I make a career change?). All of us face such battles every single day. Bhagwān Shri Swāminārāyan says, "One who is able to conquer the mind, has conquered the world.". Similarly, Shri Vāsudev Krishna says, "For him who has conquered the mind, the mind is the best of friends; but the one who has failed to do so, his very mind will be the greatest enemy." An enemy, according to the Oxford English Dictionary is, "A person who is actively opposed or hostile to someone or something," and, "A thing that harms or weakens something."[53] Sometimes our own mind works against us. It convinces us to do something, then makes us feel guilty or bad about it, often because it's gone against our values or morals. Holding on to the weight of a bad decision doesn't help you at all.

Research from Princeton University, and the University of Waterloo, has shown that the weight of a bad decision isn't just metaphorical. They asked study participants to remember a time they had done something unethical, then asked them to rate the perception of their body weight. People who had been asked to recall an unethical action said that they felt physically heavier than those who had been asked to recall a neutral memory.[54] Other times, when we want to focus on something—a project at work, an artistic endeavour, a home repair, or even a new hobby—our mind just doesn't let us. When we procrastinate, there is a conflict between what the researchers call the 'should-self'—what we feel we should do because it's good for us, and the 'want-self'—what we actually want to do in the moment. Thoughts are like clouds passing by. The self, like the sun, is always there. Remember you are not your mind; you are the passenger.

---

[52] Easwaran, E. (2007)
[53] Dictionary, O. (2012)
[54] Day, M. V., & Bobocel, D. R. (2013)

ISOLATE THE MONKEY

Visualising the mind as the monkey helps us work on our relationship with it. We have to think of it as a constant interaction to make friends, or negotiating peace with an enemy. Remember that the monkey is, for the most part, crazy. The passenger has to work and cooperate with the monkey, so that it doesn't go against it. The monkey doesn't want to listen; it goes out of control when it doesn't get what it wants. It doesn't appreciate real value, and so it reacts immediately. Sometimes, automatic reactions are needed, for example, if someone pulls out a knife on you—you would feel scared—you would probably scream, run, or both. In such a situation it is understandable. But we don't want to be controlled by automatic reactions in each and every situation of our life, nor do we want to take out the monkey altogether. The monkey enables us to be spontaneous, creative, and dynamic; all which are invaluable qualities, but when it tries to rule over us, destruction begins.

What about when the monkey is in control, or, when the passenger communicates effectively with the monkey? If this is the case, the monkey remembers to pause and assess the bigger picture. It then decides what reaction will be appropriate, and works with the passenger to propose other options. Maintaining this balance is key. The first step to understanding your mind, is to simply become aware of the different voices inside you. Starting to differentiate what you are hearing will immediately help you to think through, and then, make better decisions.

THE VEDIC MIND

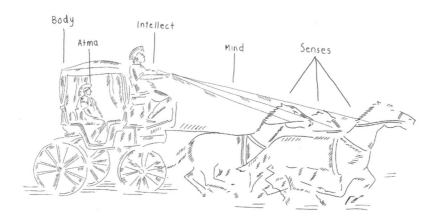

The Upanishads share an amazing analogy known as the *Ratha Kalpanā*. It compares the working of the mind to a chariot being driven by five horses. In this analogy, the chariot is the body, the horses are the five senses, the reins are the mind, the charioteer is the intellect, and as always, the passenger is the *ātmā*. Does this ring a bell? This description of the mind is a bit more complicated than my analogy, but if understood, it paints a bigger, more detailed picture.

In the untrained state, the charioteer (the intellect) is asleep on the job, so the horses (the senses) have sole control of the reins (the mind) and lead the body wherever they want. Horses, when not controlled, react to stimulus around them. If they see a field of nice grass, they'll go over to graze. If something startles them, they spook and go frantic. In the same way, our senses are activated in moments, by food, money, sex, cars, power, influence, and other such material pleasures. If the horses gain control, the chariot goes off the road, in the direction of fleeting pleasure and instant gratification. In the trained state, the charioteer (the intellect) is awake, aware, and attentive. It maintains control and does not allow the horses to lead the way. The charioteer uses the reins of the mind to carefully steer the chariot along the correct path. This is where my analogy originated from.

CONTROL THE SENSES

Think about those five horses, snorting and tossing their heads impatiently; they are harnessed to the chariot of a tired driver. The horses represent the five senses, our first point of contact with all external influences. The senses are responsible for all our desires and attachments, and they pull us in the direction of impulses, passions, and pleasures, destabilising our mind. Swamis at Sarangpur train themselves to control their senses first, in order to calm their mind.

The monkey is reactive, the passenger is proactive. How many times have you been on YouTube to watch a video, and you end up going down an endless chain. You drift from a cute animal video to a "Try not to laugh compilation," and before you know it you're watching "Who can eat the hottest pepper?" Senses are what transport our minds away from where we want to be. Don't tease and provoke your senses. Don't set yourself up for failure. We want to minimise the mind's reactive tendencies, and the easiest way to do that is for the intellect to proactively steer the senses away from external stimuli that could make the mind react in ways that are difficult to control. The spiritual successor of Bhagwān Shri Swāmināråyan, Gunatitanand Swami, says in his talks, "The mind and senses have a natural tendency of provoking desires, know this and remain distinct from them."

Begin by removing unwanted senses from your home. You can never remove all senses and triggers. Nor would you want to. The goal is not to completely silence the mind, instead you want to figure out the meaning of your thoughts, and then distinguish your Self from them. The greatest power is self-control, training the mind and inner energy, to focus it on a specific purpose.

Meditation is also a useful tool that we will explore shortly, that allows you to control sensory input, but you can also train the mind by building the relationship between the monkey and the passenger. In order to reach this level of collaboration, you must pay close attention to the automatic, reactive patterns of the mind, also known as the subconscious.

HELLO, SUBCONSCIOUS

The mind already has certain instinctive patterns that we don't consciously choose. We lead much of our lives following the same path which we've always taken, for better or worse, and these thoughts and behaviours don't change unless we actively reprogram them ourselves. Thoughts repeat in our mind, reinforcing what we believe about ourselves. Change begins with the words inside our head. We have to work on hearing, organising, choosing, and switching those thoughts.

GOODBYE, SUBCONSCIOUS

Just as you are not your mind, you are not your thoughts either. Each and every one of us has a history of pain, heartbreak, and challenges. Just because we have been through something and it may be buried in the past, it doesn't necessarily mean it's gone. In fact, it will persist in some form, often in self-defeating thoughts, until it teaches us what we need to change. If you don't deliberately attempt to rewire your mindset, you are prone to repeat and recreate the pain that you've already endured. It may sound silly, but the best way to overwrite the voices in your head is to literally start talking to them. Start talking to yourself every day. If your mind says, "You can't do this," respond by saying to it, "You can do it. You have the ability. You have the time. You will do it." Have a conversation with yourself. Talk to the monkey and also the passenger.

In a series of studies, researchers showed some volunteers collections of pictures, and then asked them to locate specific items from among those pictured. Half of the subjects were told to repeat loudly the names of the items as they searched, and the other half were told to stay silent. Those who repeated the names of the items were significantly faster than the silent searchers. The researchers concluded that talking to yourself not only boosts your memory, but it also helps you focus as well.[55] Psychologist Linda Sapadin adds that talking to yourself helps you clarify your thoughts, tend to what's important and firm up any decisions you are contemplating.

---

[55] Lupyan, G., & Swingley, D. (2012)

MINDSET SHIFT

We often look for the worst in ourselves and tell ourselves "things will never change." Begin to reframe your self-criticism and thoughts. When you hear yourself say things like, "I'm bored," or, "I'm slow," or, "I can't do this," respond to yourself, "I am working on it. I am improving." This serves as a reminder to yourself that you are making progress. Begin to build a relationship with that pessimistic monkey inside your head.

Many of the frustrations we endure can be seen as blessings in disguise—they push us to grow and develop. Try putting negative thoughts and circumstances into perspective. Many things that we think are devastating, are usually tolerable. We often magnify our thoughts and circumstances.

In a study, a group of college students spent 15 minutes a day, for four days, writing their 'deepest thoughts and feelings', about the most traumatic experience of their lives. Not only did the students say that they found the experience to be valuable, 98 percent said they would like to do it again. But they didn't just enjoy the writing, it also improved their health. Those who had written about their traumatic experiences had fewer visits to the University health centre after the study. The researchers concluded that, one of the benefits of this writing may have been in helping students write off the worst experiences of their life, as a coherent narrative[56].

Distancing from the moment enables you to to see experiences objectively and hope to put together a happy ending. When anxious thoughts crop up in your mind, instead of indulging them, respond with compassion towards them. You are defined by the narrative that you write for yourself every day.

---

[56] Pennebaker, J. W., & Seagal, J. D. (1999)

STAY PRESENT

Richard Rohr writes, "All spiritual teaching—this is not an oversimplification—is about how to be present to the moment. The problem is, we are almost always somewhere else; reliving the past or worrying about the future."

We all have nostalgic, happy memories that we enjoy revisiting, and painful memories that we can't seem to let go. But both of these can be traps. Just as the past is unchangeable, the future is unknown. A certain amount of planning and good preparation for the various, unprecedented scenarios ahead is useful, but when these thoughts sway into repetitive anxiety, stress, worry, or unrealistic aspirations, they are no longer productive.

If your mind constantly returns to thoughts of the past or the future, recalibrate to the present. Is your mind seeking to shield or distract you? Instead of thinking about what mattered in the past or what the future might hold, gently guide your monkey back to the moment. Ask yourself questions about 'right now'. Tell the monkey to focus on the road right in front of him. If the monkey is focussed, the journey will be smooth for the passenger.

DETACHMENT & SELF-CONTROL

Detachment is not that you own nothing.
Detachment is that nothing owns you.
Shri Vasudev Krishna

From a spiritual background, and also from what I understand, self-control is one of the greatest powers. Self-control is where we train our mind to focus exactly when and where we want it to be. When we are completely detached from all external ups and downs of this world and life. We can pass through the joys and struggles of life whilst maintaining a total equilibrium, without being too excited in pleasure or too depressed in pain.

We know of so many people, maybe personally too, that have got fame, but, have also been ruined by it. When we hop onto Instagram, Facebook, YouTube, or any social platform, we are drawn to how many likes people have, their life updates, how their bodies are, etc, and in reality, this is destroying us from within. Recent mental health research studies suggest that, things like isolation and over-exposure are affecting us dramatically. Statistically, we have more pain consumption in one day than we are supposed to in a lifetime, simply because of how much we are exposed to today.

Pramukh Swami Maharaj was one of the greatest examples of someone who lived with complete self-control. Despite being a swami, he lived amongst society throughout his entire life. Surrounded by all the desires and attachments that the world offered, he remained completely detached; this is true self-control. Whenever he faced honour or insult, joy or sorrow, he treated it as one. He remained stable and detached—in a state of total equilibrium.

Shri Vāsudev Krishna puts it beautifully in the Bhagavad Gītā, by saying, "Detachment is not that you own nothing. Detachment is that nothing owns you." People usually see detachment as being away from everything. But in fact, detachment is being amidst everything and still not letting it consume you or own you.

Just as you do with your actions, you must also keep control of your words. Being sensitive means to think about how the other person would feel before you say or do something. The human mind doesn't know how to discriminate between things and people. Teach the monkey how to discriminate.

DISCPLINE & SUCCESS

The majority of personal and social problems stem from our lack of self-control. Underachieving at school, procrastinating at work, resorting to alcohol and drugs, lack of exercise, an unhealthy diet, rude behaviour, explosive anger—all are connected to a lack of self-control.

Social scientists have conducted several studies to see what personality traits contribute most to success in any field of human endeavour. Many characteristics were found: positivity, responsibility, inspiration, etc, but research showed that the two qualities having the biggest correlation to success were intelligence and self-control. Those who ranked higher on both intelligence and self-control had a greater chance of success in any field of human endeavour.

Based upon Principle Three, our intellect is mostly innate. Everyone has a given level of intellect, and so there is only so much you can do to enhance it. On the other hand, self-control is totally in our hands, and it can easily be increased or decreased by our thoughts and actions. Unfortunately, this is where most of us fail. When we are asked about our strengths or qualities, we name things like kindness, humour, bravery, honesty, and sometimes humility, but we never mention self-control. In a survey conducted by researchers, people were asked to choose their strengths from a list. Self-control was on the list, but it was the least selected. Conversely, when asked to choose their weaknesses, lack of self-control was the most widely picked, topping the list of weaknesses. Today, when technology has radically changed society, the challenges of maintaining self-control has increased dramatically. When we are surrounded by temptations, just an arms-reach away, we feel much more vulnerable. We must take back control.

THE MONKEY FIGHTS

The monkey doesn't want to be controlled, and so the struggle for self-control is but a natural part of life. As humans, we possess internal instruments consisting of the senses, mind, intellect, etc. Amongst these, the intellect is rational and searches for value—intellect comes from the passenger. It analyses, "I need to work towards long-term benefits and not get distracted by short-term gratifications." But the senses and the monkey always rebel. They trap the intellect saying, "Let's indulge for now, we can look at the consequences and deal with them later if we must."

The passenger wants to use intellect to help you consider the values of any action, but the monkey wants to go crazy with the Tesla, making pitstops, delaying the journey, and indulging in immediate pleasures. Enjoyments differ from person to person. A smoker would crave for a cigarette, the shopaholic craves to throw their money about, the gambler craves for a night in Las Vegas, and so on. Whatever the attraction that the monkey sees and seeks, the passenger wants the monkey to focus on the road ahead, and reign it through the power of reason.

The monkey is on a high and wants to fight. But, if the passenger remembers he is the one who should be in control, to make the decisions (after all this is the passenger's journey), it will be able to remain firmly anchored. Thereby, forcing the monkey to drive the Tesla properly, according to the passenger's journey. Again, remember, you are not your mind, you are the ātmā.

YOU ARE DISTINCT

Detachment is an advanced form of self-control that has infinite benefits across every form of self-awareness. Its origin is always in the mind. Shri Vāsudev Krishna defines detachment as doing the right thing for its own sake, because it needs to be done; without worrying about the result, regardless of success or failure. It sounds simple enough, but think about what it takes to do the right thing for its own sake. It means detaching from your selfish interests; from always trying to be right; from being seen in a certain way; from what you want right now. Detaching means escaping the hold of the senses, of worldly desires and the material world. You have the perspective of an objective observer. The passenger observes everything. Only by detaching can we truly gain control of the mind.

Attachment brings pain. If you think something is yours or you think you are something, then it hurts to have it taken away from you. Usually people see detachment as being away from everything, or just not caring. It isn't telling you to stop caring, it is telling you to look for happiness. Again I emphasise that the highest level of detachment is being close to everything and not letting it consume and own you. That is real strength. That is the strength that I saw in Pramukh Swami. Surrounded by every desire that one can dream of, he never let any consume or own him. He remained forever distinct. I learnt from the swamis at Sarangpur that detachment is not a destination one arrives at, but, rather a process one must constantly, and consciously, undertake throughout their life.

THE POWER OF FASTING

During my research, I came across some extreme forms of detachment that individuals go through, in order to gain self-control. Obviously, we don't need to try these, but it shows the level of detachment individuals are willing to go to. Experiments in discomfort like fasting, silence, meditating in heat or cold, detach you from the body because they make you realise how much of discomfort is merely in your mind. After all, everything comes from the mind. Fasting is a powerful way to gain self-control. When we fast, we detach from the body and all the time we spend attending to its demands. When we remove eating, we can let go of hunger, pain or pleasure, and failure or success. We redirect our energy and attention to focus on the mind. I noticed this in the swamis, who go many days without eating or drinking, yet they were able to use their energy to study, research, give talks for hours, and even carry out routine chores. They do this at least five times a month. Fasting for them becomes a creative time, free of distractions. They have broken the limit that exists in their minds. Fasting is a physical challenge driven by the intellect.

Seeing the types of austerities and detachments that certain individuals choose to follow, it shows us what is possible if we are able to maintain self control and a firm resolve. One Jain monk, Shri Hansratna Vijayji Maharaj Saheb, fasted for 423 days. *Sokushinbutsu* is the name for a Japanese style of self-mummification practice where monks would eat a diet of pine needles, tree-bark, and resins, then give up the food and water while they continue to chant mantras, until eventually their bodies petrify. Don't worry, we don't need to go to these extremes. There are ordinary people as well, who use austerities to up their game. People consistently report that experimenting with extremes helps them to be more thoughtful and positive in their everyday lives.

MODERN DETACHMENT

There are infinite austerities and challenges you can try. Your boot camp starts today. Try giving up TV or social media, sweets and chocolate; take on physical challenges; abstain from gossip, complaining, and comparing. Start with awareness. Then spot the attachment. When do you experience it? When are you most vulnerable to it? Let's say you want to detach from the use of social media. Ask yourself, do you use it out of boredom, laziness, fear of missing out, or because you feel lonely?

Once you have diagnosed the attachment, the next step is to stop and rethink it. What do you want to add and what do you want to take away? How much time do you want to dedicate to technology, and in what form? Are there certain apps you want to eliminate entirely, or do you want to limit the time that you spend using your phone? The third step is to swap in new behaviour. There are two general approaches that I recommend. Some choose to fully immerse themselves. If immersions and extremes work best for you, you might commit to eliminating social media entirely for a week or a month. If you work better in slow, gradual iterations, make a small change and build on it. In the case of technology, you could limit the amount of time you allow yourself to be online, or perhaps limit, but don't fully eliminate certain apps.

Decide how you want to reuse this free time. If you want to minimise your YouTube time, look for another way to find that relaxation or decompression. I'd go to contemplation and meditation. If you are cutting back on social media, do you want to spend the time interacting with friends in real life rather than online?

At first, when we make a change, the monkey will rebel. Look for ways to ease the transition for it. If I want to eat less sugar, reading studies linking sugar to cancer strengthens my intellect and motivate me to persist. As you begin to do so, you will begin to feel the benefits of detachment. You will find new and clear perspectives; you will feel more control over the monkey, but you will also stop trying to control that which you can't control. The monkey will calm down and you will make decisions without fear, ego, envy, or greed. You will feel confident and free from illusion. You accept the circumstances and situations of life as they are, and focus on the new, clear path ahead.

MIND MAINTENANCE

Detachment doesn't mean you completely ignore your body and our mind either. The Tesla is a valuable vehicle. It contains us, as well as the passenger, so it's important to look after it. We have to take care of it, feed it, keep it healthy, but remember that the vehicle is just a carrier. What it carries holds real value, the passenger.

Going back to the Upanishads, without his chariot, horses, and reigns, the charioteer's options are limited. He is slow, he can't travel far, he can't pick up a lost traveller and help him on his journey. Linking it to our analogy, without the Tesla or the monkey, where does the passenger go? It might eventually end up going somewhere, or finding another way, but, the only way we know is with the Tesla *and* the Monkey. Again, we do not want to eliminate the voices in our heads, or the body that carries them, we just want to steer them in the right direction. This actually means that the work of the charioteer (and the passenger of course) is never-ending.

When you are hungry, do you feel guilty and say to yourself, "Oh God! I am so bad! Why am I hungry again?" Of course not. Bring the same patience and understanding when you are low on motivation, unfocused, or anxious and the passenger is weak. Waking him up is like taking a shower and feeding yourself; it is an everyday practice.

Constantly thinking about negative or sad thoughts will reinforce the sense of sadness and negativity within you. Instead, by cultivating positivity, divinity, compassion, and joy, you are able to build up a type of resilience, and you can face life with true confidence and a genuine smile. Train your brain. Train your monkey. In the end, it is your mind that translates the entire outside world into the happiness or misery that you feel inside.

Like a muscle, skills and habits grow stronger and more reliable. If we work every day to cleanse our thoughts, and gently redirect the ones that don't serve us, then our mind becomes pure and calm, ready for growth. Shri Vāsudev Krishna says, "Cultivate discriminating intelligence (*buddhi*) to discern true knowledge, and practice wisdom so that you know the difference between truth and untruth, reality and illusion, your true self and your false self, the divine qualities and the demonic qualities, knowledge, and ignorance and how true knowledge illuminates and liberates; whilst ignorance veils your wisdom and holds you in bondage."

EGO

The nature of a person is such that he only
enjoys doing that which satisfies his ego.
Bhagwan Shri Swaminarayan

The biggest obstacle on our life's journey is our ego; sometimes it even tries to overtake the Passenger, to even try and take the place of the passenger. This is a fight within our hearts. Your ego is distinct from you, and the Katha Upanishad draws this distinction:

In the secret cave of the heart, two are
Seated by life's fountain. The separate ego
Drinks of the sweet and bitter stuff,
Liking the sweet, disliking the bitter,
While the supreme Self drinks sweet and bitter
Neither liking this nor disliking that.
The ego gropes in darkness, while the Self lives in light.

As discussed in Principle Three, the ego is part of the four inner abilities. It is the 'fake image' that the mind creates to preserve your sense of being the most significant, the most important, the one who knows it all. It's your costume; the one that requires validation from the world around it. If it doesn't get the approval it seeks, it'll cease to exist. When someone hurts you, and you get upset, that isn't you getting hurt, it's your ego. When you make a statement which you think is the best, and no one agrees, and you get mad; that is your ego again. It operates according to your limited false beliefs, seeking validation from external sources; it is reactive, fear-based, and committed to keep you safely confined within the reality you have created based on false beliefs (the comfort zone). The ego lives in the past and in the future, believing you are distinct from everything around you. Your ego is the very reason you think your existence and presence on this earth is greater than others. Sorry to burst your bubble but, from a spiritual perspective, everyone is equal. You are not greater than others. Focus on becoming great for yourself. We buy materialistic things to 'show-off' to people we don't even care about; we get jealous when someone is earning double what we make annually. Mahant Swami says that your ego is your biggest enemy. It stops all rational thinking, love and understanding. The Sāma Veda says, "Pride of our wealth destroys wealth, pride of strength destroys strength, and in the same manner pride of knowledge destroys knowledge."

Sadly with time, we have made our ego our image. We cannot simply get rid of it just like that. Actually, it isn't you who has made this image. Our ego has made it for us, for its own validation. But now, we are pampering it and fuelling it. It's easy to notice when someone else's ego gets hurt because, they instantly become reserved and protective. We don't ask things because we want to know; we ask to put others down, to boost our own ego. We want people to acknowledge what we say to be true. We fear being wrong.

It isn't wrong to discuss problems or issues you are having, or to discuss what someone else is going through, but don't make it the subject to fuel your superiority and make someone look inferior to you. Keep an open mind, hear others out, but don't waste time on people who gossip about others. You will know right away when this happens, and it's a cue to steer away. It is not your responsibility or place to get involved in the issues of someone else's personal life. Bhagwān Shri Swāminārāyan says in his teachings, "One who considers himself to be superior to all remains constantly at unease, day and night. In fact, he constantly smoulders like a half-burnt log. He never experiences peace at heart."

In order to make ourselves look greater and smarter, we often hide our true nature. We are a different person at home, at work, with family, and with friends. Our image works harder to be more considerate, attentive, generous, positive, but the ego gets in the way. Our insecurities want to convince us, and those around us, that we are special. It presents an inflated self image to others, and we fuel it by doing everything we can to protect the image we want others to perceive.

Bhagwān Shri Swāminārāyan often used the word *vanity* along with ego, as they both go hand-in-hand. The majority of our effort goes into how we appear to the rest of the world. The ego finds confidence and joy in impressing others. Basically, it seems as though the ego is the internal battle of the passenger.

You might have seen the below picture before. It did rounds all over social media as a meme captioned, '$162 billion in one photo and not a Gucci belt in sight.' Don't worry, I'm not trying to suggest anything, but, if you are truly satisfied with who you are, you don't need to prove your worth to anyone else. Think about the choices that you make when no one is around, when there is no one to judge you, and nobody to impress. Who emerges at that time? That is who you truly are. A saying accredited to John Wooden goes, "You are who you are when no one is watching."

THE TWO EGOS

Our egos are a part of our identity; in fact the ego is our self-identity. Shri Vāsudev Krishna says, "A person who has given up cravings and all sense of proprietorship, who is devoid of *false* ego, he alone attains peace."

In our daily social interactions, everything we do is for our ego. Many philosophers and thinkers have described the ego in different ways. German philosopher, Immanuel Kant wrote, "The transcendental ego is the thinker of our thoughts, the subject of our experiences, the willer of our actions, and the agent of the various activities of synthesis that help to constitute the world we experience."

The Vedic texts go a step ahead and distinguish between the false ego and the true ego. The true ego is our *ātmā*, the conscious life force within us all. It is true and it is eternal. The monkey presents us with the false ego, "I am British or Indian, male or female, rich or poor." This is the false ego. To rise above this is to continuously contemplate on the nature of the *ātmā*, "I am not this body, and I nothing related to this body is mine. I am above. I am the *ātmā*."

Understandably, living in today's world, it has become so easy for us to create labels in society—British, Indian, man, woman, young, old, rich, poor, black, white, Hindu, Muslim—basing our identity on what we have, know, or feel. This excessive identification with the false ego, of 'I', you, and me', is one of the root causes of suffering. Identifying ourselves as being above this, as being inherently divine, brings a sense of peace and understanding.

EGO FRAUD

The ego continuously craves recognition, acknowledgement, and praise. It wants to be *right*, to be *more*, to put others down, and to raise itself up. The ego doesn't want to be better, it wants to be seen as the best. It also goes to extreme lengths to put other people down because, if others are 'less than' we are, then surely we must be special. Our egos accomplish this by setting a hierarchy of us and other people based on physical looks, education, salary, race, religion, nationality, the car we drive, or even the clothes we wear. It finds various ways to judge others unfavourably just because they are different from us. Again, focus on yourself, on your own life and try to improve that. You are here for yourself, to focus on yourself. We already know that life is short, and time flies quickly in this life. Let us make the most of the brief time we are here, to do something constructive, speak positively, and truly make our life greater.

In reality, we are all equal, but many factors that come into play—including success—get to our heads and we forget this. Dalai Lama says, "Under the bright sun, many of us are gathered together with different languages, different styles of dress, even different faiths. However, all of us are the same in being humans, and we all uniquely have the thought of 'I'. We're all the same in wanting happiness and in wanting to avoid suffering." Think about why it takes a global catastrophe, or a tragedy, to bring us together as humanity?

EGO & OTHERS

We try to elevate ourselves by judging others, including our colleagues, friends, and family. Do not judge others, do not make assumptions about others. A person is destroyed by holding judgements about others, only judge yourself.

Projection is the psychological term for our tendency to project the emotions and feelings, that we don't want to face ourselves, onto others. Before judging others, it's important to pause for a moment and ask: *Why am I finding faults in this person? Is it to distract myself or others from my own insecurities? Am I projecting my own weaknesses onto them? And even if I'm doing neither, am I any better than the person I'm finding faults in?*

When you're amongst a group of people, waiting for someone to finish their gossip—so that you can tell a fabulous story about yourself or make a remark—you're not absorbing the conversation happening. Your ego is waking up, ready to show others how clever and interesting you are. In this desire to show ourselves and others that we are the 'know it all', we jump to quick conclusions, fail to listen to our close friends, and miss getting insights on valuable new perspectives. Do you feel upset or grateful when you discover you were wrong about something? Are you defensive or intrigued when you find new information that goes against something you believe? If you aren't open-minded, you are denying yourself opportunities to learn, grow, and change. Your ego isolates you. Don't live in a fantasy world where you start thinking that you are so special, or that one person is worth your time and another isn't. The false self that builds you up, just as easily can tear you down. When weaknesses are exposed, the ego that once told us we were brilliant and successful, no longer has a defence. Egotism often hides, and later transforms into low self-esteem. If you don't begin to break your ego, your ego will break you.

START HUMBLE

Humility is what allows us to understand our weaknesses and strive to improve them. In the darkness of our ego, we think we are special, powerful, and significant, but when we look at the bigger picture, we see that each of us only play a small part in this world. Mahant Swami gives the example that we are like an ant in front of an elephant (the elephant here being the supreme power; *Parabrahman*).

By fixating on, and being impressed, by our own good actions, our ego grows. We should put all of these aside. Even if others treat us badly, we *have to* let go too. I know it may seem hard, but in the end, it will only do you good.

What belongs to you today, belonged to someone yesterday and will be someone else's tomorrow. Learn to detach emotionally. Spiritually, no matter what you believe in, when you recognise this, then you see that the body you identify with is nothing but a vehicle, a channel for the higher power. Detachment is liberating, and it inspires gratitude—an important quality we will look at next.

SELF-ESTEEM

By staying humble, you see your own strengths and weaknesses clearly, and can then work, learn, and grow from them. Confidence and high self-esteem help you to accept yourself as you are, whether that be humble, imperfect, or striving. It is important to note the key differences between self-esteem and ego.

EGO	HIGH SELF-ESTEEM
Wants everyone to like you.	Okay with conflict.
Thinks it knows everything.	Learns from everyone.
Wants to always *prove* itself.	Wants to *express* itself.
Pretends to be strong.	Okay being vulnerable.
Wants people to respect it.	Respects the self and others.

The ego wants to prove itself. Self-esteem wants to express itself. The ego pretends to be strong. Self-esteem is okay being vulnerable. The ego wants people to respect them. Self-esteem respects the self and others. Learn the difference between both.

GET FEEDBACK

Confidence means deciding *who you want to be* without worrying about what other people will think. It also means being inspired and led by others to become the best version of yourself.

Choose your advisors wisely when asking for feedback. We often make the mistake of either asking everyone for advice about an issue or we ask one person for advice about all of our issues. Cultivate small groups of counsel around specific areas to lean on for support. When people offer their reflections, pick and choose your options carefully. Your ego will want you to believe that only it knows best, so it will quickly push away feedback and criticism it gets. Learn to filter the feedback. Reflect instead of judging. Be curious. Don't pretend you understand everything. Ask clarifying questions.

NOW STAY HUMBLE

Some of us will reach high levels of success. We have to accept that. It could be through game, money, power, or status of some form. If you do get this type of success, instead of letting it get to your head, always try detach from it. You are not your success or your failure. Remain humble after you've achieved something too. Thank those that you need to share your success with, this keeps you humble.

Humility is ultimately unattainable. There is no end-point. The moment you feel like you have arrived at the destination of complete humility, you are only starting the journey again. It is a cycle, and there is no endpoint. Overcoming your ego is a lifelong practice, not an accomplishment. Even today, at the age of eighty-seven, Mahant Swami Maharaj still practices humility, and that is why it is so clear and evident in his way of life.

No matter how much you help others, don't let your ego get the better of you; there is so much more to be done. After carrying out so much selfless work for society, when Pramukh Swami Maharaj was asked how he managed all of these activities, he replied, "I have done nothing. It is all God's doing." This is the pinnacle of humility. The most powerful, admirable, captivating quality in any human is seen when they've achieved great things, but still embrace humility and their own insignificance. Those that are most humble are the most self-aware. Those who are most self-aware attain the highest state.

E

ENGAGEMENT

Gratitude turns what we have into enough.

Aesop

Gratitude is one of the most powerful habits that we can practice. It is the first step of engagement. It completely changes your mindset. Gratitude isn't a feeling, but rather a state of mind that can be developed, allowing you to tap into a pool of unlimited positive energy. Science has shown that gratitude has the single largest correlation with human well-being. It affects not only our mindset, but our sleep, our ability to be kinder, the feeling of being more alive; it even strengthens our immune system. Statistics show that we always gain more by being grateful as opposed to being ungrateful.

Normally, we see gratitude as saying thank you for a gift or benefit from another, but the actual definition is much broader. It goes beyond just having good manners, it is a state of *being*. Just think about how it feels when you get to really thank someone for doing something for you. The feeling is amazing on both sides. Robert Emmons defines it as "a felt sense of wonder, thankfulness, and appreciation for life."

The practice of gratitude involves focussing on the present moment, appreciating life as it is today, and what has made it so. Have you ever had the experience of eating sweetcorn, and the feeling of some bits getting stuck between your teeth? Isn't it amazing that when something like this is stuck between our teeth, our tongue automatically keeps going towards that area to remove it. It will keep doing this until it goes away. There are 31 other teeth in our mouth, but the tongue doesn't choose to go there. It's the nature of the tongue to keep going to where something is stuck. Of course, we have to deal with it, and we do. It isn't just the nature of your tongue; it is the nature of the mind too. When there is a problem in life, our mind douses to resolve it, using all the energy it can to do so. There are so many more wonderful things happening in our lives, yet our monkey mind keeps choosing to revisit the problematic areas.

Gratitude comes in handy here. It turns what we have into enough. If we count our blessings, our mind automatically begins to see the good around us. It is a tried and tested concept that we need to form into a habit to truly experience it. How can you feel bad then, if you are thankful for what you have got? I know that it is easier said than done. We all struggle to show our gratitude. We naturally focus on the struggles, just like the tongue, and we devote all our attention on the things we do not have, as opposed to what we do have.

Gratitude has been linked to better mental health, self-awareness, better relationships, and a sense of fulfilment. Scientists measured the benefits of gratitude by asking two groups of people to keep journals during the day. The first group was asked to record everything they felt grateful about, and the second was asked to record times they'd felt hassled or irritated. The gratitude group reported lower stress levels at the end of the day. In another study, college students who complained that their minds were filled with racing thoughts and worries were told to spend fifteen minutes before bed listing everything they were grateful for. Gratitude journaling reduced intrusive thoughts and helped participants sleep better.[57]

---

[57] Emmons, R. A., McCullough, M. E. (2003)

A Christian leader has said, "A grateful heart is the beginning of greatness." It is impossible to truly feel happy without being grateful for what we have. Gratefulness is key to happiness. Every day, we compare ourselves to others, and we feel that they have something more. But, flip the tables and you will see that there is so much we have that others desire for as well. Being grateful doesn't mean you keep saying 'thank you' to everyone. You need to be truly grateful in all course of action.

An ongoing study called the *Journal of Happiness Studies*, by Springer goes even deeper and suggests that materialistic strivings have been implicated as a major cause of unhappiness. On the other hand, gratitude, both in its manifestations as a chronic affective trait and as a more temporary emotional experience could be a major cause of happiness. It is important that we focus on the good that is happening in our life, and deal with the bad as we go on. Let us not consume our minds with negativity, let us consume our minds with positivity; focus on the positive, and deal with the negative. If you concentrate on what you have, you'll always have more.

People who are consistently grateful have been found to be relatively happier, more energetic, more hopeful, and experience more frequent positive emotions. They also tend to be more helpful and empathic, more spiritual and religious, more forgiving, and less materialistic than others.[58] These findings are correlational, meaning we cannot know conclusively whether being grateful actually causes positive emotions, or whether possessing traits like hopefulness, helpfulness, and religion simply makes people feel more grateful.

GRATITUDE & THE MONKEY

Gratitude helps us overcome bitterness and pain that we all carry with us. If I told you to try and feel jealous and grateful simultaneously, I'm sure you wouldn't be able to. UCLA neuroscientist Alex Korb says that we truly can't focus on positive and negative feelings at the same time.[59] When we feel grateful, our brains release

---

[58] McCullough, M. E., Emmons, R. A., and Tsang, J. (2002)
[59] Korb, A. (2012)

dopamine (the reward chemical), which makes us want to feel that way again, and gratitude begins to form as a habit. Kolb says, "Once you start seeing things to be grateful for, your brain starts looking for more things to be grateful for."

Gratitude also plays a major role in overcoming real trauma. A 2006 study found that Vietnam War veterans with high levels of gratitude experienced lower rates of post-traumatic stress disorder (PTSD). If you've been through a breakup, lost a loved one, or if anything has hit you emotionally, gratitude is the answer.[60]

Gratitude also has benefits for the physical body, not just your mind. The toxic, negative emotions that gratitude blocks contribute to widespread inflammation, which is a precursor to loads of chronic illnesses. Studies have shown that grateful people not only feel healthier, they're also more likely to take part in healthy activities and seek care when they're ill.

PRACTICING GRATITUDE

We need to be grateful in *all* circumstances, all of the time. It is hard of course, and life isn't perfect. Gratitude is built upon, through consistent practice, strengthened over time.

Brian Acton is an example of someone who has shown his conscious practice of gratitude. He worked at Yahoo for eleven years, then applied for a job at Twitter. Despite his skillset, he was rejected. When he received the news about this, he tweeted:

Brian Acton
@brianacton

Got denied by Twitter HQ. That's ok.
Would have been a long commute.

8:39 PM · May 23, 2009 · Twitter Web Client

---

[60] Kashdan, T. B., Uswatte, G., & Julian, T. (2006)

He then applied for a job at Facebook. Soon after he tweeted again.

Brian Acton ⌄
@brianacton

Facebook turned me down. It was a great opportunity to connect with some fantastic people. Looking forward to life's next adventure.

8:14 PM · Aug 3, 2009 · Twitter Web Client

He didn't hesitate to post his failures on Twitter, and simply looked at the positive side, expressing gratitude for the opportunities. He soon ended up working on an app in his personal time. Five years later Facebook bought WhatsApp, the app that Brian Acton co-founded, for $19 billion. Instead of fixating on the rejections and adopting a victim mentality, he just waited gratefully to see what might be in store for him.

Never judge the moment. When you label something as bad, your mind starts to believe it to be bad. Instead, be grateful for failures and setbacks. Allow the journey of life to progress at its own pace and in its own way. The more open you remain to possible outcomes, the more naturally gratitude will come to you. Gratitude is much more than simply saying thank you. The most important aspect of practicing gratitude is trust in life. It's about learning from the moment. Stepping back to think: *what can I learn from this moment*? Then we begin to look for gratitude.

Gratitude can also be expressed to others. A lot of the time, we feel deeply grateful, but we have no idea how to express it. Ironically, the simplest way to show gratitude is to say thank you. But we don't want to stay basic. Make your thanks as specific as possible. The minute we are given incrementally more detailed gratitude, the better we feel.

Start by keeping a log. Whether that be on your phone, or in a diary, it doesn't matter. A simple exercise is to take out five or ten minutes a day. Reflect back on the previous day and identify a few people or situations that occurred, that you were grateful for. The more detailed you are, the better. Do this every day, and once every week, create a few action points to find the people you are grateful for. Don't limit yourself, you can be grateful for just about anything, and if it repeats, who cares? You could be grateful for someone simply smiling at you, giving you a seat on the commute to work, or a colleague buying you a coffee. Gratitude is the attitude which gives us the fortitude to deal with the toughest challenges in our lives.

ACTS OF KINDNESS

The German philosopher, Arthur Schopenhauer said, "Compassion is the basis of all morality." From when we are children we have heard how important the values of kindness and compassion truly are. They aren't just simply right, good, moral, and ethical, but scientific research has recently discovered that practicing acts of kindness is not only good for the *recipient*, but also for the *giver*. Being kind and good, even when it's bad or when nothing is returned, will benefit the *giver*. Simply because being generous and willing to share makes humans happy.

Kindness and gratitude are developed together, they work in harmony. Kindness is wanting something good for someone else, thinking about what would benefit them, and putting effort into giving them that benefit. In our daily activities, we expect other people to be kind, compassionate, and giving towards us, who wouldn't? But the best way to attract these qualities into our lives is to first develop them ourselves.

Many studies have shown that attitudes, behaviour, and even health are contagious within our social networks, but what hadn't been clear was whether this is true simply because we tend to be friends with people who are like us. So, two researchers from Harvard and the University of California, San Diego, set out to find out whether kindness is contagious among people who don't know each other. They set up a game where they arranged strangers into groups of four and gave each person twenty credits. Each player was instructed to decide (in private) how many credits to keep for themselves and how many to contribute to a common pot, that at the end of the round would be divided evenly among the players. At the end of each round, the players were shuffled, so they never knew from game to game *who* was generous, but they knew *how* generous others had been to the group. As the game went on, players who had been the recipients of generosity from teammates tended to give more of their own credits in future rounds.[61] Kindness begets kindness. To receive gratitude with humility, start by thanking the person for noticing. Appreciate their attention and their intention. Look for a good quality in the other person and return the compliment.

Many writers, thinkers, and philosophers have shared this truth for centuries. "If you want to be happy, be compassionate," says Dalai Lama. A Hindu proverb says, "True happiness consists in making others happy." Happier people are more likely to describe themselves to perform more compassionate acts, to spend more time helping others, and to perform better. By performing acts of kindness regularly, people have reported feelings of increased happiness for an extended period of time. Not only that, but being kind and generous leads you to perceive others in a more positive and charitable light. It fosters a heightened sense of interdependence and cooperation within the social community. Performing acts of kindness also helps in relieving guilt, distress, or the general discomfort over others' difficulties and suffering, encouraging a sense of awareness and appreciation.

A larger impact is on oneself. By committing acts of kindness, you begin to view yourself as a compassionate and grateful person. This promotes your sense of confidence, optimism, and usefulness. Helping others or volunteering, highlights your resourcefulness, expertise, and gives you a sense of control over your life.

Helping others also leads to people liking you, appreciating you, and offering their gratitude towards you. People will reciprocate in your times of need. Helping others satisfies a basic human need for connection, winning smiles, thankfulness, and valued friendships. We often define gratitude and appreciation as what we have been given by others. But we must practice gratitude daily. Gratitude generates

---

[61] Epley, N., & Schroeder, J. (2014)

kindness and so it is a powerful quality. It brings forth all other qualities like compassion, resilience, confidence, passion. These are all positive traits that help us find meaning and connect to others.

Acts of kindness stem from a level of compassion. The Sanskrit word for compassion is *karunā*, which literally translates to 'feeling for others'. You can be sentimental, but *karunā* goes beyond just sentiments. We will explore this further in a later section of the book, but, this journey is about making an outward change, at the same time that we make an inward change. Both go hand-in-hand. Gandhi said, "Be the change you wish to see in the world."

OPTIMISM

Optimism is similar to gratitude, in that they both involve developing the habit of striving to see the positive side of a situation. Optimism is different in that, it not only focuses on the present, but also the past, and in the anticipation of a bright future. Like gratitude, optimism means different things to different people. Even psychologists studying optimism have offered different definitions. Some characterise it as a global expectation about a positive future; a belief that our goals can be accomplished. Others suggest that it is in the way that people tend to explain outcomes of situations. Optimism is not just about anticipation of "I will get there," or, "I will get this." It is also thinking about *how* it will happen.

Laura King of the University of Missouri-Columbia, has carried out an experimental study on optimism.[62] She asked participants to visit her lab for four continuous days, and to write for twenty minutes about their "best possible future selves." This was a mental exercise in which participants had to visualise the best possible future for themselves, in multiple domains of life. For example, a woman in her mid-twenties might imagine that in a decade, she will be married, have two healthy children, have an enjoyable job, and pursuing her hobbies. The professor found that the people who wrote about their visions for twenty minutes a day over several days, compared to those who wrote about other topics, were more likely to show immediate increases in

---

[62] King, L. A. (2001)

positive moods. She also found that they were happier several weeks later, and even reported fewer physical ailments several months thereafter.

By thinking optimistically about the future, you feel confident that you will be able to achieve your lifelong goals, and you will further invest your efforts in reaching them. Optimistic thoughts are self-fulfilling. Perceiving an outcome as attainable, you will persist in planning to avoid or overcome obstacles. Optimists are more likely to persevere and engage fully even amidst difficulty.[63] Evidence also shows that optimists routinely maintain relatively high levels of well-being and mental health during times of stress, and that those with frequent optimistic thoughts are physically healthier. If you have something to look forward to, you will naturally feel energised, motivated and, of course, enthusiastic. You will even be better liked by others.

The more you practice optimistic thoughts, the more *natural* and *ingrained* they become. Slowly, they become a part of you. You may be thinking that forcing yourself to 'think positive' is silly, and that sometimes we have to 'see things for what they really are'. Isn't reframing negative events into positive, or optimistic views, an anticipation of a bright future that could be unrealistic? Well, optimism isn't about deceiving yourself. I agree, the world *is* sometimes a horrible and mean place, but at the same time it is also wonderful and divine. There is no halfway point, nor is it one way or the other, it is just your perception.

To be optimistic involves a choice that *you* make on how to see the world. It doesn't mean you deny or avoid negativity, as we mentioned earlier, but trying to get in control. Research has shown that optimists are *more* vigilant of risks and threats. They are also aware that positive outcomes are dependent on efforts, and don't wait for things to just happen.

---

[63] Segerstrom, S. C. (2001)

FORGIVENESS

To forgive is to set a prisoner free,
and discover that the prisoner was you.
Lewis B. Smedes

We live in a society where we think about people in terms of their purpose or utility, and so, all our interactions with others are driven by that intention. Today, we live in a world of quick fixes; we can microwave meals, stream movies instantly, book tickets from our phones—everything has become instant. Sadly, our relationships with others don't work in the same way. Relationships are like growing a plant, where constant care is required, so that one day we see it bloom. An important aspect of maintaining any relationship is forgiveness. Forgiveness is a choice. A choice that we all make as individuals to save (or break) relationships and achieve peace of mind. It is a virtuous quality that we can practice in our daily lives.

KSHAMĀ: GENUINE FORGIVENESS

The Sanskrit word for forgiveness is *kshamā*. Contrary to popular belief, forgiveness is not an action we take for others, but for ourselves, and within ourselves, to free us from anger and negativity. Sometimes, we don't want to forgive, but, we want revenge. We want to return pain to the ones who inflict it on us. If this is the case, how can you fix yourself by breaking someone else in the process? You will only feel more pain, because revenge always backfires. Rising above revenge, we should offer *kshamā*.

Forgiveness brings peace to our minds. It actually conserves energy. Forgiveness has links to health improvements too, including less consumption of medicines, better sleep quality, and fewer somatic symptoms including backpain, headache, nausea, and fatigue. It also eases stress, because we no longer need to recycle angry, negative thoughts that bothered us in the first place.[64] Science shows that in

---

[64] Lawler, K. A., Younger, J. W., Piferi, R. L., Jobe, R. L., Edmondson, K. A., & Jones, W. H. (2005)

close relationships, there is less emotional tension between partners when they are able to forgive each other, and that forgiveness promotes physical well-being. In a 2011 study, 68 married couples agreed to have an eight-minute talk about a recent incident where one of them "broke the rules" of their marriage. The couples then separated, not from marriage of course, but for the experiment, and watched replays of the interviews. Researchers measured their blood pressure to find that in couples where the "victim" was able to forgive their partner, both partners' blood pressure decreased. Forgiveness is good for everyone.[65]

SEE THE BIGGER PICTURE

One of the most important incidents that teach us about forgiveness is from a Vedic text called the Rāmāyana. It tells the tale of Prince Rāma, who was exiled to a distant forest for fourteen years, for no particular reason other than the selfish, political motivations of his stepmother Kaikeyi. However, he did not go alone. He gave up his rightful throne and was willingly accompanied by his wife, Sitā, and loyal brother, Lakshmana.

One morning, a few years into their journey, Sitā saw an unusual, radiant golden deer prancing in the distance. Mesmerised by its beauty, she requested Rāma to capture it for her. Obliging, Rāma set off to capture the deer, but left Lakshmana with strict guidance to guard and protect Sitā while he was away.

A little while later, a voice echoed in the trees amongst the forest, "Sitā, help me!" The silence of the forest consumed the sound. "Lakshmana! Please, somebody save me!" the voice called out again. Lakshmana and Sitā were both confused. That sounded like Rāma, but he would never call out for help. They were not aware of the fact that the golden deer being chased by Rāma was actually a demon in disguise. Was the powerful warrior Rāma really in some kind of trouble?

"Lakshmana, please go save your brother!" commanded Sitā to Lakshmana, who did not budge. He knew that his brother would be

---

[65] Hannon, P. A., Finkel, E. J., Kumashiro, M., & Rusbult, C. E. (2012)

fine, he had defeated thousands of demons in the forest over the past few years, and he could handle anything himself.

"It is your duty to go!" Sitā began to panic. Just the thought of her loved one being in danger, brought an outpour of emotion in Sitā.

"Rāma can protect himself," Lakshmana replied, "But you cannot. My duty right now is to protect you. Rāma would never forgive me if I left you alone here. Who knows what lurks in this forest?"

If you know the story, you will know what actually lurked in the darkness of the forest. Lakshmana continued to stay guard of Sitā.

"We are in the middle of nowhere Lakshmana," Sitā argued, "I command you, I beg of you to go save Rāma. I sense he is in great danger!" It is said that as the last refuge in an argument, people pull their ranks, but Sitā was clearly distressed. Moments passed in silence till another shout came from the distance.

"That is your brother calling you out for help! How can you do nothing?" Sitā began to scream. "I get it. Now that Rāma will be out of the picture, you think you will have me for yourself? You want the kingdom to yourself too?" Sitā obviously knew that was not true, and that Lakshmana would have done anything for his brother, but she wanted him to react. Lakshmana hung his head in sorrow, looking down at the sand by his feet. How can someone he had dedicated his whole life in service to, make such an accusation against him? His heart was crushed. After continuous pleads from Sitā, Lakshmana made sure that his sister-in-law was safe, before running off into the forest in search of Rāma.

Now let's analyse this episode and the powerful context of forgiveness. Sitā had clearly hurt Lakshmana with her harsh words, and it changed his perspective for the events that followed. In our lives, situations will crop up where we will play the role of Sitā at times, and sometimes Lakshmana too. Our perspective too, at times like this, must remain unbiased.

What Sitā said was insensitive and wrong. But, if we look beyond the situation, that is, if you look past *what* was said, we might be able to understand *why* she said *what* she said. Sitā was going through a personal turmoil at the time. Her emotions were all over the place, speculating on what was happening to her beloved husband. We have all been victims of situations where our mind is clouded by our emotions. When this happens, we say anything and everything to try and clear our mind. But just a moment of patience, especially in moments of anger, can actually save us thousands of moments of regret in the future. In testing times, we should remain stable. When someone hurts us, look beyond the situation and think, "Are they suffering? If so, how? What are they feeling that could make them say such a thing? Is there something going on in their life that may cause them to speak like this to me?" I am not saying support and take all hurtful comments made to you by others. But, it is about seeing the bigger picture. A Sanskrit phrase says, *'para dukha dukhi'*, which means 'to feel pain when others suffer'. This is empathy, an essential component of forgiveness.

DISTINGUISH EPISODES & PEOPLE

Sticks and stones may break my bones, but words will never hurt me. It's utter rubbish; this can't be further from the truth. Words are weapons that cause emotional violence. They can leave invisible scars that can take years to heal. Making the shift from anger to forgiveness really does help. Obviously, this doesn't apply in every situation, especially those of social justice. But, in our personal interactions, for the most part, it is the way to go.

After returning from the exile of fourteen years, you would think that Rāma—now the king of Ayodhyā—would throw his stepmother out, but he didn't. He forgave Kaikeyi, who sought forgiveness from Rāma and repented her mistakes. Rāma distinguished the episode from the person. The incidents of the Rāmāyana constantly emphasise values such as forgiveness, tolerance, and unity.

We need to always be aware that everyone is going through challenges of their own, which are concealed from the public eye. This is where the lens of empathy helps, or as Mahant Swami says, the lens of divinity. Again, I am not saying tolerate abuse, or correct someone sensibly if they're wrong, but in order to practice forgiveness, we have to learn that both episodes and people are distinct.

NO ONE'S PROBLEM

Saying 'it is *my* problem' causes you to feel guilty, and over time, you may develop an inferiority complex. You may begin to think that you are not strong enough to deal with situations, and so you will be depressed over little issues. Saying 'it is *your* problem' causes you to feel angry. There will be so many occasions where you have pointed your finger at someone and said, "It's *your* problem, not mine." Blaming other people only leads to a spiral of anger. What we need to say is 'it is *the* problem'. This separates the problem from the people involved. Not only does this separation empower you to forgive the other person, it helps you deal with the problem effectively too.

SOCIAL JUSTICE

On 17th December, 2012, I vividly remember seeing a news report on TV about a 23-year-old woman by the name of Jyoti Singh, who had been brutally raped overnight and then left to die by six young men in New Delhi, India. Unfortunately, she suffered a lot thereafter and did not survive. Following the days of the attack, the media elaborated on reports of the gruesome nature and detail of the rape. The incident didn't just shock the entire nation of India, but also provoked widespread international condemnation for the ill-treatment of women in India. Protests took place across the country to ask for justice for the young woman in reform in the courts, so that women in India feel more protected. Do you think we should have forgiven the men who raped the young 23-year-old physiotherapy student?

During the great war of the Mahābhārata, Arjuna tries to convince Shri Vāsudev Krishna that the best thing to do is to lay down all weapons and not fight. Arjuna was a pacifist. "Why partake in bloodshed and sacrifice thousands of lives when we can just retreat? Surely it is better to forgive those who sin?" Arjuna argued. But Shri Vāsudev Krishna fully disagreed with his cousin and shared with him the wisdom of social justice.

On a personal level, we may be able to forgive those that hurt us; that is a personal choice, available to all of us. But, on a societal level, heinous crimes like this, if left unpunished, can wreck havoc. The repercussions of allowing individuals to break the law can be destructive. And so, Shri Vāsudev Krishna encourages Arjuna to pick up his bow and fight, not for himself, nor for the throne, but for social justice alone.

In the same way, the men who performed the criminal act of rape should always face the full force of justice, casual actions in the name of forgiveness will never help society progress. Fortunately, in March 2020, they were sentenced to death for their despicable crime. Forgiveness and justice both go hand-in-hand. Wisdom and introspection helps us to know how they should be used.

FORGIVE FOR YOURSELF

Everyone makes mistakes. You are not the only one, remember this. Dragging yourself around with guilt and self-criticism is unhealthy and pointless; it doen't do you any good. Guilt, shame, and self-criticism are some of the most destructive forces in life, which is why you *must* learn to forgive yourself. This doesn't mean that we continue to make the same mistakes again and again. When it comes to emotional pain, we wallow in self-pity, guilt, shame, and resentment, often for our entire lives. We relive our terrible moments again and again instead of letting them go. The moment you decide to forgive and let go, your negative feelings fizzle away, and you are already on the road to freedom. It's all about taking care of yourself, not the person you need to forgive. It's about putting your desire to feel good before your desire to be right. It's about taking responsibility for your own peace of mind, instead of pretending it is in the hands of someone else.

If you are having issues with someone close to you, explain how you feel without putting the blame on them, and regardless of the outcome, forgive them. If you want to be free, you have to let go. If you are feeling hurt or resentful towards someone you don't care about, free yourself and let it go instead of holding it in. Do not *want* to make others understand, pretending that it is because you want them to become a better person, that you are making them understand. Don't remain adamant. Let it go. Forgiveness isn't about being nice or caring to them, it's about being nice and caring to yourself, and for yourself.

FINALISING FORGIVENESS

I think we've spoken extensively about forgiveness, as well as the benefits associated with it. By forgiving, we begin to separate our pain from people, circumstances, and incidents; we begin to heal ourselves emotionally. Asking for forgiveness, after putting the pain and faults of others aside, is a step up. It's hard because we are so accustomed to finding the faults in others first, and then forgiving them. We aren't used to admitting our own faults and taking responsibility for what we create in our own lives.

Sometimes, we do feel shame or guilt for our past actions; but don't worry, this is actually good. We are beginning to notice that our past actions no longer reflect our current values. The reason we hurt over our past is because we are progressing. You have already begun winning the battle against the monkey.

When we accept the fact that the past can't be undone, we begin to accept our own imperfections and mistakes, we are able to forgive ourselves, and in doing so, we open ourselves up to the emotional healing that we all deserve. The pinnacle of forgiveness is to wish well of the person who has caused you pain. This is the difficult to achieve, but possible, and we will see two real examples of this shortly. If you want the negativity between you and the other person to completely dissipate, you have to wish best for both sides. You don't need to directly forgive them in person, but you can pray and wish well for them. You will only feel free and at peace when you are truly able to let go. Negativity is a natural part of the cosmic *māyā*. Negativity is everywhere, and it always will be, but we begin to let go of it through recognition and forgiveness. The less you fixate on others, the more you are able to live by Principle One and begin to truly focus on yourself.

ROUTINE & FLOW

Every day, think as you wake up, today I am fortunate to be alive,
I have a precious human life, I am not going to waste it.
Dalai Lama

The swamis wake up daily between 3 a.m. and 4 a.m. They usually sleep around 10 p.m. the night before. A few I knew before they came here, would never wake up that early—they admitted this—but here they were today, completely changed! They were committed to the process. They formed a routine. They got into a flow. I learnt here at Sarangpur, how important routine and flow was in our day-to-day lives.

Sleep researchers state that 85 percent of us need an alarm clock to wake up. When we wake up before our bodies are ready, the hormone melatonin (which helps to regulate sleep) is usually still at work, which is one of the reasons we smash that snooze button.[66]

Unfortunately, we live in a world today where, in order to be 'productive', we are encouraged to live like this. Maria Popova writes, "We tend to wear our ability to get by on little sleep as some sort of badge of honour that validates our work ethic. But it is a profound failure of self-respect and priorities." I personally know of so many people that take pride in the few amounts of hours they sleep. I'm so amazed. No, really, I am. I'm amazed as to how you can find pride in sleeping two hours and heading to work! Then, once we've woken up after barely sleeping, nearly a quarter of us do something else that is the worst thing to do to start the day—we reach for our mobile phones within a minute of waking up. Over half of us are checking our messages, snaps, and DMs within ten minutes. A majority of people go from out cold to processing vast amounts of data and information within minutes every morning.

At the time of writing, there are only six cars that can go from zero to sixty miles per hour in under two seconds. Like most cars, humans are not built for a 0 to 60 kind of transition, not mentally nor

---

[66] Roenneberg, T. (2012)

physically. Looking at your phone first thing in the morning is a personal invitation to hundreds of strangers—including those influencers—into your bedroom, before you've even peed, showered, brushed your teeth, and touched up your hair. Between the alarm clock and the world inside your phone, you're immediately overwhelmed with stress, pressure, and anxiety. And you expect yourself to have a pleasant and productive day after all that bombarding?

WAKE EARLY

The energy and mood you hold in the morning carries you through the entire day, so you have to start with fixing up your morning. We're accustomed to waking up just a while before we have to get to work, a class, a workout, or to drop the kids off at school. We leave ourselves just about enough time to shower, eat breakfast, pack up, and the rest. But having 'just enough time' means *not* having enough time. You run late. Probably not even enjoying your shower properly. You might skip breakfast. You leave the bed unmade. You can't do things with purpose, flow, and care, if you have to rush through them. When you start the morning with this type of high pressure and stress, you're programming your Tesla to operate in that mode for the rest of the day. It will follow through in your conversations, classes, meetings, appointments. Waking up early *does* lead to having a more productive day.

Tim Cook, CEO of Apple, starts his day at 3.45 a.m.

Richard Branson is up every morning at 5.45 a.m.

Michelle Obama rises at 4.30 a.m. for her workout.

Starbucks CEO Howard Schultz is up everyday at 4 a.m, and then he is in the office by 6 a.m.

Mahant Swami Maharaj, at the age of 87, rises at 3.45 a.m. daily.

Amazon CEO, Jeff Bezos makes it a top-most priority in his daily life to get eight hours of sleep every night. He says that less sleep might give you more time to produce, but the quality will suffer. So if you want to rise early, you need to head to bed at a time that allows you, your monkey, and the Tesla to get a full night's rest. If you have kids, or if you work nights, I understand it is much more difficult, but you can start with manageable increments. Just trying to wake up fifteen minutes earlier can make a difference. In those first fifteen minutes, don't pick up your phone, do something else. Say a prayer, go finish your morning routine, have breakfast, but don't touch your phone. You need to give your brain this time to set a tone and calibrate for the day ahead. After one week of trying this, add another fifteen minutes. Now you have a whole half-hour. Make it a habit, now it's up to you how you choose to spend this time.

SET A ROUTINE

Once you've created space in your morning, it is yours alone; nobody else controls it. This free time is one of the greatest gifts you now have. Use it positively, in the right away. Some health experts recommend that it's good if you park further from work, and then add a bit of a walk to your morning.

It follows that if you want a good morning, you need to start that momentum the evening before with a healthy, restful routine. So, the attention you give to yourself in the morning begins to grow and define your entire day.

Earlier sleep can put you in a better mood.[67] Have you heard of human growth hormone (HGH)? It's important as it plays a key role in growth, cell repair, and metabolism, and without it there is a chance that we might even die sooner. As much as 75 percent of the HGH in our bodies is released when we sleep, and research shows that our highest bursts of HGH typically come between 10 p.m. and midnight, so if you're awake during those hours, you're cheating yourself of HGH.[68] If you have a job that goes past midnight, or young kids who keep you up, you can ignore me here, but waking up before the demands of your day begin should not be at the expense of getting good sleep. If you spent that 10 p.m. to midnight getting proper rest, it wouldn't be so hard to make up for those hours in the morning.

Aim to simplify your mornings too. If you're spending your morning deciding what to eat, what to wear, and what tasks to handle

---

[67] Nota, J. A., & Coles, M. E. (2015)

[68] Moline, M. L., Monk, T. H., Wagner, D. R., Pollak, C. P., Kream, J., Fookson, J. E., ... & Czeisler, C. A. (1986)

first, the amounting choices complicate things unnecessarily. Finally, consider what your last thoughts are before going to sleep. Begin to make note of them. The feelings you sleep on are likely the feelings you wake up to.

Routines are what root us. Researchers at UCLA in the Department of Psychology, asked faculty staff and students whether or not they knew where the nearest fire extinguisher was located. Only 24 percent could remember where the closest one was, even though, for 92 percent of the participants, a fire extinguisher was just a glance from where they filled out the survey (usually their own office or a classroom they frequently visited). One participant didn't even realise that there was an extinguisher just inches from the office he had used for twenty-five years! Noticing what's around us keeps our monkey from shifting us to autopilot.

Routines also free our mind, but we often fear that we will become monotonous. We choose to anticipate the big events of life: holidays, promotions, birthday parties, work outings. We put pressure on these events to live up to our expectations. But, if we begin to look for small joys, in everyday things, we don't have to wait for them to come up on our calendars. Instead they will await us every day, just take the time to look for them. When we're at work, we fantasise about lying on the beach, but, when we're finally on the beach, enjoying the sun, we're frustrated that we can't get our minds off work. Allowing yourself to dream like this distracts you. Instead, living in the present is the only real way to live a rich and fulfilling life.

LOCATION & TIME

There's an obvious reason people study better in libraries and work better in offices. We came to see this during the pandemic, and we might have experienced it ourselves. Each and every environment —from the hustling metropolitan cities to the smallest corner of a study room—has its own particular energy.

Where do you thrive? In busy environments or in solitude? Do you like the safety of cozy nooks or quiet, spacious libraries? Do you prefer to be surrounded by stimulating paintings and music, or does uncluttered, minimalistic, simplicity help you concentrate? Do you like to bounce ideas off others or to get feedback after completing a job? Location doesn't just apply to our work, but in all aspects of our life. I believe that every home should have separate spaces. A place to eat. A place to sleep. A sacred space that helps you feel calm and at peace. Try create your spaces.

Doing something at the same time every day helps you to remember to do it, commit to it, and do it with increasing skill, dedication and facility. When you want to incorporate a new habit into your routine, like the ones we explore, don't make it more difficult by trying to do it whenever you have a few free moments. Allocate set times every day. Marrying habits is a way of circumventing excuses. In his book titled *Atomic Habits*, James Clear goes into great deal about the power of habits. I would recommend this read.

THE MULTITASKING MYTH

Multitasking means *attempting* to do two or more things at once. The actual word comes from a paper written by IBM in 1965, where it is defined as, "The ability of a microprocessor to apparently process several tasks simultaneously." Even computers don't *actually* process several tasks at the same time. Computer multitasking in single core microprocessors use what we call *time-sharing;* only one task can actually be active at a time, but tasks are rotated many times a second. Even this is for single-core microprocessors—one brain—just like you, me, and every other human. If you think you were watching Netflix whilst on that Zoom call during lockdown, you weren't. If you thought you were texting while driving, you weren't. You didn't do any of these things simultaneously. You took tiny breaks in between, that you may not have noticed. We ourselves create this illusion of multitasking.

Studies show that only 2 percent of us can effectively multitask; and most of us are terrible at it, especially when one of those tasks requires a lot of focus. When you think you're multitasking, what is normally happening is that you're shifting rapidly among several different things. It's known in computing as 'serial tasking'. This type of fragmented attention actually erodes our ability to focus, so doing just one thing at a time without distraction becomes harder.[69] Stanford University Researchers took a group of students and divided them into two groups—those who frequently switch among multiple streams of media (checking email, social media, and headline news, etc.) and those who don't. They put the groups through a series of attention and memory tasks, such as remembering sequences of letters and focussing on certain coloured shapes while ignoring others, and the media multitaskers consistently performed poorly. They even did worse on a test of task-switching ability.[70]

Focus on your tasks. When you're brushing your teeth, just brush. When you're showering, just shower. When you're meditating, just meditate. Don't cram tasks, it does you no good. Single-tasking as much as possible keeps your brain in the habit of focussing on one thing at a time. Pick certain routines where you always single-task, like cooking, using a certain app on your phone, showering, or doing the laundry. This will also help you to build up the skill.

DECISION FATIGUE

John Tierney, co-author of *Willpower: Rediscovering the Greatest Human Strength* says, "Decision fatigue helps explain why ordinarily sensible people get angry at colleagues and families, splurge on clothes, buy junk food at the supermarket and can't resist the dealer's offer to rustproof their new car. No matter how rational and high-minded you try to be, you can't make decision after decision without paying a biological price. It's different from ordinary physical fatigue, you're not consciously aware of being tired, but you're low on mental energy." In his book, *Paradox of Choice*, Barry Shwartz says, "The more options you have, the less happy you will be, no matter what you decide on.. The more options you have, the more difficult it becomes to choose." The more decisions we make, the more tired we will become.

---

[69] Newport, C. (2016)
[70] Ophir, E., Nass, C., & Wagner, A. D. (2009)

CREATE SPACE

Creating space is the first step to freeing yourself from the oppression of the so-called 'busy life'. If you want to channel our energy properly, you must conserve as much energy within you as possible. The more people you have in your life, and the more things you have in your life, the more energy you expend. Anyone that says that they are busy, or have a lot to do, they're talking rubbish. We don't have a lot to do, we just distract ourselves. We don't define and maintain clear priorities in life.

Simplify your life. Simplify the number of people in your life. Simplify the number of things in your life. We only have a finite amount of energy in a day, but every year we have more people in our lives. Do you see the imbalance? We have more followers online and we connect with more people, but our energy stays the same. There's no proportional growth; your energy level stays the same, but the amount of people and *things* in your life grow exponentially. The law of thermodynamics states that energy cannot be created or destroyed, but it can be transferred or transformed from one thing to another.

You must focus on *who* and *what* is important, and prioritise that. Taking that finite energy you have every day, focussing and concentrating it towards the people and things that truly matter. You will then see how your lifestyle changes for the positive, because you are investing in the people and things that matter. You want to know that the people and things you are giving your energy to, are making the most of it. Whatever you invest energy into, will grow and eventually manifest in your life.

Happiness is then a by-product. You will experience this, when you spend time with the people you love, have you noticed that you automatically feel happy? If you spend time with the people you don't like, you become unhappy. That is why I stress that we shouldn't pursue happiness, but instead pursue a lifestyle which has the by-product of happiness. To achieve this, we need to be clear of what we want to achieve in life; our purpose. We don't always know this because we don't spend enough time with ourselves. We make time for everything and everyone else in our lives, but never for ourselves. Going for a coffee with friends is not time with yourself. Going for a jog or a run is not spending time with yourself, you are watching the traffic or making sure you don't trip. Walking the dog isn't alone time, your focus at that time is your dog. Spending time on yourself is where you sit down, close your eyes, relax, not interacting with the outside world, and instead having a conversation with yourself—with the passenger. If we don't do this, we won't know what we want in life, because we don't have conversations with ourselves. It is then impossible to know what we want in life, because we can't focus that limited amount of energy that we have each day. That is why most people end up being unhappy or unsatisfied with their lives.

PROCRASTINATION IS A PAIN

Procrastination is literally the opposite of productivity. It is probably one of the worst habits to have. We often blame it on our laziness or our lack of focus. Don't argue that it is good or healthy, it isn't. There are three fundamental types of procrastinators.

- **Thrill-seekers** who enjoy the rush towards the end of any deadline, to catalyse the experience.
- **Avoiders** who fear that they will be judged for both work that is successful, and unsuccessful.
- **Indecisive** procrastinators who put off tasks to avoid the blame for a 'not-to-the-standard' end product.

Sometimes, procrastination doesn't just affect small day-to-day tasks like this, but our long-term goals too. Now, if we let our long-term goals get affected, how will we ever achieve them? Let us bring back dopamine, the painkilling friend in our body. It encourages us to take action towards reaching our goals, and gives us a feeling of satisfaction when we achieve them. When you lack any type of enthusiasm or feeling to complete a task, it means the levels of dopamine within your body are at a low. An important aspect of tackling procrastination is to get rid of distractions around you. Your environment greatly influences you. We easily get distracted by the things easily available around us, similar to binge-eating when there is food around us. Take frequent breaks between tasks and give yourself an incentive to complete the task at hand. Self-motivation really does go a long way.

DISCOVER FLOW

Have you ever experienced a time where you have been so absorbed in whatever work you are doing that you completely lose track of time? Where you have even forgotten you were hungry or that your back hurt? Where nothing seemed to matter? This crazy sensation is called 'flow'. Mihaly Csikszentmihalyi introduced this term as "a state of intense absorption and involvement with the present moment."[71] It is where you are fully immersed in what you are doing, concentrating, and often, even unaware of yourself. Flow doesn't mean the activity or work you are carrying out will be easy though. Tasks can be challenging, but they are often engrossing, stretching your skills and expertise. When in flow, people have reported feeling strong and efficient, utilising their abilities, remaining alert and in control. They perform the activity just for the sake of doing it; basically, it comes to them naturally.

This concept came to Csikszentmihalyi in the 1960s whilst he was researching the creative process. The key to creating flow is to find a balance between skills and challenges. If an activity is not challenging enough, you will become bored. Flow can come from anything, even the most monotonous and small tasks. It all depends on you. I find my flow in my spiritual and voluntary services, where I am often challenged, but enjoy what I do, paying no attention to anything else. Flow is naturally pleasurable and fulfilling. It provides you with a natural high, which makes you feel positive, productive, and in control of the experience. It is also intrinsically rewarding, you *naturally* want to repeat the activity. You should find your flow.

THE FULL SPECTRUM

So far throughout this book, I have suggested many changes that you can make in your life. But if you attempt to change everything at once, they will all become small, equal priorities. Change happens with small steps and big priorities. Pick one thing to change, make it your number one priority, and see it through before you move onto the next.

---

[71] Csikszentmihalyi, M. (1990). Flow: The Psychology of Optimal Experience

The greater your investment, the greater your return. If something is important, it deserves to be experienced deeply. And everything is important. Remember, this is a transformational journey, not an instant one.

Periods of deep focus are also good for your brain. When you switch tasks compulsively (like the multitaskers who showed poor memory and focus in the Stanford study, it erodes your ability to focus. You overstimulate the dopamine (reward) channel.[72] That's also the addiction pathway, so we are compelled to stimulate it further, to get the same feel-good hit; this leads to more and more distraction. But ironically, in the end, the feel-good of dopamine burns you out—too much dopamine can keep your body from making and processing serotonin, the contentment chemical. If you've ever spent the day jumping on and off calls, in and out of meetings, ordering from Amazon and checking the comments section on Instagram, you know that feeling of exhaustion you have at the end of it all? That's a dopamine hangover. When you allow yourself to fully immerse in experiences—whether that be through meditation, focussed periods of work, painting, doing a puzzle, doing the gardening, and many other forms of contemplative single-tasking—you are not only more productive, you actually feel better.

Over the past few years, there are a growing number of apps and magazines encouraging you to meditate for five to ten minutes a day or to 'breathe'. I am not against this, but I wouldn't be surprised if it does nothing for you. In today's world, we tend to to allocate five to ten minutes to all our daily tasks, but the truth is, you achieve very little in five to ten minutes. If you start meditating with the idea that you will instantly clear your mind, you will soon learn that immersion takes time and practice. Don't worry, meditation is coming up too.

Routines, which we have just talked about, are actually counterintuitive. When we may think of them being boring and repetitive, doing the same tasks, at the same time, in the same place makes room for creativity. Try to build routines in everything you do, and train yourself to find focus through your intention and flow.

---

[72] Lustig, R. H. (2017)

KEEP LEARNING

An important part of *Engagement* is to keep learning; to keep growing and evolving. Failure is natural, and it will happen. But rather than choosing to give up, you should learn from the lessons and move on. There is a Japanese saying that goes, "Fall seven times, stand-up eight." To make a mistake is not the end of your world, that is, unless you refuse to learn from it. Even the most successful people have failed. They simply focus on improving from the experiences and continue to grow.

Former chairman and CEO of IBM, Thomas J Watson Sr., was asked what his formula to success was. He said, "If you want to increase the success rate, double the failure rate." What he meant was that the more you try, the more you will fail. The more you fail, the more you will learn. The more you learn, the more you will succeed. The more you succeed, the happier you will be. Success lies on the opposing side of failure.

Albert Einstein is widely recognised as the greatest scientist of modern history. In 1895, the headteacher at his school in Munich wrote in his report, "Albert will never amount to anything."

Wolfgang Mozart, a musical genius, was told by Emma Ferdinand that his operas were too noisy and contained too many notes.

Walt Disney was fired by The Kansas City Star newspaper, because the editor felt he "lacked imagination and had no good ideas."

Adversity is not our biggest enemy, it is our catalyst for learning.

The Story of Jobs

Steve Jobs was born to an unwed immigrant woman. Before he was born, his mother put him up for adoption. She placed a condition that the foster parents who chose to adopt her child should be graduates. Nonetheless, a couple was found and selected for the adoption. Unfortunately for the couple, who wanted a girl, Steve emerged into the world as a boy. The couple refused to adopt him, and again he was put up for adoption. After three months, another couple was selected, but they weren't graduates. Luckily, Steve's biological mother agreed to give them Steve on the condition that they would make him a graduate.

Now, Steve's foster parents were from a poor background, but they stuck to their word. After he completed his schooling, they put him in Reed College, Portland, Oregon. It was an expensive college. Not wanting to waste his parents' money, Steve dropped out of college after just a few months. He continued to live in his friends' dorms. To make ends meet, he would collect soda bottles and sell them for whatever money he could get.

In retrospect, Steve believed that whatever happened was for the best. Since he was no longer obliged to fulfil attendance requirements, he could drop in and out of any class he liked. Reed College had the best calligraphy course in the USA, and that was where he learnt the difference between serif and sans-serif fonts. At that time, the knowledge did not have any direct relevance to his life, but later, when he developed the personal computer, Steve utilised this knowledge to offer an option of fonts in the computer software. According to him, Bill Gates copied what he did. If he hadn't received this knowledge of fonts, Apple computers would have just had one font, and Windows would've followed suit too. Steve would often mention that this incident of him dropping out of college was a blessing in disguise.

At 20, Steve had begun manufacturing computers in his parents' garage. By the time he was 33, the company had grown to annual sales of around $4 billion. But then something unexpected happened. He was thrown out of Apple Corporation. Yes, he was thrown out of the very company that he had established. The reason for this was due to the fact that some investors were brought on board as directors, and because of a difference in opinion that they developed, they chose to throw Steve Jobs out. Steve mentioned that it was a very public dismissal that felt humiliating and excruciating. He felt that he had let down innovators and thinkers at Silicon Valley and owed them a personal apology.

After a few months, he realised that he still liked doing the same thing—creating new, innovative technology. And so, he established the NeXT Corporation and took over Pixar Corporation from Lucas Corporation. This time, the corporate redcap wasn't there, and he was free to innovate as he wished. The technology developed by NeXT at the time is still used in a part of the Mac today. The first nine animation movies created by Pixar fetched a whopping $7.2 billion in revenue. Steve quoted this as another blessing in disguise. Had it not been for him to be thrown out from Apple, he wouldn't have had the freedom to innovate new technologies, that made him so successful. Later, Apple took over NeXT and Steve returned to his original company.

Even after this, Steve faced many issues in his life. He was an inspiring example of an individual who turned problems and adversities into opportunities to blossom and learn. Today, Steve Jobs is known for changing the world through his innovative technology.

If we wish to improve at anything we do, we must also be prepared for dangers to be pushed aside, obstacles to be overcome, and hardships to be faced. You pay a price to reach success.

THE AKSHARDHAM RESPONSE

Vasudhaiva Kutumbakam
The world is one family
Maha Upanishad 6.71-73

I share with you one of the most touching story, that I hold close to my heart. In this true event, my guru, Pramukh Swami Maharaj, responded to an unprecedented and horrendous incident—on his own creation—with tolerance and pluralism.

THE APPROACH

It was approximately 4.45 p.m. on the 24th of September 2002, when a white car dropped two individuals, between the ages of 20 and 25, carrying haversacks and wearing jackets filled with AK-47 guns and hand grenades at Gate 3 of the Akshardham Complex, in Gandhinagar. Avoiding security screening, the terrorists jumped the seven-foot high fence, after which the chaos began.

INFILTRATE AKSHARDHAM

The goal was simple: blow up Akshardham. They mercilessly fired rounds at visitors and pilgrims near the gift shop, as they proceeded towards the main temple whilst throwing hand grenades. One of the volunteers witnessing the shooting rushed along the 200-foot walkway, running up the stairs, closing the 15-foot doors of the main shrine, dedicated to Bhagwān Shri Swāminārāyan. The terrorists were running behind from a distance, but could not infiltrate the main temple where 35 people were peacefully offering prayers.

CHANGE TARGETS

Unable to infiltrate the main temple, the terrorists shifted their attention to the exhibition halls. Despite the volunteers having locked all the doors, the terrorists entered Exhibition Hall 1, where many people were watching the multimedia show. Upon entering, the terrorists began firing shots at the audience, wounding and killing men, women, and children. As police security guards and commandos reached the scene, the terrorists left the exhibition hall, climbing up some stairs to get on top of the outer perimeter of the temple which connected the three exhibition halls.

OPERATION THUNDERBOLT

Police and commandos escorted visitors from in and around the complex to safety, whilst volunteers aided in helping injured victims. The remaining 100 visitors in Exhibition Hall 1 were escorted to safety. As visitors from inside the main temple were being retreated, the terrorists opened fire at the commandos. They were surrounded, with no way of escape.

As NSG commandos arrived at the complex, at around 10.10 p.m, multiple strategies were reviewed and commandos positioned themselves around the complex to find the terrorists.

The stand-off continued throughout the night as the two terrorists jumped down from the rooftop and hid in the nearby bathroom. As the night progressed, the terrorists moved into a grove of trees near one of the exhibition halls, desperate and continuing to fire their rounds. At around 6.45 a.m, the 14-hour long ordeal ended with the NSG commandos shooting down the two hidden in the bushes.

AFTERMATH

Three commandos, 31 innocent pilgrims, including a swami of BAPS, were killed in this horrific incident. A further 80 individuals were seriously wounded. National and international religious, political, and social leaders strongly condemned the attack. The whole of India sank into shock and went into silence.

THE AKSHARDHAM RESPONSE

Certain leaders urged the head of the organisation, Pramukh Swami Maharaj, to voice strong protests and anger. However, Pramukh Swami chose to remain calm and composed amongst this turmoil. He walked, and urged others to, the path of prayer and forgiveness. He appealed to the state of Gujarat to maintain peace, and thus the government took the stance to maintain peace within the region and a resolve to promote solidarity.

Swamiji attended to those who came to offer their condolences and also those who came to seek solace. We do not find such equanimity in any ordinary person. The spiritual virtues and stability of an 82-year-old Pramukh Swami amazed all. He became a living proof in modern times of the highest wisdom prescribed in Vedic scriptures.

When one of his own monks had lost their lives, Pramukh Swami silently swallowed this terrible and unbearable event, preventing the news and images of the death from spreading. Swami Brahmaviharidas, who was at the scene and aiding the operation, witnessed the death of the monk before his eyes. Shattered and hurt, Swami Brahmaviharidas telephoned Pramukh Swami Maharaj, who told him, 'I know it hurts you, but contain your pain. Do not make a hue and cry. Be responsible. Keep things quiet and do not declare it in public. We cannot allow religion strife to inflame and take more innocent lives.' Pramukh Swami's emotional stability and a larger sense of responsibility to society not only kept the organisation together, but the society at large.

Even more shockingly, Pramukh Swami Maharaj had never asked for the names, origin, or religion of the terrorists. Moreover, when he came to the complex a few days later, blessing all the places of death and destruction, he asked where the terrorists had died. Swami went over to the spot and sprinkled sanctified flowers and prayed, 'May no one think of attacking anyone, any place, or any religion. May the world be freed from thoughts of terror.'

Talks of a memorial of the attack were flying around, but Pramukh Swami instructed, 'We should forgive and forget. Keep no traces or memories of the scars and hurts.' Two weeks later, on 7th October 2002, the complex was reopened to the public. Brigadier Raj Seetapathy, the NSG commando in charge of the operation, said in an interview that the manner in which Pramukh Swami Maharaj reached this violent situation impressed him. The incident turned into a case study, 'The Akshardham Response'.

'What Pramukh Swami did was unbelievable. He pieced society back together. What I observed after the operation was the calm and serenity that was quickly restored. I have faced many violent encounters in my professional life, but the Akshardham response was a great learning both from operational and philosophical points of views. Once Pramukh Swami decided to even purity the souls of the two terrorists, volunteers and devotees immediately fell silent. There was no slogan shouting, no anger being expressed for any community. It was one of the most magnanimous and exemplary acts of restraint and responsibility that foiled the design of terrorists to spark more violence.'

Pramukh Swami Maharaj's life itself was pluralistic. He didn't just preach; he practiced and lived. The magnitude of his tolerance and views on harmony are unexplainable.

S

SOCIAL LIVING

Dan Buettner is the cofounder of Blue Zones, an organisation that studies regions of the world where people live the longest and healthiest lives. In a study of diet and lifestyle practices, Buettner found that longevity was tied to several aspects of community. The community that he refers to is that which is made up of close relationships with family, who'll take care of you when you need help, and a 'tribe' with shared beliefs and healthy social behaviours. [73]Social living is fundamental to a good life. In fact, sociability is the single-largest factor that influences positive well-being.

RELATIONSHIPS

Be with someone who will take care of you.
Not materialistically, but taking care of your soul.
Taking care of your wellbeing and heart.

A mother once told her young son that happiness was the key to life. One day at school, when the children were asked to write what they wanted to be when they grew up, this boy wrote 'happy'.

---

[73] Buettner, D. (2016)

The teacher smirked and said to the child, "I don't think you have understood the question."

The boy replied, "Miss, I don't think you understand life.

Happiness is something we are all looking for in our own individual ways. We all have different perceptions and ideas of what makes us happy, but it is greatly influenced by the world around us.

In a recent study conducted by Harvard University, a group of youths were asked about what they felt was the most important goal in their lives. 80 percent said it was to become rich, and 50 percent of the same audience said another important goal for them was to become famous. We are programmed to think that becoming rich and famous is the formula for happiness. Interestingly enough, a quarter of CEOs actually suffer from depression.

People chase money, hoping for a sizeable house with a comfortable bed. Yet, 30 percent of people who have this struggle to sleep at night. People chase fame, unaware that it won't appease the feeling of emptiness within. As a society, we work hard for money to provide for our families and loved ones, yet the average family spends only 37 minutes together in a day. We take photos everywhere we go, but we do not capture the moment. Today we have fast cars and fast food, and so we have forgotten to slow down and take a moment to see the direction in which our life is moving.

Another Harvard University study on Adult Development studied the lives of 724 men across four generations, for over 75 years. In the last ten years of the study, the spouses were included as well. In the study, they tracked the health and happiness of the participants with a series of questions about various aspects of their lives such as home, work, and family life. The study concluded that it wasn't money, fame, or assets that made people healthier and happier, but it was in fact good relationships, and embracing community that kept them healthier and happier. It showed that those who had fulfilling relationships with their family and friends were healthier and happier than those who did not; regardless of how much money or fame they had. Things are meant to be used, and people are meant to be loved. But it seems that in today's society, the tendency is to love things, and to use people to obtain such things. The *things* we chase include fame, money and recognition, and we forget to balance our time for what really matters—our relationships with one another. True richness is determined by counting the number of things you have, that money cannot buy, and counting the people that are there to help you in times of need. Just as much as we invest in our education, careers, and *empires*, we need to put the same level of investment, if not more, in our relationships.

MARRIAGE

A marriage is a sacred bond; It is not a contract based merely on beauty or exterior qualities. It is important that we don't just look for external qualities in a significant other, but focus on their internal qualities too. Do they bring you peace? Do they motivate you? Do they brush off positivity onto you?

It is like a subtle thread that is bound together by loyalty and love. In any relationship, loyalty is important; to be open with one another. This doesn't mean you share all your insecurities with each other, although some partners may choose to do so. Your mind will really play games with you here. As an example, you may be angry from a frustrating day at work causing you to come home and vent that anger onto your partner. With this, there is also the possibility that you are projecting your insecurities onto them and blaming them. Either that, or, you aren't able to control yourself. Instead, learn to take responsibility for your emotions, do not take them out on your significant other.

Joy or misery, success or failure, through every moment of life, pledging to stand by one another is the purity of a relationship. The nature of one's personality is such that it will clash in any relationship, it doesn't just have to be with our life partner. Though, we must control ourselves during these times too. My guru says, "A man looks for the 'best wife', and a woman looks for the 'best husband'. Instead, we should become the best husband, or the best wife for our partner. Only then will we be able to live together in peace. We often have expectations of our partner, but we don't focus on ourselves, and how we can improve ourselves to spread our positivity and bring joy to our partner."

Another common issue of conflict within relationships is having divergent viewpoints on various issues, some of which are often of great importance. These could include financial issues, matrimonial issues, career planning, or even future life plans. However, many times there are normal issues too, such as family getaway plannings or maintaining house rules. When these conflicts arise, what should we do? In his principle teachings, compiled in the Vachanāmrut, Bhagwān Shri Swāminārāyan offers a modern solution to these conflicts by stating that mutual respect should include regard for one another's thoughts, decisions, and desires. In today's world, this would include putting aside our ego and the willingness to compromise. Such compromises are a defining characteristic of genuine love. Mahant Swami also says, "We should be willing to set aside our desires and compromise according to the wishes of our loved ones."

A key factor in maintaining intimate relationships is abstinence. When we get married, we promise each other with the vows of fidelity, and the promise that we will live together till death do us part. But sadly, in the society of unfulfilled desires, we often forget these promises, which then shatter our pledges and lead to splits in our relationships. Studies have shown that 1 in 7 divorces or separations take place due to adultery. Again, Bhagwān Shri Swāminārāyan offers several solutions for this. In one of his teachings over 200 years ago, he mentioned that we should never take advantage of unbalanced power dynamics. Fast forward to the 21st century, this sociological trend has been at the core of many of the violations that have come to light under the recent 'Me Too' campaign. When you begin a relationship, you give each other vows, including that of fidelity, to remain loyal to one another. If you make a mistake, admit your faults and be honest. By doing so, you can address them and learn from them.

Sometimes, the deepest wounds are inflicted by those closest to us, the ones we love. How can I trust her after this? How can I forgive him? Could she have done this before? These are the types of thoughts that bounce around in our mind when mistakes occur, and we struggle to forgive. Relationships are tested during difficult times. To accept someone when everything is going smoothly is easy, but to stick together when things are falling apart, that is the true test of any relationship. True love is when you have every reason to break up, but you don't. I agree that sometimes, some relationships can become toxic. You have to try and open up to each other and resolve what you can. Understandably, there may come a time where we give our all to someone, and we feel that they don't give us anything back. This leaves you with an empty feeling within. Relationships should be empowering; they should bring the best out in the both of you. It is commonly seen in toxic relationships that, we don't love the person, but we just love the idea of what they could have been. Or, in the moment that we loved them, they changed or turned out to be someone we didn't expect to be, creating a sense of appeal for to us at the time. Yes, none of us are perfect, and no relationship is perfect, but never hold on to false hope or future anticipation after warning signs. It may feel toxic or selfish to leave someone, but then think about whether or not it is more toxic to stay together.

THE THREE Cs OF TRUST

An article from *Psychology Today*, describes a field study of military leadership in Iraq done by psychologist Colonel J. Patrick Sweeney. From his studies he derived the '3 Cs' of trust: competence, caring, and character.[74] These have been identified as the qualities we look for in the people we allow into our lives. You'll recognise these people as we explore the three qualities, and most of us will know at least one person who falls into each of these categories.

Competence. Someone has to be competent if we are to trust their opinions and recommendations. This person has the right skills to solve your issue. They are an expert or authority in their area.

Care. We need to know a person cares if we are putting our emotions in their hands. Real care means they are thinking about what is best for you, not only what is best for them. They care about your well-being, not merely your success. They have your best interests at heart. They believe in you. They would go beyond the call of duty to support you.

---

[74] Matthews, Michael, D. (2016)

Character. Some people have a strong moral compass and uncompromising values. We look to these people to help us see clearly when we aren't sure what we want, or believe what is right. Character is especially critical when we are in an interdependent partnership (a relationship, a business partnership, a team). These people practice what they preach. They have a good reputation, strong opinions, and a down-to-earth personality. They are trustworthy and are able to give honest advice.

Observe people's intentions and actions. Are they in alignment? Are they demonstrating what they say they value? Do their values correspond with yours? We learn more from the behaviour of others than their promises.

One person can't be all three of these; it's very difficult to even find someone like that. These three types of trust help us remember what we can and can't expect from others. Don't expect one person to be everything for you. Even your partner can't provide care, character, and competence in all ways at all times. Sometimes we expect our life partner to be our everything, to complete us, but even within that deep and lifelong union, only you yourself can complete yourself, not anyone else. If you can't love yourself, how can you love another?

TRUST

Trust is an integral part of any relationship, and it is earned. It is a belief that a person is being honest with us, true to us, and having our best interests at heart. We *trust* someone to uphold our promises in confidence, and that they will support our intentions. We won't have the same level of trust for everyone. According to studies by Dr. Bella DePaulo, people are dishonest in one-fifth of their interactions. Yes, 20 percent of all human interaction is dishonest. 77 college students, and another 70 people from the community at large, were asked to keep track of their social interactions for seven days. They were told to record all their exchanges and to note how many lies they told. You may be thinking, "What if they lied about lying?" To encourage honesty, the researchers told the participants that there was no judgement involved, and that their response would help to answer fundamental questions about lying behaviour. They were also told that the experiment was a chance to get to know themselves better. At the end, the students reported some level of lying in one-third of their interactions. The other community members reported lying in one out of every five interactions.[75]

We've already pondered upon the ego, and how we often lie to impress, to present a better version of ourselves. One of the biggest mistakes we make when it comes to trust is assuming that everyone operates like us. We believe that others value the same things we value. We believe that the things we want from a relationship is what others want from a relationship too. We believe that when someone says the words "I love you," it means exactly what we think it means. No one is a reflection of us. Learn to see things the way they truly are. A fundamental part of trust is to accept people as they are, giving them a chance to grow with us. Long-term trust evolves naturally, but building trust is an everyday practice.

THE SIX EXCHANGES

A life without relationships is hard to imagine. A relationship, and the feeling of belonging, is an inherent universal need that keeps us rooted in life. But there is an art to maintaining them too. *Sanga* is the Sanskrit word meaning association. This does not infer to your general day-to-day associations with your colleagues or clients; I am talking about a higher level of intimacy that we share with others. Whilst exploring the Vedic text for the research of this book, I came across a text from the Gaudiya Vaishnavism branch of Hinduism. It describes relationships with six types of exchanges that create intimacy and meaning.

dadāti pratigruhnāti
guhyam ākhyāti pruchchhati
bhunkte bhojayate chaiva
sad-vidham prīti-laksanam

---

[75] DePaulo, B. M., Kashy, D. A., Kirkendol, S. E., Wyer, M. M., & Epstein, J. A. (1996)

This loosely translates to, "The six exchanges of love that develop loving relationships are the offering and acceptance of gifts, the opening of one's mind to inquire in confidence, and the sharing and receiving of food."

1. *dadāti pratigruhnāti:* means 'to offer and accept'. All levels of intimacy begin with these two. For example, when someone visits our home, we share our WiFi password with them. And the person usually reciprocates and returns the favour when we visit their home in the future. We don't offer and accept the same from just anyone we meet; it only occurs between people that we are, or wish to be, intimate with.

2. *bhunkte bhojayate chaiva* means 'to share and receive food'. This takes association to another level. Especially in South Asian culture, where those close to us invite us for lunch or dinner. When we eat together, a deep emotional bond is formed. From sharing things we have moved on to sharing food.

3. *guhyam ākhyāti pruchchhati* means 'beginning to reveal your heart in confidence'. When someone pours their heart out to us, we don't just listen to them, we feel attached to them, and begin to be influenced by their beliefs and values.

Very vaguely, we have divided and touched upon the six exchanges into three key areas. These six exchanges encourage bonding and growth. They help build upon relationships with gratitude, love, compassion, and service.

A GROWING FAMILY

Feeling connected at some level to humanity at large can be helpful, especially for those who have struggled with maintaining close relations in the past. Gandhi said, "The golden way is to be friends with the world and to regard the whole human family as one."[76] The Upanishads say, "For those who live magnanimously, the entire world constitutes but a family."[77]

---

[76] Baharati, K. S. (2006)
[77] Warrier, A. (1953)

Jean Dominique Martin says, "People come into your life for a reason, a season or a lifetime." One person might enter your life as a welcome change. Like a new season, they bring a certain level of excitement and energy to you. But we all know that seasons end at some point. Another person might come in with a reason; to help you learn and grow, or to support you through difficult times. Sometimes it almost feels like they've been deliberately sent to assist or guide you through a particular experience, after which their role in your life might decrease. And then there are those for life. They stand by your side through thick and thin, loving you and being there for you, even when you are giving nothing to them. No one relationship is equal to another.

BEING READY

The six loving exchanges we just discussed, lay a foundation for any close relationship, but most of us endeavour to look for 'the one'. The Harvard Grant Study followed 268 Harvard undergraduates for seventy-five years, collecting large amounts of data about them throughout their life. When researchers analysed the data, they found a single factor that reliably predicted the quality of participants' lives—love. Participants could have every other external marker for success; money, a thriving career, good physical health—but if they didn't have loving relationships, they weren't happy.[78]

In *How to Love,* Thich Nhat Hanh writes, "Often, we get crushes on others not because we truly love and understand them, but to distract ourselves from our suffering. When we learn to love and understand ourselves and have true compassion for ourselves, then we can truly love and understand another person."[79] Nobody completes you. You are not half. You don't have to be perfect, but you have to come to a place of giving. Begin to complete yourself first, and then you can look towards others.

---

[78] Shenk, J. W. (2009)
[79] Hanh, T. N. (2016).

HEARTBREAK

Never attach yourself, or obsess over one person, regardless of the situation or time spent with that person. No one deserves any type of abuse; be it verbal, emotional, or physical. If you are placed in this type of situation, believe me, you are better off alone. Don't allow any type of abuse, manipulation, or toxicity to remain in your life, not even to transition to a friendship. I know I have said that no relationship is perfect, but if you are not content to a certain level, or even worse if you are being emotionally drained, do you think that will change without effort from both sides? This is a difficult choice, but one we all must often make—learn to accept it and move on. Obviously it isn't easy, especially when you've spent quality time with someone, investing in them, giving yourself to them, making memories with them, then it is hard to let go. But don't mistake attachments for love. Often, we are just attached, well not always us, but the monkey is for sure. Remember that attachments are a cause of suffering. The more we grasp, the more we are afraid to lose, leading to suffering. The same applies with people, the more we hold on to the wrong person, the more we suffer. Sometimes, we just need to learn to let go.

You may try to distract yourself from heartbreak, but the fixes will only be temporary. Researchers followed incoming college freshmen to see how well they adapted to their transition. They found that those with a tendency to suppress their emotions had fewer close relationships and felt less social support.[80] Think about how the other person made you feel. Articulate your feelings into some form of writing or recording. Read what you've written and listen back objectively, noticing patterns. Then learn from the situation. You may undervalue yourself in the moment of a breakup, or you may feel guilty too, but your value shouldn't depend on someone's ability to appreciate you. If you expected the person to fulfil all your needs, then a vacuum will remain. Now that you are alone, use the time to make yourself whole again. Be someone who makes you happy. Don't rush into anything new before you are truly ready.

---

[80] Srivastava, S., Tamir, M., McGonigal, K. M., John, O. P., & Gross, J. J. (2009)

ROUNDING UP RELATIONSHIPS

Maintaining a healthy relationship is a difficult task, but it is one we all take on. As Mahant Swami said, "Marriages and partnerships are sacred." Romantic attraction will come and go, but a substantial relationship is built on the foundations of shared values. These include respect, loyalty, trust, and shared beliefs—all that work both ways. Give time and appreciation to your relationships, particularly your family. Everyone is already going through enough with work, children, and other mounting responsibilities; don't let anyone feel neglected, spend quality time with one another. This applies to children too. They require special attention. You may not realise the dire consequences of neglecting a child or just shoving an iPad in their hands, until it's too late. Children that are deprived of receiving consistent love try to make up for that love by rebelling, turning to drugs and alcohol, indulging in sexual behaviours, seeking the wrong friends, and even criminal activity. Children that feel neglected may also suffer from low self-esteem or depression, these will destroy them for life. Be careful.

Always be careful not to take the ones closest and dearest to us for granted. Appreciation and affection that isn't expressed, is rarely understood. Happiness of the heart is the happiness that we share with others.

Studies have shown that if you want to predict how happy someone is, or how long they will live, you should find out about their social relationships. Having strong social relationships strengthens the immune system, extends life (more than by quitting smoking), aids speedy recovery from surgery, and reduces risks of depression and anxiety.[81] This doesn't just apply to the sociable; but even introverts that are forced to be more outgoing. They too usually enjoy it and report after that it actually boosts their mood. We need to interact and intertwine with others; we need to give *and* take, each and every one of us needs to *belong*.

---

[81] Cohen and Herbert, 1996

INVEST IN CONNECTIONS

Simplicity is the key to brilliance.
Bruce Lee

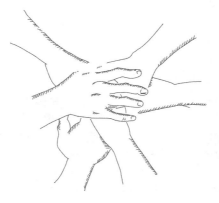

The importance that social connections have to our health and ability to experience *ānanda* are overwhelming, and I cannot stress this further. The relationships you have with others constitute as the single most important factor responsible for your overall well-being. Happy people have better relationships. Investing in relationships is a directly correlative strategy on your path to *ānanda*. Let's look at two key ways in which we can strengthen our social connections.

NURTURE RELATIONS

At the beginning of the book I explained how happier people are more likely to get married, as well as have fulfilling, long-lasting relationships with their partners. They are also more likely to feel satisfied with their family life, social activities, and will receive more emotional and tangible support from those around them. This causal relationship works both ways. Social connections make people happy, but it also means that happy people are more likely to gain better social connections. It is a continuous loop.

A classic article of social psychology, titled *The Need to Belong,* presents a persuasive case that humans are greatly motivated by a drive to seek out and maintain strong, stable, and positive interpersonal relationships.[82] Without a sense of belongingness, humans suffer various negative consequences, both mentally and physically. This has held true since the time humans first appeared on Earth. They hunted together, ate together, fought enemies together, lived together, and thus formed social bonds. They wouldn't have survived or reproduced without this motivation.

A key function of any social bond is the inherent support received in times of stress, distress, and trauma. People with strong social support are actually healthier and live longer.[83] A study on the communities of the long-living populations; Sardinians in Italy, Okinawans in Japan, and Adventists in Loma Linda, California, revealed that they all had five things in common. Topping the list were 'putting family first', and, 'keeping socially engaged'.

Make time for the people who take interest in you. Friends become as much a priority as other areas of your life, but don't overdo it either. Be helpful, supportive, and loyal to friends who need it. William Shakespeare said, "Keep thy friend under thy own life's key."

FIND TRUE FRIENDS

Finding true friends is guaranteed to bring positivity into your life. We often believe that the more people we 'know', the higher our social status. But, not everyone you call your friend is actually your *friend*. Tell me if I'm wrong. Some may say that they value your honesty and that they are your true friend, but then that same person turns around and lies about you behind your back, often to make themselves look better or to feed their ego.

Keep your friend circle simple. Stay around those who add value and meaning to your life and steer away from those who don't. Our friends have an immense influence on who we are, who we become, and how we mould our mindset. Their comments will matter, their opinions will matter, their actions towards us will matter—positive or negative. If our friends don't understand and accept us for who we are,

---

[82] Baumeister, R. F., and Leary, M. R. (1995)

[83] House, J. S., Landis, K. R., and Umberson, D. (1988).

we tend to change ourselves in order to fit into their expectations. We allow our lives to be moulded by useless comments and social manipulation.

Even more so today, with the continued growth and influence of social networks, how we define a 'friend' is constantly changing. Nowadays, friends come in the form of strangers who we have never met. The way we label a friend has become so loose, we have lost touch with true friendship. How many of these friends can we really rely on in our time of need? We live in a society where friendships are becoming less focused on emotional and life-based connections, and instead becoming all about short-term mutual gains. Many friendships today are based on bad habits such as drinking and smoking, which will definitely have a negative affect on you. I am not saying that short-term friendships are bad; each and every person that comes into our life serves a purpose. But we shouldn't expect things from everyone around us, this is more likely to cause you unhappiness.

Jealousy and competition sometimes infect friendships too. If you sense this, move straight away. Trust me, you are not in the right circle. Genuine friends will always support you and want the best for you. Success is shared, not stolen. Accept the fact that not everyone in your life is here to stay. Some people are just temporary, whilst others stay for life. We outgrow and move on, moulding ourselves and growing from within. Everyone is on their own journey, and this is all part of the greater plan.

LONELINESS

We can cure any physical disease with medicine.
But the only cure for loneliness is love.
Mother Teresa

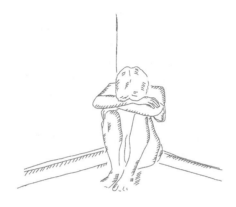

We know that diabetes can cause death, and that cigarettes can reduce life expectancy. But, what many of us don't know is that loneliness has similar effects on health. On 14th February 2018, the BBC launched the largest ever *Loneliness Experiment*, with 55,000 people from across the globe participating. In this interesting experiment, loneliness was found to be as bad for our health as smoking fifteen cigarettes daily, and that it can reduce your life expectancy by up to eight years. The epidemic of loneliness is spreading so rapidly that it is estimated to affect 1.1 million British people, and up to fifty per cent of all Americans. In the USA, one in every four people have said that they have no one to confide in.

Loneliness isn't the feeling of being alone, it is more the feeling that you aren't connected or loved by the people around you, even though you may be surrounded by people. You may have experienced this. You have so many contacts in your phonebook, followers on Instagram, countless Snapchat streaks, tons of WhatsApp groups, but you can still feel disconnected within. Whether that be in a relationship, friendship, or even marriage—you feel that pain deep within your heart, but you never share it or make it public. Loneliness stems when you rely on other people for your happiness, to make you feel complete. This is not a trait that you want to hold onto for prolonged periods of time, especially when seeking inner peace.

You can't love someone else before you learn to love yourself. You can never find the right person before growing, developing, and being the best person for yourself. If you love and put yourself first, then you will never feel lonely. We have become so busy trying to build new relationships and connections that we have forgotten the most important relationship and connection—the one with ourselves. Happiness is how you feel about yourself, when you are by yourself. We feel amazing when we are surrounded by our friends, family and colleagues. But when we are alone, we feel completely disconnected and lonely. This is when we realise that how we feel about ourselves is much more important than how others feel about us.

It is your responsibility to get your *space*, however you choose to do so. You also need to realise that your words and actions have the same impact on your inner self as they do on others. Other people are also dealing with a lot that we may not necessarily be aware of. The smallest thing can trigger the greatest reaction. The root of our disconnection from others is a disconnection from ourselves. When we are not in touch with ourselves, it is very easy to feel alone, even when we are in the physical company of others. We spend so much time following others on social media, but less time discovering ourselves. We spend time taking selfies, but less time becoming self-aware. We are prone to superficial relationships with others, because we have a superficial relationship with ourselves. We cannot have true exchanges of love, because our own hearts are empty. Although, when we dig deep and connect with the true self within, we can access the foundation of love which lies in each one of us, allowing it to flow into every part of our life. Remember, no one is coming to save you, you must save yourself. No one will change your life, you need to ignite that spark within yourself.

OVERTHINKING

Psychologists call it self-focussed rumination, but most of us know it as overthinking. All of us do it—we think too much—needlessly, passively, and endlessly; on meanings, causes, and consequences, of our thoughts, feelings, problems, and character. Why am I so unhappy? What will I be doing next year? Will I pass my exams and interviews? Will I get a promotion? Why did they break up with me? Will I ever get married? The list is never-ending.

Overthinking isn't bad, as it is the monkey's natural way to anticipate future obstacles that may come our way, and look at possible solutions. But, it's constant overthinking that fuels sadness, fosters negatively biased thinking, impairs your ability to solve problems, sucks up motivation, and has a major interference with concentration and initiative.[84] Some think that by continuously overthinking, it helps them get a stronger insight into themselves and their issues, but this is also a misunderstanding. Instead, what you gain is a pessimistic perspective on your life. Combining overthinking and negative moods is also toxic. Research has shown that people who overthink when they are already sad are likely to feel powerless, self-critical, pessimistic, and negatively biased. Evidence that shows how overthinking is damaging continues to grow. If you continuously overthink, you will never be able to experience true peace or *ānanda*, that is until you break this habit. Learn to reinterpret and redirect your negative thoughts into more optimistic ones. We accept that in every day life minor hassles and failures occur, but those who react strongly to these minor ups and downs, are among the unhappiest people in the world. To become happier, you must learn to disengage from rumination over both major and minor negative experiences. Do not let any type of negativity affect how you feel about yourself or your life as a whole.

---

[84] Lyubomirsky, S., and Tkach, C. (2003)

COMPARISONS

In our everyday lives, we can't go without seeing our friends, colleagues, family members, and even celebrities that are richer, more attractive, healthier, funnier, and happier than we are. Some research does indicate that comparisons can be useful in helping us to strive for ambitious goals or to improve upon our weaknesses, but the majority of observations suggest otherwise. Some comparisons can lead to feelings of inferiority, distress, low self-esteem and so on. The more comparisons we make with others, the more likely we are to encounter unfavourable comparisons, and the more sensitive we will feel, leading us to suffer more from negative consequences. People who continuously compare find themselves chronically threatened, vulnerable, and insecure about themselves. The happiest people take pleasure in the success of others and show concern in the face of others' failures.

POSSIBLE SOLUTIONS

Stop. I know that as simple as I make it sound, it really isn't. But when you do begin to overthink, you must tell the monkey to stop immediately, or to stop comparing yourself with others. The monkey needs to understand it isn't about how fast the Tesla is going, it is about ultimately reaching the destination, safely and peacefully. Distract the monkey. Distract it with happy, curious, peaceful, and amusing thoughts. Redirect its full attention somewhere else. I do it by reading a book or an article or watching a memorable video. You can do it by listening to music, meeting a friend, getting some fresh air. It really doesn't matter what you do, as long as it absorbs you and distracts you from overthinking.

Another way you can 'stop', is by simply telling the monkey to "Stop!" I mean, if you are alone, you can literally shout it, but just be careful if you're in the middle of a supermarket. The people that I see embodying *ānanda* set out twenty to thirty minutes daily to do nothing but think and contemplate, especially the swamis in Sarangpur. You must face the negative thoughts that push and pull you throughout the day and try to work on improving them, but only do this when you are not sad or distraught. Bhagwān Shri Swāminārāyan calls this concept *antardrashthi*; literally translating to turning your gaze inwards, or more accurately, self-contemplation. In his teachings, ge even goes on to suggest to his audience that everyone should contemplate daily. Today, research backs this up, saying that by doing so you begin to notice that most thoughts are just passing and will have very little effect on you. You could also write down the thoughts that are burning within, spilling them onto paper, and allowing them to pass.

ANTARDRASHTHI

Make a note of various thoughts that have come across your mind today. This is a form of journaling, that will help you distinguish between positive and negative thoughts. It is usually performed mentally, but you can start by noting them down.

THE CATALYST OF DRAMA

Speak less. Use words sparingly,
as you would use milk, not like water.
Shri Yogiji Maharaj

It has destroyed empires, toppled governments, ruined marriages, stamped on careers, caused heartbreak, nightmares, suspicion, generated grief, and made the innocent cry late at night into their pillows. What is it? It is gossip and drama. Office gossip, shopping gossip, family drama, work drama. It doesn't just create headaches, it creates headlines too.

In our lives, we all find ourselves in some form of gossip or drama. Often, we don't even realise it. Mahant Swami Maharaj says that the worst part is that, we enjoy the drama and gossip. We see it as being playful and completely harmless banter. In fact, we see it as being a normal part of our everyday lives. I mean come on, we all need some excitement and juice in our boring lives, right? The reactions we get or give when we hear the gossip just adds to the flavour!

Gossip evokes gossip, it allows us to keep track of everyone's reputation without actually seeing the good or bad they are doing personally. We enjoy juicy gossip because it makes us feel more powerful, we feel we know best about what is right and what is wrong, and we feel closer to those who we are gossiping with.

Today, when this world is filled with loose, fragile relationships, it has become a sport—a seemingly enjoyable pastime. Yogiji Maharaj used to say that a man gets more taste out of gossip than he does from a sumptuous feast. Someone who gossips, or likes to indulge in it, lives on a diet of other people's faults and scandals. We shape our opinions about someone based on what someone else tells us. Often, we don't even check whether it is true or not. What gives us the right to form an opinion in this way?

Three-Filter Test

Socrates was once sitting in Athens, Greece, and a man came up to him and told him that he wanted to talk about Socrates' friend. Socrates said, "For sure tell me, but only if it passes the three filter test. First, whatever you tell me about my friend, is it good or is it bad?"

The man replied, "It's bad."

Socrates said, "Then I don't know if I should listen. But anyway, tell me if it is true or not?"

"Well, I haven't verified that!" the man responded.

Socrates asked, "Whatever you want to tell me, is it beneficial or not to either me or him?"

"Neither."

Socrates then told the man to leave.

You too can use the three-filter test for yourself, when people try to tell you gossip, or when you find yourself amidst it.

First, is it good or bad? If it is bad, don't bother lending your ear, unless you are genuinely seeking out to help that person.

Secondly, is it true or false?

Third, is it beneficial or not?

If it is beneficial, hear it out, otherwise avoid it.

The media profits from gossip, from publicly exposing people's poor luck. We buy into this, and so it appears today that it has become socially acceptable to discuss the lives of others. What if someone gossiped about you? How would you feel if you were the topic of discussion? I'm sure the tables would turn then. Stay away from gossip and drama. If you are amidst it and can't move, change the topic, make it positive. The ones who engage in gossip are the ones who aren't happy. If you gossip, you too won't be happy. Don't give yourself unnecessary stress and drama. We do it because it's all about inferiority in power. It feeds our ego. Sorry to be blunt, but we do it to make ourselves feel better, because we think we are superior to others. Unfortunately, we aren't. Regardless of your social position or background, no one is superior to another.

Spreading negativity through our talks will only bring negativity back to us. Don't think you are immune to it. Begin with controlling your speech. Use your tongue to give life, not death.

H

HEALTH & WELLBEING

Eat to live.
Don't live to eat.
Benjamin Franklin

Let's begin with diet. It plays a very important role in your life. It's simple, if you don't have a good intake of food and drinks, you won't feel good. Have you noticed that when you eat certain foods, you feel fatigued and sleepy? When you feel like you're lacking the energy to carry out any activities? Most of the time these are junk foods and sadly, they are not necessarily good for us, but are simply modified to taste and look good. Because of this, we tend to become accustomed to these types of food. This not only has a negative impact on our mind and thoughts but also on our body, making us more prone to diseases.

In her book, *Deep Nutrition - Why Your Genes Need Traditional Food*, Dr Catherine Shanahan observes, "Whether by intent or simply fortuitous coincidence, today's definition of a healthy diet enables corporations to sell us cheap, easily stored foods that will put more money in their pockets and more people in hospital. By denying our bodies the food of our ancestors and severing ourselves from our culinary traditions, we are changing our genes for the worse."

Fortunately or unfortunately, because of my previous diet I now suffer from a chronic condition. I used to eat a very unhealthy diet of junk food, spicy food and fizzy drinks. I felt like I was invincible to gaining weight, and I still feel like I am, but I didn't realise that other parts of my mind and body were being affected in the process. Thankfully, following the guidance of my guru, and other senior swamis and consultants, I am now following a strict diet regimen. Although I am not fond of being restricted to what I can and cannot eat, I can wholeheartedly say that I feel much healthier and happier.

Just to give an idea, I follow a strict Ayurvedic diet comprising of a low-fibre, low-grain, plain diet. Ayurveda means the science of living and it is the world's most ancient holistic health care science, originating in the Atharva Veda. Ayurveda combines diet, herbal remedies, yoga, lifestyle practices, detoxification and rejuvenation. It is not just a 'quick-fix' solution, it is a way of life. Ayurveda promotes a vegetarian diet, with food intake to be that which controls the three 'dosha'. A dosha is one of three primary energies that exist within your body. They are namely:

- Vata (air)
- Pitta (fire)
- Kapha (water & earth)

The ideal diet comprising of all three at a balanced level, plays an important role in mental, emotional, and physical characteristics. Your mind, body, and soul must be functioning in order to have all three of these in proper synchronisation. This is something you would need to look into yourself, as it a detailed science which we could talk about all day,, and it will differ from person to person. But it is a science, with proven results, that your diet can affect not just your body, but also your mind and mental state.

Organic food is probably the way to go. Yes, it can be costly, but is anything more important than your own health? You don't want to sacrifice your health from eating unhealthy foods. Even Ayurveda promoted quality organic products, as this is the optimal way in order to keep you feeling rejuvenated and vitalised.

Another important part of any diet and lifestyle is water. Around 70 percent of your body is composed of it, which is why it is so important. Water keeps your vital organs and body hydrated and gets rid of those nasty toxins. If there is an imbalance of water in your body and it falls below the amount that your body needs, your body will react, often negatively. You will notice this because you will lose focus, start getting headaches, feeling dizzy and you may even faint! Try to take fresh, filtered, warm water. I used to drink chilled water with plenty of ice until I began my diet. I learnt that when you boil water, it gets charged with heat.It then becomes what we call in Sanskrit *sukshma*, meaning sharper in quality. This sharpness allows the water to cleanse our channels and penetrate deeper levels of our physiology.

Some other tips I learnt about drinking water, which still help me today include:

- Sit down and drink water, as opposed to standing
- Don't chug, take small sips
- Drink room temperature water, warm is better, cold is worse
- Drink only when you are thirsty
- Drink water first thing in the morning

It really helps, but it takes a while and needs to be integrated into your lifestyle. It may be hard, so try starting with organic foods and warm water. I won't even force you to stop eating junk food, but I wish I did earlier. Ideally, I'd say that The Keshav Way is to follow a diet enriched with organic foods which will help the three 'dosha' energies within your body, and that will help move you towards maintaining a positive mindset and lifestyle. Because we really are what we eat.

Exercise is also important. Without the right diet, there isn't any point in exercising. But, when our diet is correct, we can look at exercise benefitting us. Researchers from Pennsylvania State reported in the *Journal of Sport & Exercise Psychology* that, "People who are more physically active have more pleasant-activated feelings than people who are less active, and we also found that people have more pleasant-activated feelings on days when they are more physically active than usual." Start with a speed walk, or a light jog, and notice the changes in yourself. The American Psychosomatic Society published a study showing that a three-minute speed walk or jog improves recovery from clinical depression. Yes, that's right, clinical depression.

One of the most impressive studies on exercise was published in the *Archives of Internal Medicine* in 1999.[85] Researchers recruited men and women aged fifty and over, all of them suffering from clinical depression, and divided them into three random groups. The first group was given four months of aerobic exercise, the second group were given four months of antidepressant medication (Zoloft), and the third group both. The aerobic exercises involved three supervised 45 minute sessions per week of cycling, walking, or jogging at moderate to high intensity. Shockingly, by the end of the intervention, all three groups had experienced their depressions lift and reported fewer dysfunctional attitudes and increased happiness and self-esteem. Exercise was as effective as the medication used to treat depression, or as a combination of both exercise *and* medication. Exercise is less expensive, and has little to no side effects other than tiredness. Six months later, when researchers looked at the participants again, those who had recovered from depressions were less likely to relapse if they were part of the exercise group, compared to the medication group. The researchers named this study the Standard Medical Intervention and Long-term Exercise study. SMILE. This study shows the multiple benefits that physical activity can have on health and well-being. Physical activity reduces anxiety and stress; it lowers your risk of succumbing to numerous diseases, increases your quality of life, improves your sleep, protects against cognitive impairments, and helps control your weight.

It isn't just the self-confidence and self-esteem that makes people happier. Physical activity also extends opportunities for social contact, lifting the burden of loneliness and isolation. Exercise has been shown to elevate levels of serotonin, similar to the effects of Prozac.[86]

---

[85] Archives of Internal Medicine, 159: 2349–56.

[86] Meeusen, R., and De Meirleir, K. (1995)

WORRY

Worrying about how things might go wrong,
doesn't help things to go right.

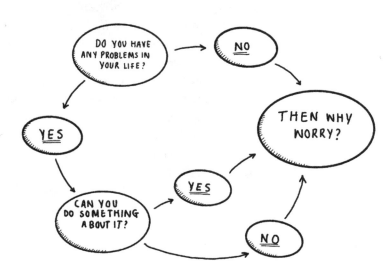

This is one of my favourite diagrams, and it is quite popular so you might have seen it before. As mentioned earlier, there will always be difficult situations and problems that occur in our life, that may well be out of our control. Whether or not we can do something about it, your response should never be worry or anxiety. Detaching yourself from situations that are outside of your control is a prudent skill, taught by Shri Vāsudev Krishna, for your personal growth.

I am not saying you should just sit back, relax, and do nothing. If you can, you must do everything within your power to try and solve a situation or a problem, but after that, take your attention away from it. The majority of things that occur in life will be out of our hands, so we should never judge a situation by its face value. Analyse every situation and see if it is within your control. Regardless of the answer, your reply should always be, "Why worry?"

STRESS & TRAUMA

Take a deep breath.
It's just a bad day, not a bad life.

Stress develops when we are attached to a particular outcome and we worry that things may not turn out as we desire. But, it is a normal, healthy reaction that is meant to make us feel uneasy. It is the natural way to react when told that something is wrong, and we need to act on it. Stress manifests in a number of ways—aggression, impatience, mood swings, anxiety, and so on. When you are stressed, your body releases chemicals to alert you, with adrenalin and cortisol playing important roles. Stress can be both physical and psychological. An example of physical stress is dehydration. The body reacts by making you feel uncomfortable and thirsty. You drink some fluid and this balances the situation and stress is removed. When faced with stress, you are given two choices, to either react or to deal with it. No matter what type of stress hits you, there is always a way of dealing with it properly. What often happens is that, when we suddenly get stressed, we react emotionally and sometimes we don't have time to think.

Managing Stress

There are seven key steps to help you deal with minor crises and immediate, instant stress. We will look at each one in turn.

Step 1: Recognising for Change

First, you must recognise that you are suddenly stressed. Certain feelings warn you. For example, feelings of anger, unease, butterflies in your stomach, apprehension, etc. This is when you must remind yourself, "It is time to change."

Step 2: Press Pause

Once you have recognised that it is time to make a change, stop yourself from thinking emotionally and allow yourself to calm down for a few moments. Breathe. Pause. This allows you to get involved in proper decision-making process to deal with the stress.

Step 3: Set Yourself Free

Try your best, if possible, to distance yourself from the situation. This will help give you much needed space. The best space is physical space, but if you can't leave the place, then try to relax, close your eyes and go into your own world within your headspace. If you are with someone who has annoyed you, explain to them that you want some time out to think before you respond. It may sound dumb or inferior, but it is the most sensible approach.

Step 4: Helicopter Perspective

Imagine yourself on a helicopter, looking down from above at the situation. Try to gain some perspective on what is happening. Try to put the situation you are in, on the timeline of your life, asking yourself how important this situation will be to your future. Is it going to last forever, or will it pass? Remind yourself that most things in life just pass. Soon this moment will be nothing but a distant memory. The majority of things that occur in life have very little importance in the long run.

Step 5: Game Plan

Then, you move on to form a plan to remove the stress. Start by asking what you can do to respond, rather than react. Would this help? Are you able to change the way that you see the situation and would this alter your response? Next, analyse the situation and circumstance to see if this can be changed. What can *you* practically do to alter things and what things do you have to accept and work with? Work out what is in your control, and what isn't. Normally, you can control everything about yourself and your reactions, you can control a little part of the situation or circumstance, but you cannot control other people. Accept this fact.

Step 6: Reflect

Always reflect before you act. Don't just sit back and be passive. There is nothing more destructive than someone who makes themselves a victim. If you really struggle, then I suggest you seek out someone appropriate to help you.

Step 7: Smile

When you can, smile. Depending on the seriousness of the situation, try to see the lighter side. Obviously if the situation is critical and life-changing, then you must allow yourself to grieve and receive the support of your friends. There is nothing wrong with grieving; it is a healthy way to come to terms with disasters and heartbreak.

AMPlified Stress

Accept. Accepting something unpleasant, helps to get it off our chests. Never bottle up your emotions. This is the worst thing you can do, as it will come back to attack not only you, but others too. It isn't clever; it's stupid. Remind yourself that'life is unfair, don't just say it, but also live by it.

Moving On. When you want to move on is a decision you must make yourself. Don't stop until you are ready to do so. When you are ready, ask yourself what you want to do now. Either stay where you are and keep the same problem alive, or, cut whatever has been lost and form a new plan and move forward. It is, as always, your choice.

Plan. This is a key part of moving on. How can you move on without a plan? You will just return to the same problem, with the same emotions and the same situation all over again. Your plan will take you forward and give you a sense of acceptance. It must address how you will alter your 'emotions' as well as the practical aspects.

Causes of Stress

A key reason for stress is that people don't accept that life and the world is in a constant state of flux. We've all heard of Heractilus' famous quote, "The only thing that is constant is change." And he's right—things never stay the same, they always change. One of the best examples of this is relationships. Every day your relationship with someone changes slightly because your circumstances (as well as you) having changed it slightly. Expecting any relationship to stay the same as the day you met is a recipe for chaos, and will probably leave you ending up feeling upset or disappointed. This is largely due to the unrealistic expectations we hold on relationships that we don't acknowledge changing over time.

Jobs are similar to this, they are also never constant. People often get angry or frustrated when they are not offered job security or a fixed job role, but this is very unrealistic, especially in today's world. The main point here is that if you hold an expectation that any thing in your life will remain the same and constant, then it is very likely to be a source of stress for you. To remove this stress, you need to try to live *here and now*, and accept that changes is normal.

CHRONIC STRESS

Take responsibility to find solutions.
Start by looking within, and not blaming others or circumstances.

What is Chronic Stress?

Being stressed for prolonged periods of time, and becoming used to living with it, is what we refer to as chronic. Chronic stress has been found to directly make changes to our physiology, hormone, and chemical systems, resulting in the damage of health and weakening the immune system, thus making us more susceptible to illness. It also leads to depressive illness and anxiety a lot of the time. Removing chronic stress is key, and if you believe you are seriously stressed then you should consult a medical expert for help.

Common symptoms of chronic stress include constantly feeling tired, short temper, lack of a sense of humor, worrying for no apparent reason or trivial reasons, inability to relax, paranoia, feeling tearful or depressed, inability to face work or friends, small tasks seeming difficult, or disrupted sleep patterns.

Some of these symptoms are also due to other reasons, but if you are constantly having these symptoms, you must address the cause. When trying to prevent chronic stress think about using time sensibly, maintaining realistic expectations, taking responsibility, addressing problems as they occur, recognising your limits, seeking help, talking out stressful situations. Chronic stress occurs primarily because we fail to deal with stressful situations when they occur, and begin to accept them as normal. This type of thinking is destructive and unhelpful.

How do we deal with it?

Write down anything that you notice causes or contributes to any underlying stress. Simply trying to unravel complicated situations in your mind normally ends in vain unless done regularly. You will end up in a continuous cycle, instead of actually dealing with specific factors that contribute to the problem.

The solution should be made up of three areas, namely, your own perceptions and attitudes to the problem, the circumstances and setting of the problem, and others involved in the problem. When you look at these three aspects individually, you will find many reasons as to why the stress occurred in the first place, and then work towards the solutions to help eradicate the stress. If you are not prepared to change your behaviours and beliefs when stressed, it is almost certain that you will continue to be stressed in the future; you have to accept that sometimes change is required.

Where does it come from?

Creators of Our Own Misery

We will always find people who create their own misery and fail to realize that they are responsible for this. For example, Alex is rude to people that he meets. He then begins to complain that he feels alone and that no one cares about him, which makes him stressed. He fails to recognise that it is his own behaviour that's causing the issue. Remember: friendly people have friends.

Excuses, Excuses, Excuses!

Alex is feeling stressed because he is struggling to complete his degree course, and is continuously failing assignments. He says that it is because he has to work part time in the campus coffee shop and that his tutor is not good. Even though this may be somewhat true, he is not realising that these excuses, and the required effort, is beyond his capabilities and/or he does not know how to study effectively. Excuses are stopping him from facing the real source of the distress.

Mushrooms

Mushrooms compete for space as they grow. One will inevitably try to take over another. This is usually the largest mushroom, so when you pick out this mushroom, the empty space is occupied and filled again, and this continues. There is always a mushroom on standby, ready to come and fill the gap.

Some people suffer from the Mushroom Syndrome, but instead of mushrooms they grow worries. Even when there is nothing to worry about, they overthink and find something. This is a destructive habit that you have grown to learn. It is tiring not only for you, but others around you as well.

Most worries are trivial in the long run and often take care of themselves. Needless worrying doesn't do any of us any good, and worrying is an option that you can choose not to take up. The majority of chronic stress often starts in our own minds.

Circumstances, Events & Others

I know it is difficult to learn to accept a situation for what it is, but often we don't have much choice. For example, having regular migraines is a difficult issue to face but accepting that recovery is possible if you follow your doctor's guidelines, is the only constructive choice we have.

People in our lives can also cause us to feel long-term stress, and this happens in many ways. Back to Principle One, always look to yourself first when dealing with others. Not every discussion is a 'win or lose' situation. Set time aside to think through your plan of action and make sure the solution is focused. Also, accept that some individuals are not accommodating, and won't want to work with you to resolve any differences. When you cannot resolve differences with another person, seek mediation or support from a neutral third person if you wish to resolve the issue at hand. If you really don't want to do that, or cannot get along, then be rational and practical, and try to minimise contact with them.

Breathe Out

Everybody suffers and reacts to stress in a bad way, at some point in their lives. The majority of us never deal with stress very well. We are all in this situation, but, we can all learn to improve on how we deal with stress. Never beat yourself up for handling situations or stress badly. Try to smile, relax, and come back with enthusiasm. You can only do your best, the rest is *out of your control*. Don't ask *why*, instead ask *how*. For example, don't ask yourself, "Why do I feel sad all the time?" These types of questions are demotivating and unconstructive. Instead ask, "How will I deal with my sadness?" This in turn, is constructive and will help you look at how to move forward.

Again, it is all about constant contemplation. Talking your stress out with those who are able to listen and understand is a powerful means of pinpointing what is bothering you and you are able to confide in someone. It can also help you gain insight into solutions. Rely on your *true friends* for this.

TRAUMA

Around 50 percent of US adults will experience a severe traumatic event during their lifetime. When it happens, many become stressed, depressed, fearful, or confused. They find it difficult to get on with daily tasks, and struggle to sleep and even eat properly. Some trauma is long-lasting and intense, and sometimes people are unable to return to their previous selves even years later. Coping is what people do to alleviate hurt, stress, or suffering caused by some negative event or situation. There are many problem-focused and emotion-focused strategies for coping including behavioural and cognitive therapies, as well as engaging in pleasant activities.

Seeing the silver lining in the negative event can also often change the perspective, and see life to have a greater value, for your own personal growth. Psychologists have observed that there is actually benefits in believing that life has improved, or will improve after a major trauma. Studies have also been carried out on the likes of bereaved individuals, cancer patients, stroke victims, and HIV-positive men. 70 to 80 percent of people who have lost loved ones report finding some benefit in the experience.[87] A groundbreaking study found that female breast cancer survivors reported that their lives had been altered (usually for the better) after developing the disease.[88] Seeing benefit in negative life events is an effective coping strategy, involving seeing value in a loss or trauma. It can influence your physical health and well-being.

---

[87] Tennen, H., and Affleck, G. (1999)

[88] Taylor, S. E., Lichtman, R. R., and Wood, J. V. (1984)

MEDITATE

Be in harmony with yourself,
and the world will reflect it.
HH Mahant Swami Maharaj

We are living in a world where instant satisfaction and rewards are expected. The reality of the fast-paced world makes it that if we don't move fast, we risk falling behind others. Along with managing our emotional stability, the mental, physical and emotional stress we experience can cause damage to our mind and our body. Happiness is an emotional or mental state, which includes positive emotions that can lead to a joyful life. A sound mind resides in a sound body. Gunatitanand Swami says in his teachings, "The mind is like a restless monkey, it isn't peaceful, so it needs to be controlled."

If you were told that there was some medication that you could take once a day, and it will reduce your anxiety and increase your level of contentment, would you take it? What if you were told it would also increase your self-esteem, empathy, improve trust and memory? More so, if the pill is natural, has no chemicals, and costs nothing. Would you take it? That pill is meditation. Meditation is a form of discipline that can help you to control your mind. Modern science has recognised the huge benefits associated with meditation: relieving us of stress, giving us a sense of purpose, allowing us to be more creative, among many other benefits. Agreed that we may exercise on a daily (we should be anyway), but, our mental stability is just as vital to avoid the harmful effects of our negative thoughts, and to ensure that we can remain in a balanced mindset. Our mental peace plays a vital role in maintaining happiness. The truth is, we already have contentment—it is within us. We have just not tapped into it. Meditation alone doesn't work. It is all good closing your eyes and doing some controlled breathing, but that will only give you an external experience of peace. We want to tap into, and communicate with, the passenger within us to experience true peace within. Anger wrecks havoc. It is not the answer. Not for you, nor your body.

Studies show that anger results in increased blood pressure, directly affecting your heart. This causes the release of cortisol (a steroid hormone) in your body, which shrinks memory cells in the brain and reduces your lifespan. Remaining calm boosts our physical being, whilst being angry or stressed, and manifesting negative emotions causes a lot of harm and imbalance within your body.

Researchers have studied the bodies of individuals when they meditate, and have confirmed that during meditation they have reduced respiration rate, and gained a heightened state of awareness and alertness. Meditation interventions have also been shown to be effective in patients with heart disease, chronic pain, skin disorders, and a number of mental health conditions such as depression, anxiety, panic, and substance abuse.

A research team from Massachusetts General Hospital studied the brain scans of people before and after participation in a mindfulness meditation course. The results are published in *Psychiatry Research*. What did it show? After completing the course, parts of the brain associated with compassion and self-awareness *grew*, while parts associated with stress *shrank*. Further studies report that meditation can actually permanently rewire your brain, and raise your levels of happiness. My gurus also teach that along with meditation, we need to have faith in the higher power. When these two are combined, we can experience the true fruits of meditation and progress towards living in peace and tranquility, irrespective of whether we are passing through favourable or unfavourable situations. Thus, we are able to remain calm. This was evident in the swamis at Sarangpur. For me, meditation has formed part of my life since 2007, but I never really practiced it properly. It was more of a 'close your eyes and sit there' scenario. It was ten years later, in 2017, when I seriously began meditating every morning as part of my prayers. It started off as a 'chore' in a way, but slowly I began to enjoy it. I didn't meditate for long, maybe 10 minutes in the morning, but it was enough for me to notice a change in myself. I noticed that for the rest of the day I could control my anger more and remain calm in stressful situations. It allowed me to take a step back from my day-to-day life, particularly in my years at university where I had to balance my studies, work and spiritual activities. It allowed me to remain calm and at peace, even amidst the hustle and bustle of life. I realised that I was able to have more control over my thoughts and decisions, and inevitably, I felt more at peace.

When meditating, try to do it in a peaceful and quiet place, in a cross-legged position, on the floor. Keep your head upright and your posture too. You then begin by focussing on your breathing. Notice when you take deep breaths in, and when you breathe out. Imagine your lungs filling with all the air as you breathe in, and then it all emptying as you expel. It is a natural process of withdrawing your attention from the surrounding environment and focussing both your physical and internal processes and consciously directing them inwards to a chosen point of attention. Only find a point of focus once you have control over your breathing though. I choose for that to be my Guru. Basically, your mind should focus solely on one thing. You choose what that is for you. Then, try to release any thoughts that come into your mind and refocus on your breathing or focal point. Keep your mind clear or on the point of focus. Don't stress too much if you can't, you don't need to over-complicate it; being aware of your breathing is enough—that is still a start to meditation.

The benefits drawn from meditation are many, from stress reduction to strengthening the body's immune system. It also helps to give more orderly thinking, improving your power of concentration and ultimately the slowing of the biological ageing process. From a spiritual perspective, it reinforces our vital life energy. Giving our attention to what we have as opposed to what we don't, keeps us content in life and helps us live peacefully. Remember, everything we need to attain, we already have done so.

Meditation helps you take control of the power your ego tries to have. It calms the monkey and reinforces your true identity with the eternal *ātmā*. Meditation doesn't have to necessarily be done in the morning, you can do it at any time, but research has shown that in the morning our mind is most calm. People think the aim of meditating is to get rid of all the thoughts bouncing around in our heads, but that is wrong. Meditation is to concentrate, to wind down. It helps you become consciously aware of the present—focussing on now, and that is the most powerful focus to have; focussing on the present.

MANTRA

Incorporating sound into your meditation practice enables you to connect with the higher power. Sound transports us. Ancient spiritual texts known as the *Purāna* discuss the why and how of chanting, suggesting that the repetition of sound purifies us. Sounds are immersive, like giving our souls a regular bath. Recognising the value of sound has carried through to modern times. Nikola Tesla said, "If you want to find the secrets of the universe, think in terms of energy, frequency, and vibration." Tesla experimented extensively with machines that created healing fields using vibrations. This might strike you as a bit woo-woo, but modern science is actually resurrecting Tesla's research on vibrational healing. Modern brain research is also starting to uncover scientific explanations for the healing power of ancient healing rituals, like a repetitive drumming and singing, which open pathways to the subconscious.

Swamis harness the power of sound by repeating affirmations or mantras during meditation. I recommend adding a mantra to your meditation practice. *Mantra* in a deep sense means to "transcend the mind," and it should be a spiritual sound expressing thoughts and meaning that summons a power greater than ourselves—we connect to the higher power. The oldest, most common, and most sacred mantra is Aum. In Vedic texts, *Aum* is given many shades of meaning, from infinite knowledge to the essence of everything that exists to the whole

Veda.[89] It comprises of three syllables, A-U-M. In Vedic tradition, this is important because each sound embodies a different state (wakefulness, dreaming, and deep sleep) or period of time itself (past, present, and future). You could say that the word *Aum* represents everything. The vibrations from *aum* have been shown to stimulate the vagus nerve, which decreases inflammation. Vagus nerve stimulation is also used as a treatment for depression, and researchers are looking at whether chanting *aum* may have a direct effect on mood. It's already been shown to calm one of the brains emotional centers.[90] There are many powerful mantras affirmations out there, the ones that I use regularly are below.

Aum Aksharam Aham Purushottama-dāso'smi
I am the eternal Akshar (Brahman),
a servant of Purushottam (Parabrahman—the ultimate entity)

Aum Lokah Samastah Sukhino Bhavantu
May all beings—everywhere—be happy and free.

---

[89] Gerety, F. M. M. (2015)
[90] Kalyani, B. G., Venkatasubramanian, G., Arasappa, R., Rao, N. P., Kalmady, S. V., Behere, R. V., ... & Gangadhar, B. N. (2011)

A

AMBITION, PURPOSE & MEANING

One whose happiness is within;
who is active within, who rejoices within
and whose aim is within; is actually a perfect yogi.
Such a person ultimately attains the Supreme.
Bhagavad Gita 5.24

To seek genuine happiness, we must focus on ourselves. Based on the first principle, you need to make yourself a priority. It may seem selfish, but it is the truth. It doesn't mean that you shouldn't pay attention to your family and friends; you must do that, as we all need to play our role within society. Say you have a family dinner and you've ordered a takeaway pizza. You open the box and the pizza has been cut into eight slices, with a slice for each of the eight people at home. In that moment, it would be selfish to have an extra slice. It is all a matter of context, and you must understand the difference. The difference is simple: *d*on't be selfish for yourself, be selfish for the betterment of your Self. This moulding—this personal journey—will be a continuous process throughout your life. It will take time to get to the point where the circumstances and situations around you no longer affect you. Where the behaviour of those around you doesn't affect your mental peace and stability. Only when you are able to be there for yourself, can you truly be there for others.

Care for your roots, care for your trunk.
Only when your roots are in place,
Can the crown give to others.

One of the most important things about any tall and beautiful tree, are the roots. No one notices the roots, everyone only sees the tree above the ground. Vaguely put, any tree has three key areas to it. One is its roots; second is the trunk; and the third is the crown of the tree.

Starting with the roots, any healthy tree must have healthy roots. Again, the deeper the roots, the more 'rooted' and stronger the tree. It can then stand against nature's way of tornados, cyclones and storms. Though, we do not see these mighty roots. These roots are comparable to the moulding of your Self. People only see the fruits of your achievements such as their wealth or status. People see your charisma and success. What cannot be seen is your roots—your internal development. If you cannot work on the roots of yourself, the unseen, you can never sustain what is seen, or what is yet to grow.

Pramukh Swami Maharaj once visited the house of a devotee in London. A very wealthy man, and the world saw him as a successful and happy individual. The sheer luxuries they saw at the house of the man astonished the other swamis travelling with Swamiji. That same day, the man met Swamiji in private and completely broke down. In the lap of his guru he cried, revealing his issues and confusions of life. The world saw his wealth, his luxuries and his popularities. They saw the trunk and the crown of the tree before their eyes, but what they couldn't see were the roots of the tree underneath the soil, which are invisible to the eyes. These are the roots of inner development; the roots that mould our Self.

Unless we do this, the tornados, cyclones and storms of life will shake us and could even tear us down completely. Strengthening our roots comes from connecting; to our own self, the higher power, and connecting with our *ātmā*. When these roots become strong, the trunk remains steady and stable. Our physical and emotional well-being is the trunk of the tree. This can only happen though if the roots are deep and strong.

The last part of the tree is the crown. The crown is what you give out to the world. Where the fruits of our actions are seen, where the leaves, flowers, and fruits of the tree flourish. These fruits are for others, the shade of the leaves are for others, the flowers are for others; it is always about our contribution to others. It will take time to get there, but when we do, we will automatically love all the people around us, with no expectations or conditions. Like my guru, Mahant Swami Maharaj says, "When we see all as divine, we become divine."

PURPOSE

The swamis at Sarangpur spend their entire day in service. This is part of the spiritual process. They do whatever is asked, however difficult or uneasy it may seem, without choosing any favourites. They rotate through various activities from cooking, cleaning, gardening, looking after the gaushālā (cow shelter), adornation of deities, studying, meditating, teaching, etc. Everyone works as a collective body, to get all tasks complete. This really got me thinking. How can those that were just millionaires yesterday, come to this remote village and clean the toilets? There had to be some underlying purpose. They had realised a higher purpose. They gave all their time and energy for this purpose; they had discovered something bigger than themselves. The tasks weren't seen as 'chores' or 'jobs'. They performed any 'chore' with a smile on their face. Their purpose became their way of life.

If we only feel excited when people say nice things about our work or achievements, it's a direct sign that we're not passionate about the work itself. And if we indulge our interests and skills, but nobody responds to them, then our passion is without a purpose.

When people fantasise about what they want to do and who they want to be, they don't often investigate fully enough to know if it suits them. People think they want to be in finance or law because they know it's lucrative and well-paying, or, they want to be a doctor because it's respected *and* honourable. But they go on with no idea whether those professions suit them.

According to *Forbes* magazine publisher Rich Karlgaard, the majority of us don't hit our stride quite so early, but society's focus on academic testing, getting into the 'right' colleges, and developing and selling an app for millions before you even get your degree (if you don't drop out to run a multimillion-dollar company) is causing high levels of anxiety and depression not only among those who haven't conquered the world by age twenty-four, but even among those who've already made a significant mark.[91]

---

[91] Karlgaard, R. (2019)

Shri Vāsudev Krishna says that it's better do one's own work imperfectly than to do another's perfectly. Steve Jobs said something along these lines, in his 2005 Stanford commencement address, "Your time is limited, so don't waste it living someone else's life."

Our society is set up around strengthening our weaknesses rather than building upon our strengths. In school, if you got three As and a C, all the adults around you are focussed on that C. Why did you get a C? It doesn't seem to matter about the other grades we get.

Identify your passions. Identify the activities you love and those that you are naturally inclined to do. Instead of making a huge career change, look for smaller opportunities to do what you love in life. According to researchers, we can re-engineer our tasks, relationships, or even just how we perceive what we do. The intention of our approach to work has a tremendous impact on the meaning we gain form it and our personal sense of purpose. Learn to find meaning right here, right now, and it will serve you all your life.

GOALS

*Those who love peace, must learn to organise
as effectively as those who love war.*
Martin Luther King Jr.

It is important that you give time to yourself. When we get caught up in a hectic lifestyle, we struggle to make time for ourselves. We get so overwhelmed with what is around us that we forget who we really are. We must unwind and spend time alone. Now, when you are living with children, a partner, and other family members this may seem selfish. Though sometimes, you need a break and time to recharge to focus on you for the betterment of those around you.

A mind-blowing study asked whether men and women would want to be alone with their thoughts for fifteen minutes, or receive an electric shock. Sixty percent of men and thirty percent of women said that they would rather get an electric shock. We often refuse to be alone with our thoughts, it scares us.

Today, social media has given us the 'filler' to stop us from being alone with ourselves. Have you ever taken your phone out of your pocket and then put it back, wondering why you took it out in the first place? We try to convince ourselves that we were just checking the time, but in reality we don't even remember the time. On average, a person checks their phone every twelve minutes, burying their heads in their phones about eighty times a day. Taking a break doesn't mean endlessly scrolling through Instagram, or checking your friend's Snapchat stories. You need to set your phone aside, away from all the noise. It is all about self-discipline. There will always be a way that capitalism and consumerism will try to control us.

Try spending some time outdoors, go for a walk. I don't think I must tell you the positive benefit of going outdoors. It helps rejuvenate your entire body. A 2018 study showed that environmental exposures including natural viewing, outdoor walks and exercises, or gardening, all play a role in reducing stress, heart rate, and blood pressure. Allowing your body to absorb rays of sunlight helps to boost vitamin D and levels of serotonin, the natural 'painkiller' in your body. What you do in that time is up to you. But this is probably one of the first steps you must take to discover your happiness. I choose to self-introspect. You may choose to just take a breather or read something. Again, I leave this totally up to you.

Having goals also gives you a sense of purpose and a feeling of control over your life. But they must be meaningful, to stimulate your confidence and keep you striving. Pursuing goals adds structure and meaning to our daily lives. Many psychological studies have shown that across cultures, people whose primary goals are intrinsically (from within) rewarding obtain more satisfaction and pleasure from the pursuits. Intrinsic goals are ones that you pursue because they satisfy you from within and are meaningful to you, allowing you to grow and develop emotionally and maturely, and contribute to your community.

In constrast, extrinsic (external) goals reflect more of what others approve or desire from you. Examples include making money, feeding your ego, seeking power or fame, or submitting to peer pressure. These are not useful in the long run. Researchers have shown that pursuing intrinsic goals is more likely to fulfil needs of autonomy (control), competence, and relatedness.[92] This doesn't mean extrinsic goals are bad, because they too often help to pursue intrinsic goals. But the priority should always be intrinsic goals. Social psychologists have found evidence that by just doing something can change how you feel about it.[93] For example, raising money for a charitable cause can lead you to believing more firmly in that cause. So, take actions towards your goals, putting aside any doubts.

---

[92] Kasser, T., and Ryan, R. M. (1993)
[93] Myers, D. G. (2005).

INTENTION

As long as the influence of the gunas remain
within a person, happiness can never be experienced
Bhagwan Shri Swaminarayan

Around ten years ago, the Satyam scandal shook the corporate world of India. It was perhaps one of the biggest corporate fraud to take place on Indian soil. Satyam Computers had been at the foreground of India's IT revolution for a number of years. Chairman of the company, Ramalinga Raju, was found to have exploited the company of over 10,000 crore rupees (around £1 billion). A high-level inquiry revealed that for years, he had been offshoring funds through fraudulent means such as blank employees and company payroll, loans to family, insider trading, and improper acquisitions. With this bundle of wealth, he had purchased villas and properties in over sixty countries. Sixteen luxury cars and 300 pairs of shoes were found in his possession. This fraud shook the corporate world in 2009, leading to collapse of the company's empire. Raju was convicted in 2015, but surprise surprise he paved his way out on bail. But we don't want to go into that now. Undoubtedly, Raju had talent and intelligence. He did his MBA from Ohio and was enrolled in the Owner/President Management programme at Harvard Business School. His amazing management skills, foresight, and immense desire to succeed is what propelled Satyam to the forefront of IT worldwide. What he lacked was the purity of intention.

Raju's case is an extreme example of intention. What if he hadn't done anything illegal and used his talents and hard-earned money to have a comfortable life? Would that still be labelled as an impure intention? When is an intention considered to be impure, and how does impure intention harm us? If Raju was asked about the intent behind his crimes, he would more than likely say he wanted success and happiness, or, he may say he was securing the success he had already built over the years. Success, for Raju, meant financial abundance, corporate dominance, and societal prestige. Can we blame him for intention to succeed? The issue was that his definition of success itself was perverse, and that is what led to his downfall. Our intention can only be considered pure when our definition of success is pure, and we continuously and sincerely strive to achieve it. In our minds we all have an image of an ideal life. Certain goals captivate us, and we design our entire lives around achieving them because we think they will make us happy. The word *dharma* comes from the Sanskrit root word *dhri*, meaning 'to hold, maintain, or keep'. In its noun form it also means, 'that which is rooted and cannot be taken away'. Put simply, *dharma* is your actions and duties. The purity of our *dharma* is defined by the purity of our intentions.

THE WEB OF MAYA

The Vedic scriptures emphasise that desire is what motivates all human actions. The Rig Veda even goes as far as saying that desire was the first seed of the mind. Desires are fuelled when we chase personal gratification. Our desires of adventures, pleasures, and comfort often take the form of material goals. "I *want* a five bedroom house. I *want* a Ferrari. I *want* financial freedom." I can almost guarantee that if I told you to write down your goals, you will often give answers describing what success means to you.

We think that success equals happiness, but this idea itself is the illusion. The Sanskrit word for illusion is *māyā*. It is believed in Vedic tradition to be the creative power of the Supreme, that binds all of creation. In simple terms we can see it to mean believing in that which is not. When we let achievements and acquisitions determine our course, we are living in the illusion that happiness comes from external measures of success, but all too often we find that when we finally get what we want, when we find that success, it doesn't lead to the happiness we were expecting. Jim Carrey once said, "I think everybody should get rich and famous and do everything they ever dream of, so they can see that it's not the answer."

Tara Bach, founder of the Insight Meditation Community of Washington DC, writes, "As long as we keep attaching our happiness to the external events of our lives, which are ever-changing, we will always be left waiting for it."

Mahant Swami Maharaj also says, "Humans crave for power, intelligence, and the like, but none of this gives them peace. It is an illusion. The pleasures of the world are like a baby's dummy."

Money and fame are also a facade. Our search is never for a certain *thing*, but for the feeling we think it will give us. We already know this, because we see wealthy and famous people who seem to 'have it all'. Despite having *everything* they have bad relationships or suffer from depression, and it's obvious that success didn't bring them happiness. The same is true for those of us who aren't rich and famous. We quickly tire of our smartphones and want the next model. We receive a bonus, but the initial excitement fades surprisingly fast when our lives don't really improve. We think that a new phone or a bigger house will somehow make us feel better, cooler, or more satisfied, but instead we find ourselves wanting more. Material gratification is external, but true happiness is internal. Kabir, a famous fifteenth-century poet of India, tells the story of a musk deer. The musk deer picks up an irresistible scent in the forest and chases it, searching for the source, not realising that the scent comes from its own pores. It spends its whole life wondering fruitlessly. In the same way we search outside for happiness, finding it elusive, when it can be found within us. Happiness and fulfilment come from mastering the mind and connecting with the *ātmā*. Success also doesn't guarantee happiness, and happiness doesn't require success. While having more money can contribute to overall life satisfaction, the impact levels off at a salary of around $75,000 (which we've already explored). In other words, when it comes to the impact of money on how you view the quality of your life, a middle class citizen fares about as well as Jeff Bezos.

Success is earning money, being respected at work, executing projects smoothly. Happiness is feeling good about yourself, having close relationships, finding a higher purpose, making the world a better place. What we see popular culture celebrate today is the pursuit of success. Media today, aimed at adolescents, focus more on image, money, and fame. Popular songs and books use language that promotes self-achievements over community connection, socialising, and self-acceptance. It's no surprise that happiness rates have consistently declined globally.

THE MAYA OF HAPPINESS

Happiness can be elusive. It's hard to consistently sustain a high level of joy. To feel a sense of *meaning* shows that our actions have purpose. What we do matters, so we matter. The Atharva Veda states, "Money and mansions are not the only wealth. Hoard the wealth of spirit. Character is wealth; true values are wealth; and spiritual wisdom is wealth."

Purpose and meaning, not success, lead to true contentment. In Sanskrit the word *sankalpa* is an intention that is formed by one's own heart and mind, that one strives for a goal. Your intention is who you plan to be in order to act with purpose and feel that what you do is meaningful. When you keep digging, very often you will find that what you are ultimately searching for is an internal feeling such as happiness, security, confidence, or the like.

I saw in the swamis at Sarangpur, that everything they do, they see it to be spiritual. A senior swami I conversed with about my personal flaws, mentioned to me, "Whatever activity you do, whether that is showering, eating breakfast, driving, working, studying, anything... Everything should be spiritual. See God in all your activities. This must be firm within your mind." This intention for building spirituality into my life, is today the principle intention that allows me to remain positive and at peace, giving me a sense of purpose too.

Nobody is going to create our lives for us. That is why I don't believe in wishful *manifesting*, the idea that if you simply believe something will happen, it will. Martin Luther King Jr, said, "Those who love peace must learn to organise as effectively as those who love war." The broadest intentions often drive efforts to help and support other people. Time and again we see that if we are doing it for the external result, we won't be happy. We've already established this a few times already. But with the right intention to serve, we can feel meaning and purpose every day. Letting go is what truly allows us to grow.

THE THREE GUNAS

The three *gunas* (the modes, or qualities, of *māyā*) are invisible powers that we tune into dependent on our current frame of mind. It is determined by our choice of words and actions, and we come under the influence of each *guna* accordingly.

The first is *sattva*, meaning goodness or reality. Those influenced by *sattva* lean towards purity, truthfulness, knowledge, peacefulness, and a level of happiness. The second is *rajas*, meaning passion. Our passion compels us to work hard and strive to achieve as much as we can; it is what increases our eagerness for challenge and reward. The third is *tamas*, meaning ignorance or darkness. It pulls us towards envy, hatred, anger, indifference, violence, depression, and so on.

We respond to situations and circumstances based on the influence of the *gunas*, that is why different people respond to same situations differently. The three *gunas* pervade all of *māyā*—all matter in physical, gross and subtle form. Just as the three RGB primary colours (red, yellow, and blue) mix to produce the wide spectrum of colours we see, similarly the three *gunas* mix and blend to produce numerous combinations of influences on what we see and how our behaviour and attitude is towards the world.

The most obvious way for us to see the influence of the *gunas* is in the food we eat. We talked about how our diet affects our thinking, and this is what I meant. Shri Vāsudev Krishna says in the Bhagavad Gitā, "Food in the mode of goodness increases duration of life, purifies existence, give strength, health, happiness and satisfaction. Such food is juicy, wholesome and pleasing to the heart. Foods that are too bitter, too sour, too salty, too hot, or too pungent are in the mode of passion. Foods that are stale, decomposed, or putrid, are a product of bloodshed are in the mode of ignorance."[94]

Another example is in places we visit. A place can easily be influenced by the three modes too. In the university library our mind is calm and we are able to concentrate; it is designed in this way to be clean, quiet, serene, and well-lit. These are inherit *sattvic* qualities. A

---

[94] Bhagavad Gita 17.8-10

rajasic place would be in a restaurant; if you were studying with the smell and views of food around you, your mind wouldn't be focussed on the studies. There is a reason that at times I chose to write parts of this book at mandirs, or amidst swamis. A *tamasic* place would be a nightclub—could you study in a nightclub filled with alcohol, shishas and dancers? People who meditate naturally tend to look for quiet places like in a garden, or a quiet room. Meditation is a sattvic practice.

We can be influenced by any three of the *gunas*, but for the most part it is a mixture that reflects our interests and aspirations. With contemplation and reflection, we are able to identify which modes most affect our behaviour. The important part is the intent behind our actions, rather than the action itself, that defines each quality. Bhagwān Shri Swāmināryan defines a liberated soul, and the ultimate aim of spiritual life, as rising above the three *gunas*, or to become *gunātit*. Yes, it is difficult, but it is the essence of his teachings. The mode of *sattva* is the first step. Stay clean—mentally and physically, eat pure food, use your tongue wisely, and associate with pure souls.

INSPIRATION

Make your own future,
Be your own hope,
Above all, have faith in God.

Inspiration plays a very important role in our ambition and purpose. Inspiration can come from a wide range of places. Some are inspired by movies, books, and some by certain people. I am inspired by my Guru, the way he lives his life and what he teaches. This gives me strength to keep me going. The added benefit of being able to talk, write, call, meet and spend time directly with him only inspires me more. There have been several incidents in my life, in the past six to eight years, when I have felt completely down and lost, without a sense of direction.

There was a time I questioned a lot of things in life, including my faith which was supposed to be the base of my life. I doubted myself and this led to a deep feeling of sadness, a sense of being unfulfilled, and anxiety. I knew that staying this way without seeking a solution would only do me more harm than good. I tried various thought practices, read numerous books, consulted a number of experts, listened to audiobooks on positivity and mind management, watched talks and inspirational videos online, and even followed motivational pages on Instagram. Little did I know that the answer to my issues were right in front of me the entire time. He was there. Being able to communicate with the one who inspired me, and to whom I looked up to, really helped me see life from a positive perspective, and approach the situations in life from a different angle. Hearing the stories of tough situations that individuals had been through and the hardships they had to face, even the hardships he faced himself, changed my entire outlook on life. "Life has its inherent difficulties," he said, "This is *samsara*. But, it isn't the end, look at your attainment, this creates your character. Believe God to be the all-doer; whatever he does is always for the best. Have faith in him and remain firm."

Luckily, I had him to guide me on my path of life and he continues to do so even today. When you find something to inspire you, you automatically discover a drive within. You feel that you have a clear aim of where you want to get in your life, and what you want to get out of it. The possibilities become endless. Everyone gets inspired in different ways. For some, external rewards are enough to fuel enthusiasm and inspiration. For others, internal motivation is needed. The ones who are motivated from within are able to create inspiring thoughts, values, beliefs, and goals within themselves. Whatever the external circumstances may be, whether favourable or unfavourable, it doesn't matter to them. Find your inspiration. Why not use Ikigai from Principle Five?

SAVOURING

Savouring can be defined as any thought or behaviour that generates prolonged, intensifying enjoyment. It requires to step out of yourself and review an experience. Several studies show that people who are inclined to savour moments and past experiences were more self-confident and gratified, they were less hopeless and neurotic. Those able to capture joys of the present moments, and hang on the these *good feelings* are less likely to experience depression, stress, guilt, and shame.

In a set of studies, depressed people were invited to take a couple of minutes daily to relish an ordinary thing they might do, such as eating, having a shower, walking to the bus. When they had done that, they were told to write down in what ways they experienced the event differently, compared to if they rushed through it.

The studies showed a significant increase in happiness, and a reduction in depression. Relish the normal experiences. Enjoy the little things, for one day you may look back and realise they were the big things. Engaging in positive reminiscence can also provide pleasure and solace when you need it most. A study that successfully taught people how to travel to an experience that recalls positive images and memories boosted happiness in several ways.[95] It reinforces your sense of identity, you gain insight into yourself, boost self-esteem, and present a positive self-image about yourself. It also helps to produce pleasure and enjoyment of its own, reliving the memory for you, providing a sense of comfort when you need it most.

---

[95] Bryant, F. B., Smart, C. M., and King, S. P. (2005)

SERVICE

In the Joy of Others, Lies our Own
HH Pramukh Swami Maharaj

The highest purpose is to live in selfless service, or in Sanskrit, *sevā*. In the joy of others, lies our own. The majority of us may be resistant to this idea. We all want to help by selflessly serving, and we might already be, but we often feel limited by our busy lives and work. Some people think that they have too many issues of their own that need dealing with, and that these should take precedence over everything else. Is it true then that we should figure out solutions for ourselves before we devote ourselves to helping others? We've all come across these types of thoughts, and I agree, it is hard to think about selflessness when we ourselves are in a place of struggle. But I assure you, it is the optimal route to inner peace and having a meaningful life.

The Shrimad Bhāgavatam shares a powerful example of service, "Look at these fortunate trees. They live solely for the benefit of others. They tolerate the wind, rain, heat, and snow, but still provide shelter for our benefit. It is the duty of every living being to perform welfare activities for the benefit of others with his life, wealth, intelligence and words."[96] The only way to be one with all of creation, as well as the higher power, is to serve. This is evident in the life of my gurus, who throughout their lives have literally done nothing but served others. The swamis at Sarangpur also dedicate their life to selfless service.

Service is the essence of The Keshav Way. This world is impermanent, perishable, unreal, and the source of all suffering and delusion. If sense gratification was the sole purpose of our lives, then everyone would never be happy; but wherever we look, we see suffering, pain, and dissatisfaction. It is service that leads to inner fulfilment and true happiness.

---

[96] Srimad Bhagavatam, Canto 10: 22.32, 22.35

SERVICE: THE TESLA & PASSENGER

Service fulfils us on many levels, beginning with the simple belief that we are born hardwired to care for others, and so service does us a lot of good. This instinct is most obvious in children, who don't get distracted by the demands of others on their time and attention. An image that went viral a few years back shows a little girl, probably around two years of age, watching a politician crying on Japanese TV. She takes a tissue, goes up to the TV, and virtually wipes away the politician's tears. Such things go viral because we recognise, and perhaps miss, the little girl's compassion for another person, even a stranger.

In his autobiography, *Long Walk to Freedom,* Nelson Mandela writes, "No one is born hating another person because of the colour of their skin, or his background, or his religion. People must learn to hate, and if they can learn to hate, then they can be taught to love, for love comes more naturally to the human heart than its opposite."[97]

Linking service with our goals, studies show that when we pursue 'compassionate goals'—those aimed at helping others or otherwise helping to make the world a better place—we are less likely to have symptoms of anxiety and depression than when we focus on improving or protecting our own status or reputation.[98] The act of giving to others activate the pleasure centre of our brain. This may be why those who help others tend to live longer, be healthier, and have a better overall sense of well-being.[99]

Service connects us. When you serve, it's hard to be lonely. In most scenarios, you have to go out into the world to help other people. Service amplifies gratitude. Service gives you a broad view of all that you have. Service increases compassion. When you serve, you see that the world needs what you have to offer. Service build self-esteem. Helping others tells you that you're making a difference in the world.

---

[97] Mandela, N. (2013)

[98] Erickson, T. M., Granillo, M. T., Crocker, J., Abelson, J. L., Reas, H. E., & Quach, C. M. (2018)

[99] Post, S. G. (2005)

You have a sense of meaning and purpose. The word *sevā* itself means selfless service. Vedic teachings and teachers throughout millennia have promoted the concept of *sevā*. We have seen how happiness and gratitude can spread through communities. The same is true of service. When you serve, you may mention it to your friends. You might bring someone else with you. Someone joins you, and they talk to other friends. When you participate in service, you do your part to spread the value of service in your culture and community.

SERVICE TODAY

Out in the modern world, no matter how much we want to help others, we are distracted from the service mindset by the desire to be financially and emotionally stable and secure. If you are lost and disconnected, then service will feel cumbersome and less fulfilling. But when is the time right to serve? Will it ever be right? Internal exploration has no endpoint. It's an ongoing practice. Your problems will never be completely solved. They will keep on firing towards you. Yes, by all means take care of yourself, but don't wait until you have enough time and money to serve. You will never have enough. Let me share a story with you.

A young girl was born in a poor area of Maharashtra, India. She had no formal education, her family made her take care of the buffalos on the farm instead. At the age of ten, she was married to a man who was thirty years old. By the age of twenty, she had three sons and was pregnant again. A mafia leader was exploiting the people of the village and forcing the women of the village to work tirelessly for hours on end, paying them practically nothing. Everyone was afraid of this man, but this woman informed the district collector, who overlooked the police, about this individual. The mafia leader was stopped from carrying out his dirty work, and so he became furious. He went and told the woman's husband that was is a fool. He also said, "Your wife is having affairs with so many men. In fact, the child that is in her right now is my child, it isn't even yours. If you don't kill her and the child, I will kill you."

Enraged with anger and shame, the husband kicked the young woman in the stomach repeatedly, hoping to kill her and the child. She fell unconscious on the floor. Thinking that she was dead, he dragged her to a cowshed where a herd of cows were kept. He thought that if people found her, they would just assume the cows trampled her. She laid there unconscious. When she woke up, she said she found one cow standing right above her, protecting her. If it weren't for the cow, the buffaloes, oxen, and cows would have trampled her. But the cow protected her. Even when her in-laws came to check if she was dead, the cow chased them away with its horns. After coming to consciousness, she gave birth to a baby girl under the cow. She took a rock and cut her umbilical cord. For hours, the cow protected her. When the woman got enough strength, she embraced the cow and promised, "Just as you protected me when I was in great need, I will protect others in need too."

A lengthy story, but as we can see, no one would have had her back. Her own family rejected her; yes, her own biological family that she was born into. A foolish tradition at the time meant that after marriage, a woman couldn't (and shouldn't) return home. In order to ensure she wasn't exploited further, she slept in a crematorium with her little baby child. She collected wheat that people put around the dead bodies and mixed it with water that she would cook on top of the fire of the dead corpses. Her life had become quite depressing. Then she decided that she didn't want such a life for her child. With her child in her arms, she went to the railway track and laid waiting for the train to come and crush them both. As she lay there; she heard someone crying in anguish. She got up and saw an old crippled man crying out. He was crying out for some food and water, so she went and played the role of a beggar in order to get him food and water. In the old man, she believed that the higher power was speaking to her. She believed that it was telling her that she had a higher purpose in life other than to commit suicide; that she had something more to do; to really contribute to the world. Later that day, whilst she was sitting in a field, she wondered what she would do. She had nothing and no one. How could she even begin to think about helping anyone?

Sitting under a tree, she saw that there was one branch that a woodsman had violently cut with an axe. The branch was barely hanging off the tree, but it was enough to give her child shade. This was her answer. She thought, "However much I have been beaten down, I can still do something for others." She started her search and began to find homeless, abandoned, and orphaned children. She became their mother and took care of them. She learnt to sing beautifully, and through singing and begging she made a basic livelihood to provide for her children, and kept them safe. After some time, people saw what a difference she was making to the lives of so many children and they built an orphanage for her.

Over the years she has had about 1,500 children, and over 1,000 grandchildren. She has made a tremendous difference in their lives, as well as her own. All of her children are given a good education. Many are doctors, lawyers, and farmers—some of the things that she never had the opportunity to pursue. She has won many awards internationally for her accomplishments. But what is the most meaningful and fulfilling accomplishment of her life?

A few years later, after the President of India, governors of states, and many more, gave her international awards, an old frail man arrived at her orphanage. He was starving, sick, and homeless; desperately in search of shelter. After a few minutes she recognised that this man was in fact her ex-husband. The one who tried to brutally murder her. She said to him, "When you left me to die, I was homeless in rags. Today, you are the one who is homeless and in rags. Today, I have a pleasant place to stay with so many loved ones."

She said that the most meaningful accomplishment in her life was when she chose to forgive him. She told him she would give him shelter, not as a spouse, but as a mother. From then, whenever people visited the orphanage, she would introduce him as her eldest son. Her daughter, born under the cow, is now a medical doctor and runs one of the orphanages. Today, she considers all the tragedies in her life to have been gifts to empower her and make a difference to others. She considers it all to be the grace of God. She says that although her life has been a road with many thorns, she has *chosen* to make friends with those thorns. Her life became beautiful, and so, she was able give beauty to the lives of so many other people. This is the true story of Sindhutai Sapkal, also known as the 'Mother of Orphans' throughout India and the world.

The power of compassion is far greater than anything that money, fame, or status can get you. Every one of us can have an influence in the world when we strive towards gratuity. Genuine satisfaction and happiness lies in giving to others; in the joy of others. Regardless of who you are, where you come from, how clever you are, or even how rich you are, everyone is inherently special and there is nothing, or no one, that can take that away from you.

In a series of experiments, researchers at the University of California, Berkeley, found that those with less money actually tend to give more. People were given $10 and told they could choose an amount to share with an unknown stranger. People who were lower in socio-economic status were more generous than wealthier participants.[100] These findings are further backed up by a survey of charitable giving in 2011, which showed that Americans in the bottom percentage of income gave, on average, 3 percent of their earnings to charity whereas people in the top 20 percent gave half that—around 1 percent. (Just to be fair, and so we don't think all rich people are full of themselves, the wealthy are still responsible for over 70 percent of all charitable contributions.)[101] The question to contemplate is, who is wealthier? The one with money or the one who serves?

---

[100] Piff, P. K., Kraus, M. W., Côté, S., Cheng, B. H., & Keltner, D. (2010)
[101] Greve, F. (2009)

BEING SELFLESS

You may wonder how, throughout this book, we have predominantly discussed about *us* and how we should be focussing on ourselves. So now why are we talking about others and being selfless? I think the example of the flight emergency is suited here. When you board a flight, the cabin crew announce, "If there is a lack of oxygen supply in the cabin the oxygen masks will drop from above. Pull the mask towards you sharply, placing it over your nose and mouth, secure the elastic band behind your head, and breathe normally. *Ensure your mask is securely fastened before you help children, infants, or others."* How selfish right? Surely we should help others before we help ourselves? But, understand it as such, unless you help yourself and breathe oxygen first, what real help can you be to anyone else? Similarly, you can only love others and be compassionate to others, when you know what it feels like yourself. You can only truly share that what you truly possess.

If you continuously try to help others without being satisfied and balanced yourself, the consequences can, and will be, devastating. It is destructive to care too much and be preoccupied with the suffering of others. So, you must be slightly selfish at the start of the journey to ensure that you can later be selfless without causing damage to others, as well as yourself. In fact, both go hand-in-hand. You must find your balance.

Service helps to transform negative emotions like anger, stress, envy, and disappointment into positive ones through perspective. Research published in *BMC Public Health* points out that volunteering can result in lower feelings of depression and increased feelings of overall well-being.[102] One can serve with a mixture of intentions. We might do it to be liked, to feel good about ourselves, to look good in front of others, to connect with other people, or to receive some kind of reward. But true service—real *sevā*—is that which is performed without any expectations. Fortunately for us, service does often yield happiness, as both Vedic teachings and science show. If I do something

---

[102] Jenkinson, C. E., Dickens, A. P., Jones, K., Thompson-Coon, J., Taylor, R. S., Rogers, M., ... & Richards, S. H. (2013)

to serve you, you're happy. If you're happy, then I'm happy. But is service selfish if it brings you happiness? The problems that most of us face are mental, such as anxiety, depression, and loneliness. Whereas for many of the people in need of service, the greatest challenges are mainly basic—food, clothing, shelter, and the likes. We can heal our mental challenges by helping others with their physical needs. Service is a reciprocal exchange. You're not saving anyone by helping them; you need help as much as they do. You are saving yourself in the process.

An infinite number of people and causes need our help now. We need each and everyone in the world to serve in some way. Choose where you want to serve based on your own compassion, beliefs, purpose and values. Service helps other people and it helps us. We don't expect anything in return, but what we get is the joy of service. It's a universal exchange of love.When you're living in service, you don't have time to complain and criticise. When you're living in service, your fears go away. When you're living in service, you feel grateful. Your material attachments diminish. You feel fulfilled.

And so, service is a direct path to a meaningful life.

Service that brings joy to others, brings joy to us too.

Ultimately, it is selfless service that brings joy to one and all.

Because, in the joy of others, lies our own.

VEDIC HAPPINESS

Nobody wants to fail. The universal intention of humankind is to succeed. The problem is that our concept of success is wrong, and so our efforts are often misdirected. A prime example of this is Howard Hughes, an American film director and philanthropist, known as one of the most financially *successful* individuals in the world. Yet, when he died from his mental misery, he secluded himself from society due to depression and paranoia. His story shows that even if you possess all the wealth in the world, without a stable mind, you can never be happy. We've already explored how fame doesn't necessarily lead to the type of success we are talking about. Elvis Presley was a cultural icon of America, as well as the most celebrated solo artist in the entire history of recorded albums. The sale of his albums almost reached a billion. Yet, he struggled with depression and died at a young age from a drug overdose. The Oxford Dictionary gives two definitions of success as 'the attainment of fame, wealth or status', and, 'the achievement of an aim or purpose'. We can probably rule out the first definition, and focus on the second one alone. Famous writers and thinkers also define success in a similar way.

- Warren Buffet, entrepreneur and business tycoon, says, "I measure success by how many people love me."
- Stephen Covey, author of the *Seven Habits of Highly Effective People*, looked on success as deeply individual. He said, "If you carefully consider what you want to be said of you in your funeral experience, you will find your definition of success."
- Deepak Chopra, famous writer and wellness coach, writes, "Success in life can be defined as the continued expansion of happiness in the progressive realisation of worthy goals."
- Richard Branson, billionaire business tycoon, says, "The more you are actively and practically engaged, the more successful you will feel."

All of these thoughts help us get a glimpse of the meaning of success, but they don't provide a comprehensive definition of it. The Vedic scriptures state that all humans have three common yearnings: to be good, to do good, and to feel good.

Based on this, success in life can be measured against three criteria: be the best that you can be, do the best that you can in the work you do, and then experience *ānanda* and satisfaction in life Regardless of our behaviour and attitude, we always expect compassion and justice from others. We always want others to understand us. A prime example of this is that from the Mahābhārata. During the war, when Karna's chariot wheel got stuck in the ground, he jumped down and attempted to dislodge it. At that time, Shri Vāsudev Krishna instructed Arjuna, "Shoot Karna in the back! If he faces towards you, it will be impossible for you to kill him!"

Karna heard these words and responded, "Oh Krishna! You are said to be the Supreme Lord, and you are teaching Arjuna to cheat? You set the *dharma* (duty) for this war, you set the rules, yet today you are teaching a*dharma* (antonym of *dharma*) to Arjuna?"

Kshatra-dharmavekeshava
What is the dharma of warriors, Krishna?

Shri Vāsudev Krishna replied:

Kva dharmaste tadā gataha
Karna, what dharma did you follow at the time...

Krishna then continued to elaborate on all of Karna's lapses in dharma. If Karna was so fond of dharma, why did he fight on the unrighteous side of the Kauravas in the war? Where was his dharma when Draupadi was humiliated? Where was his dharma when Duryodhana tried to usurp the shares of the Pandavas? All his life he had sided with the unrighteous Kauravas, and demanded righteous behaviour from the Pandavas. This story illustrates that even those who wrong, do not wish for anyone to wrong them. We always expect others to be righteous towards us, regardless of what we do. After all, life is ultimately about our *ānanda*, and so we are naturally inclined to this type of behaviour. This principle was well understood by Aristotle, and 2500 years ago he said, "We choose honour, wealth, and prestige because they bring us happiness. But we choose happiness for itself and never with the view for anything further."

Amazingly, 2500 years before Aristotle, Veda Vyāsa, the compiler of the Vedas, also stated[103]:

Sarveshām api bhūtānām
nrupa svāmaiva vallabhaha
itare 'patya-vittādhyās
tad-vallabhatayaiva hi

Everyone loves their happiness.
It is only for the sake of self-happiness
that they love their children, wealth, etc.

No one ever taught us to seek happiness, we never learnt it. It almost seems that we are intuitively born to decide what bliss means to each of us as individuals. The Western philosophers weren't the first to pinpoint this quest for happiness, despite them getting a lot of credit for it. Many believe that this search for *ānanda* began only a few hundred years ago, but the real quest began almost 5000 years ago, rooted in the Vedic scriptures.

Ānando brahmeti vyajānat
Ānandādhyeva khalvimāni bhutāni jāyante
Ānandena jātāni jīvanti
Ānandam prayanta-bhisan-vishantīti[104]

Brahma is bliss; for from bliss,
indeed all beings originated; having been born,
they are sustained by bliss;
they move towards and merge into bliss.

Ānandamayo 'bhyāsāt[105]
Brahma is bliss

---

[103] Shrimad Bhagavatam 10.14.50
[104] Taittiriya Upanishad 3.6
[105] Brahmasutra 1.1.12

The Vedas classify two kinds of happiness, *shreya* and *preya*. *Shreya* is described as the kind of happiness that seems like bitter poison to begin with, but turns out to be like sweet nectar later. For example, waking up at 6 a.m. and going to the gym may seem extremely painful to practice, but when your health improves as a consequence of it, you realise that the benefits were well worth the hard work and sacrifice made. On the other end of the spectrum is *preya*. This is like having what seems like nectar at first, but later transforms into poison. For example, feasting on large cups of cookie dough ice cream every day may give you immense pleasure momentarily. But, when the body's physical parameters inevitably go out of control, that initial joy turns into agonising misery. Describing *shreya* and *preya* in further detail, the Kathopanishad states:

> anyachchhreyo'nyadutaiva preyasteubhe
> nānārthe purusham sinitaha |
> tayoh shreya ādadānasya sādhu bhavati
> hīyate'rthādhya u preyo vrinite
> shreyashcha preyashcha manushyameta stau
> samparitya vivinakti dhirah
> shreyo hi dhiro'bhi preyaso vrinite
> preyo mando yogakshemād vrinite[106]

Putting this simply means, "There are two paths—one is *beneficial* and the other is *pleasant*. These both lead humans to very different ends. The pleasant is enjoyable to begin with, but always ends in pain. The ignorant are snared to the pleasant and perish. But the wise are not deceived by its attractions. They choose the beneficial path and finally attain true happiness." The reality is that pleasures which will damage us in the long run are easily available, whilst the worthwhile pleasures seem distant. They require hard work and earnest efforts, which is why we need discipline and self-control. These are some of the secrets of happiness according to the Vedas.

---

[106] Kathopanishad 1.2.1-2

PERSONIFY KESHAV

There has always been discussion and hesitation on whether spirituality and science can mix. Religious beliefs can't be empirically tested or falsified, but that doesn't mean that the *products* and *consequences* of religious beliefs cannot be studied. A growing number of psychological studies are suggesting that religious people are happier, healthier, and are better at recovering from trauma than non-religious people.[107] In another study, parents who had lost a baby were interviewed three weeks after the loss, and again after eighteen months. Those who attended religious services regularly, and reported religion as being important to them, were better able to cope eighteen months after the loss, showing relatively less depression and greater well-being than the non-religious parents. [108]

Other studies show that those active in their religions live longer even with various diseases, and are healthier in general. Many religious groups encourage positive, low-stress lifestyles, advocating moderation and harmonious family life. The social support and sense of identity provided by belonging to a religious group helps in offering friendship and companionship. Again, humans have naturally evolved to live in hives, and religion supports this basic human need.

An even more interesting finding is that believing God has a purpose in everything helps to find meaning in every event of life, including the traumatic ones. Believing God to be the all-doer can change thinking critically. Regardless of whether you belong to a religious organisation or not, your health and overall well-being may simply benefit from having this form of faith. In a study carried out on patients undergoing chemotherapy, those who believed that God had control over their cancers had higher self-esteem and were rated as better adjusted by their nurses (e.g. they were more happy, serene, and active, and also related better to others).[109] This belief helped cancer patients cope better than the belief of personal control.

---

[107] Ellison, C. G., and Levin, J. S. (1998)

[108] McIntosh, D. N., Silver, R. C., and Wortman, C. B. (1993)

[109] Jenkins, R. A., and Pargament, K. I. (1988)

Faith also gives rise to a number of positive emotions and experiences associated with *ānanda*, and this could explain why religious and pious individuals are happier than others. One such attribute is forgiveness. A number of studies have shown that highly religious and spiritual individuals see themselves as more forgiving and that they also value forgiveness more than others.

DIVINITY EVERYWHERE

A genuine sense of meaning in life must come from your own thoughts, feelings and experiences. A universal way to practice religion or spirituality is praying. Almost seven out of ten Americans report praying daily, and only 6 percent report never praying.[110] Another important habit to cultivate is to see divinity in every thing. This links hand-in-hand with altruism, the practice of concern for happiness of others. My guru, Mahant Swami Maharaj continuously emphasises on seeing divinity in one and all. He teaches that every being is inherently divine, but we fail to see this. When we are able to see divinity in others, we are also able to see divinity in ourselves and the world around us. Scientists no longer ignore the powerful influences that spirituality and religion have on health and well-being. In the US alone the vast majority of individuals, about 95 percent, believe in God.[111] If you choose to harness the benefits of faith, it can greatly improve your well-being and your life too.

SPIRITUALITY THROUGH THE VEDAS

Throughout this book I have referred to the Vedic scriptures many times. In fact, a lot of the thoughts that make up The Keshav Way are based upon Vedic philosophy. The reason for this is that they are believed to be amongst the oldest known scriptures to humankind. The Vedas are not simply a collection of books, they are the oldest known religious texts believed to be direct knowledge from the Higher Power. They are known to be *apaurusheya*, meaning 'not created by

[110] Blanton, D. (2005, December 1)
[111] Hoge, D. R. (1996)

anyone'. The texts were compiled by Veda Vyāsa, through oratory tradition, dividing the entire body of knowledge into four Vedas: *Rig, Yajur, Sāma, and Atharva*. But, Veda Vyāsa is never declared as the author of the Vedas, only the compiler. The word Vyāsa is itself the Sanskrit word for 'compiler'. And so, Veda Vyāsa means 'the compiler of the Vedas'.

This knowledge was further elaborated upon in other scriptures. These include the two *itihās*[112] (*Rāmāyana* and *Mahābhārata)*, eighteen *Purānas, Shad Darshan* (six treatises on philosophy), many *Smritis* (books of dharma) and thousands of *Nibandhs* (philosophical thesis by the great sages). Together, this entire body of literature is known as the Vedic scripture.

Consolidating all of this knowledge is the *Vachanāmrut*, which translates to 'talks of nectar'. They are the direct teachings of Bhagwān Shri Swāminārāyan, based upon his vast knowledge and deep studies of the Vedic scriptures. He presented the teachings in a concise and understandable manner, using powerful analogies. Kudos to the *Vachanāmrut*, that stands to answer the majority of the questions in my life. If you haven't got the *Vachanāmrut*, I would recommend you get a copy. The Vedic scriptures are vast, and we will probably never get through them all. The Vachanamrut consolidates all of this knowledge through concise, relatable means.

Even Western philosophers have shown admiration for these scriptures. Arthur Schopenhauer said, "The Vedas are the most rewarding and most elevating books in this world."

Max Müller said, "There is no book in this world that is so thrilling, stirring, and inspiring as the Upanishads.

Ralph Waldo Emerson wrote, "In the great books of India, an empire spoke to us, nothing small or unworthy, but large, serene, consistent, the voice of an old intelligence, which in another age and climate had pondered and thus disposed of the questions that exercise us." It is within these ancient Vedic scriptures that the ultimate truth is shared.

---

[112] Meaning 'history'

THE ULTIMATE TRUTH

The Vedic scriptures contain an immense bank of knowledge. By reading them alone they cannot be understood or imbibed. It takes a lifetime to go through the Vedas and properly understand them. Many of the swamis at Sarangpur take up the challenge of studying the Vedic texts throughout their lifetime. The Vedas themselves have informed us of what needs to be done. They instruct us to understand them through the guidance of a *guru*. The word guru has become somewhat taboo these days. There are love gurus, tech gurus, cooking gurus, and so on. But the original meaning of the word stems from two Sanskrit root words: *gu* and *ru*. Putting both words together gives *guru* meaning "one who brings a being from darkness into light." Don't take this in the literal sense; it is a metaphor where darkness refers to ignorance, and light refers to the ultimate truth and clarity. A true guru is one who takes us away from ignorance, and brings us towards the truth. The Mundaka Upanishad states:

tadvijñānārtham sagurumevābhigachchhet
samitpānih shrotriyam brahmanishtham[113]

To understand the Truth, approach a spiritual guru, who is both well-versed in the theoretical knowledge of scripture, and embodies it through his practical life.

The Shrimad Bhāgavatam states:

tasmād gurum prapadyeta jijñāsuh
shreya uttamam shābde pare cha
nishnātam brahmanyupashamāshrayam[114]

One who is desirous of the highest welfare should surrender to a true guru. Such a guru should be both theoretically knowledgeable and realised.

---

[113] Mundaka Upanishad 1.2.12
[114] Shrimad Bhagavatam 11.3.21

The Vedas have emphasised the need for a guru numerous times, as without a true guru the absolute truth cannot be acquired. The most prominent scripture of modern-day Hinduism is the Bhagavad Gītā. It is the conversation between Shri Vāsudev Krishna and Arjuna, that took place on the battlefield of Kurukshetra during the great Mahābhārata war. In Chapter 4 of the Gita, Krishna says:

tad viddhi pranipātena pariprashnena sevayā
updekshyanti te jnānam jnāninas tattva-darshinah[115]

Learn the Truth from a spiritual master.
Inquire from him with reverence and render service unto him. Such an enlightened sadhu [guru] can impart knowledge unto you, for he has seen the Truth.

From the above verse, we understand three things:
1. Approach a spiritual master (true guru)
2. Inquire from him submissively (with reverence and respect)
3. Render service to him (the Sanskrit term is *sevā*)

Based on all this, the secret of the Vedic scriptures is clear. To understand divine knowledge and personify spirituality in our lives, we *need* to find a true guru and surrender to him. The true guru gives inspiration, strength, faith, and belief. Ultimately, the true guru embodies *ānanda* perfectly. He is the embodiment of *param ānanda*. He is the embodiment of *sahaj ānanda*. He is Keshav personified.

---

[115] Bhagavad Gita 4.34

V

VINAY'S THOUGHTS

PAIN & STRUGGLE

God only gives his toughest battles to his strongest soldiers.
Moses

Major concern in psychology has been in the way that people cope with adversity and get back to normal functioning. Researchers today have studied people facing many kinds of adversity—including cancer, heart disease, HIV, rape, assault, paralysis, infertility, housefires, plane crashes, and earthquakes. They have studied how people cope with the loss of their strongest attachments—children, spouses or partners, and parents. A large body of research shows that although traumas, crises, and tragedies come in various forms, people actually benefit from them in three primary ways.

The first is that rising to a challenge, and taking up the challenge, changes your self-conception. None of us knows what we are really capable of enduring. You might say, "I would die if I lost A", or, "I could never survive what B is going through", yet, the statements are spun out of thin air by the monkey. If you did lose A, or if found yourself in the same position as B, your heart would not stop beating. You would respond automatically and eventually adapt. People sometimes say that they can never recover after terrible loss of trauma. But after a few weeks some degree of normality returns as one struggles to make sense of the loss and altered circumstances. One of the most common lessons people draw from bereavement or trauma is that they are much stronger than they thought, and this new appreciation of their strength then give them confidence to face future challenges. People who have suffered from battle, rape, concentration camps, or traumatic personal losses, often seem to be immune against future stress. They recover more quickly, in part because they know they can cope. Dalai Lama has said, "The person who has had more experience of hardships can stand more firmly in the face of problems than the person who has never experienced suffering. From this angle, then, some suffering can be a good lesson for life."

Often, struggle and adversity also become filters for a higher degree of life. When someone is diagnosed with cancer, or a couple lose a child, some friends and family rise to support and look for ways that they can express their support and be helpful. Through this, we often develop love for them as they show care, and we carry forward the love and gratitude towards those who cared for us in a time of need. In a large study of bereavement, Susan Nolen-Hoeksema and her colleagues at Stanford university found that one of the most common effects of losing a loved one was that the bereaved had a great appreciation of and tolerance for the other people in their life. This relates to the third common benefit, trauma changes priorities and beliefs towards the present and towards others. Adversity *can* lead to growth, strength, joy, and self improvement, by the three benefits described above.

Remember that the pursuit of happiness is like a blind man in a dark room, searching for a black cat that isn't even there! Some think happiness is within sight, but beyond reach. Many feel that they must find a way to avoid pain in their lives. But pain is a part of what we must accept. We should not waste time and energy trying to avoid pain; accept it as a part of life. Nothing happens without purpose. Pain is a call from the higher power, an inherent element of the cosmic *māyā*. It is an opportunity to learn and grow from the experience, nothing else. If you accidentally put your hand on the stove, you get burnt. It's not the stove punishing you, it is telling you to take your hand away quickly before more damage is done. When someone gets pain in their abdomen, and they find out it is a kidney stone, is it punishing them? No, it is simply telling them to get a grip on their body and diet. The world is letting us know that we are searching for happiness, but in the wrong places, and we must change that quickly.

In our lives, when a door to happiness closes, another one opens, most often a better one. Stop looking back at the closed doors and turn your attention to the one opening. Reassess how lucky we truly are. None of us are victims, we are all winners on an amazing journey. My gurus, Pramukh Swami Maharaj and Mahant Swami Maharaj continuously teach that whatever happens, happens for a reason, and that God is the all-doer. Whether you believe in God or not, you can still apply this teaching into your life. Every experience you have is there to mould you, improve you, and to make a better *you*.

You are the stone; You are the chisel; You, and you alone, are the creator of your own happiness. This teaching by my gurus is not just a preaching, they live by it. Whatever experiences they have gone through in their lives, positive or negative, they have remained stable, at an equilibrium.

Every experience is a fresh opportunity for us to grow and to improve, it is not suffering, our perception makes it suffering. I am not saying that you shouldn't be sad, or that you shouldn't feel pain, that again depends on the seriousness of the situation, as well as other factors. But you cannot always play the victim game when life doesn't go as planned, which it won't. Don't let situations and circumstances define who you are, or who you will become.

AFFIRMATIVE THOUGHTS

You must know what you want to achieve, and how you will go about achieving it. When you go out for desserts, you don't say, "I will have a milkshake." You know, and specify, exactly what type of milkshake you want. Likewise in life, if you are confused about what you want to achieve, the results will also be confusing. The goals you want to achieve should reflect who you are within. They should define how you can improve yourself, as well as the quality of your life.

I won't even say that having desires for materialistic objects is bad; do it if you must. Maybe only transcended souls have no desires. But behind every desire, there should be a positive purpose. For example, you can wish for a nice car, or a bigger home, but, for the reason of wanting to raise your children in a happy and comfortable environment. At the peak of The Keshav Way, we must have zero desires to truly live in *ānanda*. I know it won't be possible straight away, but to take the first step is in your hands now.

Note your ambitions, write them down. Be honest with yourself and write exactly what you want, let nothing hold you back. It is fine to have huge ambitions, but think about how you will get there too. What you want to strive to achieve, must also be in the present tense. Don't use "I want to become a successful accountant," instead write, "I am a successful accountant."

Say them to yourself, adjust them and amend them. Situations and factors will affect your goals, but don't be let down and completely change them either. We have planted the seeds, don't uproot them. Remember that your motivation should come from within, not outside. Don't set ambitions for *others;* set them for *yourself.*

MY AMBITIONS

KESHAV IS WITH YOU

Swami Vivekananda, a great visionary and philosopher of India, used to say, "All power is within you. You can do anything and everything." The answer to life lies within you. We cannot pin down exactly what the answer is, but again, I believe that it is something truly divine. So for simplicity, let us say that Keshav is with us all. It isn't perceivable because we haven't reached that state yet. But through our life, words, actions, deeds, emotions and beliefs, we can truly experience the Keshav within us.

You must put in effort; ambitions aren't met or attained just like that. If the intention is there, you can achieve it; with the help of the Keshav that resides within you. But you must take action. If you don't take the first step, you will miss out on many opportunities. Don't expect changes to just happen, especially if you don't want to put in the work yourself.

You must step out of your comfort zone. To be honest, if you just want to sit back and do nothing, then you might have wasted your time with this book. Don't be reactive; be proactive. Sometimes we wait until the situations get so dire before we choose to change something about it. But what if we made the change at the beginning? We can only do that if we make ourselves aware. You can only grow when you are challenged, not when you are in comfort.

The truth is that extraordinary people will get things done even when they don't feel like it, because they are fully committed to their goals. My guru, Pramukh Swami Maharaj, was the prime example of this. Difficulties came his way too, but his vision was clear which is why he was able to achieve it.

BEAUTY WITHIN

You should always take care of yourself. Feeling comfortable with who you really are is a very important trait you must have. Recognising and accepting your beauty is part of the self-love process, but it is surely a difficult one to grasp. Especially in today's world where social networks and the media bombard us with false perceptions of beauty. We naturally compare ourselves to attractive people and so we define our physical traits against these 'perfect' people. Do not set benchmarks for yourself, because by doing so you will begin to perceive others in a different light too. In 1998, 947,000 females and 99,000 males in the USA underwent cosmetic surgery in a bid to improve their appearance. In the same year, $234 billion were spent globally on cosmetic products.

Don't believe the lies defining your beauty. The size of your jeans doesn't define you. The colour of your skin doesn't define you. The numbers on a scale don't define you. The marks on your body don't define you. No one's expectations can define you. No one's opinions can define you. Your life isn't for anyone else. No one is perfect and no one will ever be. Perfection is subjective and solely based on an individual's perception. Be happy with your own imperfections. They are what make you stand out. Never underappreciate yourself. Someone who accepts themselves as they are, can inspire the entire world. Make that you. Show the world an example on how to attain happiness through self-acceptance.

My guru, Pramukh Swami Maharaj, was known for his beauty from within, as well as his beautiful actions towards humanity. This is very rare, but attainable. Inner beauty is defined by unconditional love and kindness. The definition of beauty we know is external, and we never see it to define 'inner beauty' because people are only interested in materialistic successes. When we learn to see the inner beauty in people, we too will be able to focus on our inner beauty. True beauty is so much more than just physical features. Internal beauty lasts for life, and even beyond. You should spend your life building your character, not your physical appearance. You can get plastic surgery, but you can't buy character. Beauty is not just about external looks. It is about a genuine heart that loves, cares, and feels for the pain of others. That is

284 · The Keshav Way

what makes a person truly beautiful. Let me remind you that beyond the differences that divide us; nationality, religion, gender, race, appearance, or health, lies the common essential qualities that we all share—we are all divine and also have the inherent ability to love.

YOU ARE UNIQUE

When you compare, you experience misery. Comparisons are the fastest way to take the fun out of life. You may have done something that you are proud of and feel you are the best at; that is until you see someone else has done something similar, or better. I agree that it is very difficult to not compare, but seriously, it isn't any of your business what other people are doing. Again, it is another natural tendency. When we were children at school and our friends had better shoes than us, we wanted them too. Children gain the habit of comparing themselves, and that trait only grows with age. Parents play a crucial role in this. Never compare your children to other children, appreciate them for who they are. Don't say things like, "Have you seen Sam's grades?" This is scarring for a child and will leave a lasting impression on them to feel worthless and 'not good enough', possibly for the rest of their life.

Corporations and brands also play a role in the reason we compare by encouraging comparisons non-stop. Not got an iPhone? Catch up! Not got a Porsche? You're not up-to-date! Not wearing what a celebrity is wearing? How lame! Tactics like these are referred to as manipulative marketing strategies which are planned to prey on an individual's fear and low self-esteem. This gives us the tendency to compare and perceive others to be doing better than us but, what we don't notice is those who are struggling compared to us. This the reason we never truly feel grateful for what we *actually* have.

As social media influence also increases, comparisons will prove more and more problematic. We can see that from young children through to adults, as everyone is heavily absorbed in it. Little do we know, this is feeding us a sugar-coated version of an ideal lifestyle, a fiction, or a delusion. We present our 'ideal' lives on social media, a montage of a fake identity to hide our insecurities and seek validation. We quench our thirst through people's likes and comments praising us, but we always end up seeking more and more. Comparing our lives with others on social media is a total waste of time. During my research, I was shocked to find that some people create fake relationships, to build their 'public profiles'; with a fake show of love and affection in front of the camera, to make thousands per photo. With endless filters and mind-blowing captions, they make everything seem amazing. The reality could obviously be different. Studies show that engaging in social media allows for the brain to release dopamine, the hormone that makes us feel good. But did you know that the release of dopamine can be addictive too?

I am not asking you to get off social media, because not even I can do that. I have tried, and I have just been pulled back again. But what we can do is ensure that we don't let it invade our lives. Be the best version of yourself by keeping the focus on your own life and the ambitions you set to achieve. For sure, look at the lives of other people, give them recognition, and be part of their successes. Then, go back to focus on yourself, and continue to pursue your own journey.

There is nothing more gratifying and fulfilling as living a life where you are *you*. There is a psychological concept known as 'social proof', which suggests that people tend to follow the crowd. When the large majority of people are doing something, we automatically assume it is the right thing to do. The people around us affect our actions more than we think. Take slavery for example. When it was legal everyone assumed it was fine. Though today, everyone agrees that it is degrading, inhumane, and immoral. Self-introspect and question your actions from the day. Why did you do what you did? Why did you choose what you did? Was it right? Or were you simply following the crowd? When you self-introspect, you will realise how you are living, and only then will you be able to make changes. If you become a slave to what other people say and do, you will lose control and your life will spiral down a deep hole.

Fear controls society. People steer towards living a life dictated by the beliefs and choices of others, instead of living their life for themselves. Never do this. You should never feel you are living to meet someone else's expectations nor to gain appraisal from others. Accept your uniqueness. Life should be unlimited. Let's try something. You might have have heard or done this before. If a red house is made with red bricks, a blue house is made with blue bricks, and a black house is made with black bricks, what is a greenhouse made with? Did you say 'green'? If you said 'glass', well done. If you said 'green', you are wrong. This technique is a psychological technique known as *priming*. I primed you to say 'green' as opposed to 'glass'. This technique is used by marketing companies globally to boost sales. We allow the world around us to control us.

True genuineness is very hard to find today, especially when we are influenced to meet the needs of another person, or a large corporation. Accept your own uniqueness. Don't let society's needs determine who you are. That is wrong. Don't get trapped; be free. Live your life today as most people won't, so that you can live the rest of your life as most people can't. Don't follow the crowd, be yourself. You don't need to grow to suppress the rest of the world, but grow so that the rest of the world doesn't suppress you.

LOOK AFTER YOU

I have never allowed my mind to become fixated,
even on what will happen one second from now.
Learn to live in the present.
HH Mahant Swami Maharaj

Often our subconscious tries to change our self-perception. The subconscious is the part of our mind that isn't fully aware, but which influences an enormous part of our actions and feelings. To keep it simple, it is the brain of the monkey. Sometimes it discourages us, as well as what we do, "Why are you failing?" or, "Why aren't you good enough?"

With regular practice of the ways shown in this book, you will be able to have control over your subconscious. Lots of people will try to bring you down, but try not to bring yourself down. Don't punish yourself for your mistakes. Mistakes allow us to better ourselves. Learn to self-forgive for your past and present mistakes, but don't use it as an excuse to make more. Learn to let go, accept whatever has happened. We are human, mistakes happen, and we continue with our journey. If people judge you for your past, that is their problem, not yours; you must focus on your present alone. Don't let others use your past to judge you either. This not only holds you back from a happy tomorrow, but also a joyful present. When you learn to forgive people, including yourself, you don't just improve the past, you improve your now and tomorrow too. It will give you a sense of peace and bliss. No one can dictate your destiny, but you.

LOVE YOURSELF

Your time is limited,
don't waste it living someone else's life.
Steve Jobs

What other people think about you has nothing to do with you, but everything to do with them. We tend to neglect self-love. We are programmed to care more about other people's opinions, rather than our own self-perception. Sometimes, the negativity within us stems from the dissatisfaction we have with ourselves. Our *ātmā* is buried deep within us, trying to reach out to us. We must take the proactive initiative to connect. This doesn't mean that you ignore everyone; constructive criticism is good. But how you take it is up to you. Constantly evaluate yourself—both the good and bad.

In today's world, we continue on a thriving mission to impress others, to prove ourselves best. We limit our financial capacity by buying materialistic things that we don't need, just so we can impress those who wouldn't give a damn about it anyway. We change ourselves in order fit in, rather than changing our perception of the world by being ourselves. We stride on a journey to meet our external needs whilst we neglect our inner needs. Purpose coach, Jay Shetty, refers to the idea of 'the perception of perception'. It's the idea that, if I think that you think I'm a genius, then I would feel like I really am a genius, and vice versa. We base our self-worth on a perception of a perception. Focus on your intention as it is very easy to lose yourself. It's not about how others describe you in three words, but more so about how you would describe yourself in three words.

Love, humility, and service are the most important things in this world. But you must also love and be kind to yourself. Don't change who you are as a person, but instead accept who you already are. If we don't do this, we become insecure, this affects our confidence, mindset, and health. People will naturally accept you if you love yourself. Self-love is important to build and maintain firm relationships. Buddha said, "You can search throughout the universe for someone who is more deserving of your love and affection than you are yourself, and that person is not to be found anywhere. You yourself, as much as anybody in the entire universe, deserve your love and affection."

It all starts with accepting yourself for who you are, giving focus on your own joy, health, and wellbeing. Though people may not accept this, knowing your own self-worth is crucial and so, sometimes you shouldn't care what others think. When people struggle to accept themselves, they search for faults in others.

STARTING HABITS

I want to share a set of powerful habits with you. Some ideas are repeated from previous parts of the book, but this is just to consolidate the points and emphasise their importance. These ten habits, derived from part of my research, have been scientifically proven to help your brain become faster, smarter, and better. They have been proven to not only optimise your brain but also your health and well-being. It is important for you to try out all of these habits and not just some, to understand which one gives the best results for you. It is known as the Pareto principle, or the 80/20 rule. It states that 20 percent of causes can give 80 percent of effects and results.

Your Food

We've all heard the phrase, *you are what you eat*. What you eat really matters, specifically to your mind, body, and especially for your Keshav. Certain foods are important in maintaining a positive and strong mind. There are specific foods that actually boost your brain activity.

Turmeric contains curcumin, which has been shown to cross the blood-brain barrier, meaning it can directly enter the brain and benefit the cells within your brain. It is also a potent antioxidant with anti-inflammatory compounds which benefit the memory, eases depression, and helps new brain cells grow.

Avocado has been shown to reduce blood pressure and maintain healthy blood flow, as they provide monounsaturated fat.

Blueberries are also powerful brain food. They contain an antioxidant known as anthocyanin, which reduces inflammation and oxidative stress, which effect brain ageing. Studies show that they also help with memory.

Broccoli contains glucosinolates, broken down in the body into isothiocyanate, which reduces oxidative stress, and lowers the risk of neurodegenerative diseases. It also contains high levels of vitamin K, known to improve cognitive function and memory.

Green, leafy vegetables like kale, contain antioxidants, vitamins, and minerals—all of which are very powerful in reducing brain ageing and improving memory.

Dark chocolate contains cacao (cocoa), which contains flavonoids that improve cognitive function. Chocolate, as bad as we're told it is, helps us to focus and concentrate, stimulating endorphins. The darker the chocolate the better, as it has less sugar.

Soy Products are rich in certain antioxidants called polyphenols that research has shown links to a reduced risk of dementia and improves cognitive abilities in regular ageing processes.

Nuts & Seeds. We are all aware of the benefits of this for our body, but they also have many wonderful benefits for the mind. Particularly walnuts which provide high levels of antioxidants and vitamin E, that protect your neurons against brain ageing.

Water. It's obvious, 80 percent of our brain is water. If you don't have enough of it in your body, it will lead to fatigue, slower reaction and thinking, and studies have shown that those who are well-hydrated score better on tests of brainpower.

Your Thoughts

In the earlier chapter on emotions, we looked at ANTs—Automatic Negative Thoughts. We must observe our thoughts and understand what, and how, we are feeling. Just as we have seen how we can cleanse our diet with rich foods, we must cleanse our thoughts too. Try to go 21 days without complaining. We are addicted to the likes of complaining and moaning, so I think that would be a good start. It will work through the law of action, rewiring your mind.

A coward dies a thousand deaths, a hero dies but once.
William Shakespeare

Your mind cannot differentiate between the imaginary and the actual reality. So feeding negative thoughts will manifest the negativity. Remember that your mind is the most powerful tool you have. Rehearse positive thoughts in your mind, to manifest positive energy, not the negative ones.

Your Nutrients

Nutrients like Omega 3s, DHAs, Ginkgo Biloba, Vitamin B and B12s are all important. Today, when our diets are becoming more fast-food based, particularly with our lifestyles, we are lacking certain supplements. I am not a nutritionist or a dietician, but I regularly get tests done and I see that there is more than what meets the eye; maybe you should too. Being low on certain vitamins and nutritions can have a major impact on your cognition and long-term health.

Your Positivity

Who you spend time with is who you become. Within our brain, we have what we call mirror neurons, that work with the nervous system. It's like when you watch a movie and something bad happens to a character, you feel it too, like a sense of empathy. We imitate people; those who we spend time with are who we become, because we imitate their habits, behaviours, thought patterns, and everything else.

You're the average of the five people you spend the most time with.
Jim Rohn

We have been talking about our biological networks and our neurological networks, but we must also analyse our social networks. An example is smoking; it has less to do with our neurological network, and has more to do with if our friends, or those around us who smoke. How you do one thing is how you do everything. Be clear on whom you want to meet and be around. A reminder that your circle influences you.

Your Environment

A clean environment helps your mind stay clean. When we are studying and our desks are clean, we experience our thoughts getting more clarity. I am not just talking about the physical environment, I am also talking about clean water and clean (fresh) air.

Your Sleep

Sleep is one of the most important habits that we all must improve on. Not just for your brain, but for your overall well-being too. Studies have shown the benefits of sleep shown time and time again. In sleep, we convert our short-term memory to long-term memory. Regardless of what you think, all-nighters do not help. You need good sleep. Millions across the globe struggle to sleep. It is assumed that we all know how to fall asleep. Researchers have found that sleep helps with controlling the natural brain ageing processes. A lack of sleep can lead to higher chances of dementia and similar disorders. We also *need* to dream. I know right now you are thinking, "Wait, what?" Well, you read it right. Your mind needs to dream. Our best ideas come to us during our sleep. Mary Shelley created Frankenstein from her dreams, Paul McCartney came up with 'Yesterday' in his dreams, and Mendeleev came up with the periodic table in his dreams. What is it we are dreaming about at night? When our brain is working all day and we come to sleep, the brain doesn't switch off. In fact, it is when it works most actively.

Your Mind

Research is still ongoing, and there no conclusive evidence, but electromagnetic fields can harm your mind. Our mind wasn't designed to take in this much exposure of electricity from devices like phones, tablets, and laptops. And it is right there, closest to our brains. 90 percent of those under the age of 18, sleep with their phones under their pillows. We do not know the effect that this is having on our minds, maybe we will find out towards the end of our lives; or you can avoid it now, and shield your mind.

Your Knowledge

There are two fundamental aspects that make up brain capacity. Namely, neurogenesis and neuroplasticity. Neurogenesis is where you can create new brain cells until the day you die. Neuroplasticity is where your brain has the ability to create new connections. For example, Einstein didn't have a bigger brain than us, he just had more connections than most people. Again, this links to nutrients and novelty. Your mind needs stress and stimulus through the likes of exercise, nutrients, and new learning. The famous study we looked at earlier, found that the nuns remained agile as they grew old, partly because of their faith and also because they were lifelong learners.

Your Stress

We've detailed stress in-depth in an earlier chapter. Stress can be dangerous. It releases cortisol and adrenaline. We don't realise it because it is invisible, until we are on a holiday, or getting a massage, because it is there all the time. When your mind becomes free and relaxed, it begins to wonder. Some people wake up anxious or stressed, and they don't know why. Let me ask you, what do you do before you sleep? Are you checking your emails? Scrolling through social media? Watching scary movies or reading books? These things can lead to restless sleep, which leads on to the effects you experience in the morning. A good way to manage stress is preparing to go to bed. To start, stop all work at least half an hour before going to bed, including looking at your phone. Turn off your emails, don't go on social media, don't watch videos. Just completely shut off, go take a shower, and then relax. Once you get to bed, sit up straight and take a few deep, relaxing breaths. If you do this every night, then within a few days you will feel more relaxed and have comforting sleep.

Another important point in managing stress is what you do when you first wake up in the morning. Do you roll over and pick up your phone? Maybe to turn off the alarm, but then do you end up on social media? Repeat the deep breathing when you wake up, closing your eyes and reflecting on yourself; the Keshav within.

Stress emanates from day-to-day dealing and disturbances. It is important to know that stress isn't bad. It adds a sense of spice in life, complete freedom from stress comes only at death. You cannot live without stress, you must learn to live with it. It is like fish; they don't see water, because they are in the water all the time. Today, when we are all the more stressed than ever before, managing it is even more crucial. The best way to do that for you is through the likes of meditation, relaxation, and yoga.

FAITH OVER FEAR

Whether exploring unfamiliar terrains, running races,
or worshipping God, faith in others, faith in oneself,
and faith in God is essential.
Life is full of such challenges and it is faith which
fuels all our endeavours to tackle them.
It is with this dynamo which drives our actions.
It is by faith that any task can be accomplished.

Fear is programmed into our minds. Everywhere we go, there is fear. We continuously scan the world for problems because that is what keeps us *surviving*. Our brains are constantly looking for problems to try and solve. It's exactly what they have been trained for. Aristotle has said, "Happiness depends upon ourselves." And today, we have scientific evidence that shows how important our attitude and certain actions are in order to manage that attitude. Mahant Swami Maharaj often shares Charles Swindoll's quote, "Life is 10 percent what happens to you, and 90 percent how you react to it."

Casting our mind back to Part 1, the research published in *The How of Happiness* by psychology professor Sonja Lyubomirsky, from the University of California, says that it is actually only 10 percent of our happiness that is based on the circumstances of our life. That is to say, 10 percent of our happiness is what happens *to* us. This means that 90 percent of our happiness isn't based on what's going on in the world around us. It is based on what is going on in the world *within* us.

Faith is a matter of choice. It is a strong, unshakeable belief in the higher power, oneself, and others to help accomplish tasks successfully. Fear is also a mechanism to help us avoid the struggles of life. Both faith and fear are beyond our perception. We cannot see faith or fear, but we can experience them. You may fear the deep waters of the ocean because you don't know what lurks deep under. We make fear-based assumptions many times. Learn to replace your fear with faith. I am not saying it will make everything easier, but it surely makes this journey easier. It is an indispensable quality to have, that can lead us to success.

The battle of the Mahābhārata is about to begin. Thousands of warriors have their weapons to hand, ready to fight. But Arjuna breaks down, terrified. He sees his family and friends on either side of this battle, and knows that many of them will die. Arjuna, struck with fear, drops his bow.

Arjuna was probably the most talented archer, not only in that battle, but, arguably, who ever lived. Yet, fear causes him to totally lose connection with his true abilities. This happens to us too. We have so much to give to the world, but fear and anxiety disconnects us. I can almost guarantee that as you grew up you were taught, either directly or indirectly, that fear was a bad thing, and you were told things like, "Don't be scared!" Fear is seen as embarrassing, humiliating, and so it is often an attribute we try to conceal.

Truthfully, we can never live fully without some level of fear or anxiety. Fear is nothing but a warning sign in our Tesla. The monkey is obviously the first to notice it. The importance lies in what you choose to do when you see that warning signal. Sometimes fear is a critical warning to help us survive a real danger, but for the most time, the monkey has been messing around, and the anxiety we feel is related to daily concerns about money, our job, our family, and relationships. Unfortunately, this *is* our fault; we allow anxiety to hold us back by blocking how we truly feel. The longer that we hold onto these negative feelings, the more they grow like a cancer, spread, and become toxic. Fear is useful in helping us identify and address certain patterns of thinking and behaviour that don't do us any good. We often let fear drive us, but that isn't even the actual issue. The actual issue is that we fear the wrong things. We fear change and challenges, unaware that it is these that actually make us stronger.

Dealing with Fear

Studies have shown that being able to successfully deal with intermittent stressors, like managing a large work project or moving to a new home, contributes to *better* health, along with greater feelings of accomplishment and well-being. When you deal with hardship, you realise that you are capable of dealing with *that* hardship. This gives you a certain level of confidence that when bad things happen, you *will* find ways to handle them. To close the gap without fear, you must acknowledge its presence. Face your fear. Become familiar with it. In this way you bring yourself into full presence. We often distract ourselves from fear. These patterns for distracting ourselves from fear are set when we are young, and are deeply ingrained. So it will take some time and effort to uncover them. Recognising fear patterns help us to trace it to the root, and that's when we can begin to uproot it.

The Cause & The Cure

You are distinct from your fears and anxiety. Fears come from the monkey. Similar to an emotion, when we talk about them, we usually say that we *are* the emotion. I *am* sad. I *am* scared. Remember, fear is not us, it is just something that we experience, another passing experience. It's the same with our emotions; they are fleeting feelings that we feel, but they are not us. Shift from 'I *am*' to 'I *feel*'. I *feel* sad. I *feel* angry. I *feel* scared. Some of us may already do this, but this helps to put emotions in their rightful place, and then we can work on dealing with them. Fears are closely related to attachment. Humans seem to have this need to own and control things. It's actually the monkey that attaches over everything; the passenger really doesn't care. The passenger is detached. It realises that it is just a visitor, and everything that it *owns* is actually *borrowed*. It knows that true happiness is derived from the moment, accepting things the way they are. Clinging to temporary things gives them power over us, and they inevitably become sources of pain, fear, and anxiety. The majority of pain, fear, and anxiety stems from our attachments. When we *accept* the temporary nature of everything and everyone in our lives, we feel gratitude for the good fortune of getting to *borrow* them for the duration. We explored the story of Alexander at the start; think about him again. This is one of the things I noticed in the swamis. Their detachment from objects and people, is what allows them to be free from fear and pain. I want to point out that this doesn't mean you should be careless when it comes to certain fears. If the doctor tells you your health is poor, and you will probably get diabetes if you don't make changes to your lifestyle, you will have some fear. But you must alter your lifestyle to free yourself from that fear.

According to Santideva, an Indian Buddhist monk, "It is not possible to control all external events; but if I simply control my mind, what need is there to control other things?"[116] *This is the answer, and I saw it in the swamis. All around me, I saw that they were able to detach from the situations and focus on their responses. They realised that their response had more to do with the outcome, rather than the situation itself. They continuously practiced controlling their emotions, and it was obvious in the stability of their mind and the purity of their character.*

I don't want you to have a misconception about attachments. You may feel that I am talking about ridding everyone from our life, but this isn't the case, and it's practically impossible. It is more about seeing everything as *borrowed*. When you lease a car, do you tell yourself that you own it? Of course not. You know that you only have it for a certain period of time, but you still enjoy it; you are grateful for the chance to drive it. Similarly, when we acknowledge that all our blessings are like the leased car, we are free to enjoy them without living in a constant fear of losing them. We are all guests here on this planet. Literally, we are the passenger on this journey.

Short-Term Fears

I've first-hand observed short-term fear in those around me, particularly when it comes to studies and jobs. Jobs give us security, and we are all naturally attached to the idea of providing for ourselves and our loved ones. When someone loses their job, they panic out of fear. When you panic, you start to anticipate outcomes that have not yet manifested. Fear makes us all writers. When we begin to ruminate of what could be, we spiral off, devising possible future scenarios. When you anticipate future outcomes, you imprison yourself, the monkey child-locks all the doors. Seneca observed this and said, "Our fears are more numerous than our dangers, and we suffer more in our imagination than in reality."

Learn to reframe the situation. I know, it's hard to do this, especially in the moment, to remain open to opportunity when the

---

[116] Wallace, A., & Wallace, V. (1997)

unknown future spins in your body and mind, like a tornado. In adverse times we don't think of these responses, and we make quick judgements, but there are strategies to help us amend this panic and fear too. Sometimes when we panic we freeze. Panicking and freezing are a disconnect between the monkey and the Tesla; the body and the mind. Either our bodies go on high alert and rush ahead of our mental processes, or, our minds are racing and our body starts to shut down. Sometimes closing your eyes, and taking a deep breath, can help relieve such situations. They are usually fleeting. When we go through a period of instability, we fear what lies ahead. In the moment, we struggle to see the complete picture, but we know that when the episode passes, we will never look back to learn from the experience. Life isn't a collection of unrelated events, it's a whole narrative that stretches into the past and the future. The Stoics taught that when we learn to stop segmenting experiences and periods of our lives, and instead see them as scenes and acts in a large rnarrative, you gain perspective that helps deal with fear.

Long-Term Fears

On the flip side of the coin is long-term fear. It is much harder to work with this. Usually we bury it or run away from it. This is what most of us do with fear. Instead of assessing and responding, we deny or abandon the situation completely. Relationships are a space where we commonly use this 'solution'. Let's say you are having some major conflict with your partner. Rather than sitting down with them and talking about what's going on, or even trying to figure out that it may be best to part ways, you pretend that everything is fine. It's like that elephant in the living room. When you hide fear, your problems follow you. In fact, they are probably growing bigger and bigger. But trust me, at some point they will explode and you will be forced to deal with them.

Arjuna's response from the start of the battle teaches us how we should be dealing with failure. In the moments before the battle starts, when Arjuna is overcome by fear, he doesn't run from it or bury it like most of us would. He is a brave and skilled warrior, yet in the moment it is fear that causes him, for the first time, to reflect. It's often said that when the fear of staying the same outweighs the fear of change, that is when we change. He asks for help from Shri Vāsudev Krishna in the form of insight, enlightenment, and understanding. Right from that moment, he started to shift from being controlled by his fear to understanding it. He chose to face and confront it.

Whereas when you suppress them or run away from them, your fears and your problems remain with you, and they accumulate. It's like the landfill sites. The world used to think that it didn't matter how much rubbish we dumped without caring for nature or the environment. If we couldn't see it or smell it, it would take care of itself. Yet before regulations came into play, landfills polluted water supplies, and even today they are one of the largest producers of human-generated methane gas in the United States. In the same way, filling a landfill of fears within us isn't a solution.

Going through the process of acknowledging fear, observing your patterns of dealing with it, addressing and amending those patterns helps to reprogram your fear from something that is inherently negative to neutral, or even indicate an opportunity for change. Fear motivates us. Sometimes it motivates us towards what we want, but sometimes, if we aren't careful, it limits us with what we think will keep us safe. Choose faith. Have faith.

PART FIVE

CONCLUSION

LIVE KESHAV

Man sacrifices his health in order to make money.
Then he sacrifices money to recuperate his health.
Then he is so anxious about the future that he does not enjoy the present;
the result being that he does not live in the present or the future;
he lives as if he is never going to die, then dies having never really lived.
Dalai Lama

The first verse of the Ishā Upanishad, from the Yajur Veda, says:

Ishā-vāsyam idam sarvam yat kim cha jagatyām jagat
tena tyaktena bhunjīthā mā gridah kasyasvid dhanam

This entire creation—static as well as dynamic—is pervaded by the Supreme.
Hence, enjoy the pleasures in a detached manner.
Do not be greedy. This wealth does not belong to anyone.
Yajur Veda 40.1

This mantra itself is the foundation of all positive philosophies and ideas of the world. If you continuously contemplate on this message, which is further emphasised by my guru, Mahant Swami Maharaj, in Satsang Dikshā, "This body is a means for liberation, not merely a means for indulgence in sense pleasures."[117] It provides the ideal approach to living your life *The Keshav Way*. It is the first step to

---

[117] Satsang Diksha 2

attaining peace and happiness. It teaches us that the world around us is not ours. It belong to the owner—the Supreme Being or higher power, referred to in Vedic tradition as *Parabrahman*, who pervades every point that is His. Because we don't own this world, we should use the facilities of this world without believing ourselves to be the owners. This doesn't mean you should refuse to use the facilities of this world. We should definitely make the best use of them, but by remembering it isn't ours, and our true path is something greater. The Upanishad mantra also mentions that we should not harbour greed, which is the highest level of foolishness. We don't own anything in the world, nor will anything come with us at the end of our journey. Running after what we will eventually have to leave behind is truly foolish. We are no longer going to be Alexander.

Let me touch upon detachment again too. You cannot truly enjoy life without detachment. In fact, the only way to enjoy the true nature of this world, and our life, is by remaining detached from it. I know that this may seem counterintuitive, but believe me, it isn't. Think for a minute how everyday, we obsess ourselves over the things that we own, and this inevitably causes worries and miseries. Every worry starts from the desire of belonging. We worry about how we will get what we want; we then worry about how we will maintain the security and continued association with that object; finally, when it is time to wave goodbye, we regret losing it.

This is the dilemma of life. It is like chasing after your shadow. I don't want you to continue glamorising and idolising those who earn fame, wealth, power, and status. Don't aspire to be like them. This hunger will never end. You will continue to run on this treadmill all your life without really getting anywhere. You will never feel that you have achieved enough, and suddenly when the light switches off at the end of this crazy race called life, the show well and truly does end. When this show ends, we are all at the same level, we're all finished. The 'toys' that we collect in this world—name, fame, wealth, power, status, or whatever it may be—we never actually own, nor take any of these with us. We foolishly assume that we own what we have forever, but they will go within a blink of an eye. We are back to square one. So what do we do? Some suggest to live life in the present moment without worrying about the future. Others suggest we should enjoy life to the fullest. Face the future, problems, illness, or death, when it comes, there is no need to worry about it all now. Some even argue that death is simply prolonged sleep, so why worry? Let me clear this up for you too. How many thinkers, speakers, and philosophers do you think would enjoy their marvellous speeches if they had a gun held to their head? Elusive ideologies and concepts like this, that fear to address the fundamental underlying issues, will only provide a temporary escape; they serve only as attention diverters.

We touched upon death at the very start of the book, and that, it is natural we all fear death and want to avoid it. If death was truly painless, why would there be a natural repulsion to it? Why does society consider murder or manslaughter to be the most heinous crime? This fear of death is intuitively built within us, and has spread rapidly throughout society. In all our actions throughout life, we try to avoid death. When you associate the fact of death with all the running around that you do, to seek gratification through temporary pleasures that you indulge in, deep down you know that you are being foolish.

The solution is simple. Instead of trying to pursue what we can't obtain forever, pursue what is permanent and all-pervading, within us and outside. Pursue divinity. There is divinity all around—within us, around us, in everyone, and everything. Begin with ourselves. See divinity within yourself, and you will begin to fill the entire world with divinity.

BEGINNINGS

We live in a quick-paced, complex world. With 195 nations, countless cultures, thousands of languages and dialects, numerous religions and philosophies—all mixed with many superstitions, stereotypes, and biases. Every person on this planet may be a unique individual, on their own unique journey, but the destination is the same. We may not know that destination for sure, but the passenger does. You must go on your own journey and live your life in such a way that you begin to feel Keshav within you. Yes, consult others but leave the ultimate choices to yourself. You alone must decide what is right and what is wrong for yourself. You alone must decide, in every given situation and circumstance, what is bad, good, better, and best. Get rid of the tension and anxiety that come from others people's comments. Have faith in God, Guru, and yourself.

In life we will all face difficulties of all sorts. Everyone does, rich or poor, famous or common—no one is exempt from these difficulties; it is the very nature of *māyā*. Add value to your life, find your passion and purpose, and be at peace with yourself. Take everything in small steps, don't jump straight into the deep end. Reflect back on when we began this journey together.

We are all made to believe that happiness is based on factors such as people, places, and objects. That once we achieve our goals like getting our dream job, finding our life partner, buying a nice home, or travelling the world, only then will we be happy. Temporary happiness is futile and damaging in the long run. Humans are programmed to want more and more. Money too is seen as happiness. But remember that the richest and most powerful have stumbled and fell; their lives have ended in misery and pain. No one or nothing has control over your happiness. Only you control your happiness.

Imagine if you could be happy all the time? Isn't that why you came this far into the book? Being happy for every moment, at every second of your life. Everlasting bliss and happiness. Happiness is not a journey outwards, but a journey inwards to discovering yourself; discovering the Keshav within. Every one of us, regardless of our differing beliefs and values, are on a spiritual journey with empowering thoughts over our limited ones. We must develop positive habits and learn to also let go. We mustn't live in the past, nor should we ponder excessively about the future; we must live in the present. Stop comparing, stop complaining, and love everyone in this world. Have no expectations of others; have expectations of only yourself. Embrace the world and the divinity around you. Begin with yourself. Begin today.

This journey will last your entire life. Be patient and take it a step at a time. Anything and everything, good or bad, that happens in your life is a lesson to learn and grow from. Stay strong and rooted, and keep on moving forward. Most important of all—have faith. Let go of your fears and live a life filled with faith and trust.

You and I have been put on this planet with an intention far greater than we can ever comprehend. We must begin to love, assist, help, and serve. Inspire others, put a smile on someone else's face. Make a difference in this world by making a difference to yourself. Make your lives Keshav and inspire others to become Keshav too; this is *Keshav Jivan*.

I thank you for taking the first step with me on this journey, and I offer my sincerest prayers for you in seeking true bliss and happiness. When you find it, please remember me keep me in your prayers.

Before I share my final thoughts with you, I would like to share a secret. The secret to fully achieve the epitome of *param ānanda* (eternal happiness). This journey only really begins once you discover your inner Keshav. When you do, I will share the secret to connecting your inner Keshav with the outer Keshav. Yes, you heard me right, the next step is to connect with the living, breathing Keshav. But that is a conversation that you and I will be having another day…

FINAL THOUGHTS

Happiness means something different to each and every person on this planet. We must explore our own definition. For some, it is a state of flow, for others it is satisfaction. For some people, it's a feeling of peace and contentment. I truly believe that happiness (or more accurately, *ānanda*) is the original state of the *ātmā*. This original state can be discovered when we eliminate the idea that something is missing in life. In all seriousness, nothing is missing, so why do we ruminate over the past? Why do we ponder about the future, or regret something we have done, or that we plan to do?

Happiness doesn't come from positive thinking or positive actions alone. After thorough research, reading, and experiences of myself and others, I think it is right to say that, with all positivity comes negativity. Saying you are happy means you were sad at some point. Every positive thought has a negative seed, every negative thought has a positive seed. Greatness comes through suffering; to appreciate positivity, we have to experience the negativity too.

True happiness is neither about positivity or negativity; it is about eliminating desires. The fewer desires that you and I have, the more we can accept life as it is, the more stable our mind becomes. The mind enjoys going back to the past and projecting into the future. By being present in the now, you are able to feel happier and content. It is within our minds that we create notions of happiness and unhappiness, of perfect and imperfect, of joy and sorrow, and these all stem from desire. The world is a reflection of our mind. The world is as we perceive it to be. This is *māyā*—the universal material source of creation. We are born, we have a set of experiences and stimulations, we suffer, we die. This is the history of humankind. How we choose to live the life in-between birth and death is up to us, that choice is ours. Happiness is your choice; when we believe it as such, we can begin to work on it. We are only here for a short period of time, so why waste it?

Our mind is just as malleable as our body. We dedicate so much of our time and effort to changing the world around us, changing the people around us, changing the circumstances around us, as well as our own bodies. The same needs to be done to our minds. Happiness requires you to live in the moment. Projecting yourself into the future and living in delusions, can destroy your happiness. Don't ponder or ruminate on the past. Let it go. Don't cling to bad memories. Don't cling to regrets. Don't cling to people of the past. None of it. Unhappiness comes from comparing 'now' to 'back then'. A person who is happy doesn't necessarily have to always *look* happy. One who effortlessly accepts life as it is, and still remains elevated, never loses their innate peace.

The most common mistake humanity keeps making is believing happiness comes from the externals. We know this. It's nothing new. Looking externally for anything is a delusion. We are humans, creatures of desire, and we naturally *want*. But to believe that peace, joy, and happiness comes from external circumstances, that something out *there* will make us happy is a delusion that leads to suffering.

When we are young, we have time. We have good health too, but we have no money. When we reach our mid-forties, we have money and fairly good health, but we have no time. When we retire, or get close to retirement, we have money and we have time, but our health is all over. We spend our whole life like this.

The words 'should' and 'need' pull us down. They are associated with guilt and social programming. Doing something because we 'need to', or, because we 'should' means we really don't want to do it. This is making you sad; get rid of 'shoulds' and 'needs'. Life is not a multiplayer game, it is a single-player game. We come alone, we die alone, all our thoughts are our own, reality is our own. We don't know who was around from our family four generations from now, it will be the same for us. We will be gone, all memories of us will be gone. Before we were here, nobody cared. After we are gone, nobody will care. Seek something higher, it is there.

Happiness and peace are skills we can develop. We are not born happy; it isn't a natural birthright, but it can be developed. Nutrition is a skill, working out is a skill, reading is a skill, building relationships is a skill, maintaining them even a more difficult one. Learning skills is what we do all our life. Put your intention and focus on this. Build good habits. Not consuming alcohol will keep your mind stable. Controlling your diet will keep your mind stable. Simplifying your life with limited technology will keep your mind stable. Stop feeding the monkey dopamine, it's loving it, and when it gets withdrawal symptoms, it'll go crazy. Life is about replacing these bad habits with good habits; they become natural thereafter. When we were young, we didn't have many habits. With time, we learnt new things and gradually developed habits. Today, we have become self-conscious in many habits and routines. We can do the same for happiness and peace.

In any and every situation in life, we only have three choices: change it, accept it, or leave it. If we want to change a situation, that is a desire; it will lead to suffering if not changed. We must be careful on what we choose to change. Unless it is prudent to change something, stay away. It is always best to accept, regardless of the outcome. My spiritual belief is that whatever happens is God's wish, and this has given me immense inner strength and courage in times of my mental and physical health difficulties. Life doesn't always go to plan, but when does it anyway? We must learn to take a step back and look at the grand design. Whatever happens, happens for the best. The sooner we accept the reality of the situation, the sooner we adapt, and we will. It'll take time, but we will be able to achieve acceptance of situations beyond out control. I didn't believe it to begin with, but as I began to take a step back and analyse the situation, now my brain seems to do it automatically.

Above everything else, we must look after our spiritual, mental, and physical health. Spiritual health is what the *ātmā* quenches for; it is a requirement for a fulfilling life. Mental and physical health ensure that the monkey and the Tesla continue to run in this journey of life, that is, until we reach the end destination. Everything else should come after. Today, humans do not live how they are meant to live. We eat what we aren't supposed to eat. Our visual cortex is exposed to much more than it evolved to see. Humans aren't meant to walk in shoes; a lot of back issues arise from wearing shoes. We're not meant to sleep warm at night. We're meant to be exposed to the cold to strengthen our immune systems. Humans didn't evolve to live in 100 percent sterile and clean environments. Today, more and more people are becoming ill from the basic of illnesses. Our immune systems aren't being trained for what they were *created* for. Humans aren't meant to check their Instagram or Snapchat every five minutes. It is seriously time for us to take a step back and look at the bigger picture.

Ultimately, the mind should work for us, don't let it become the boss. The mind is a muscle, and so it can be trained, conditioned and reprogrammed. Unpack your thoughts. Unpack your emotions. Unpack your reactions. There is no endpoint to this journey. It is a lifelong process that we just keep getting better at.

Success, money, fame, or pleasures won't give you happiness. Happiness is being satisfied with what you have right here, right now. I have firsthand spoken to, and know of, people who have it all— material success and social success—yet they admit it hasn't given them happiness, they are not *more* happy than they were in the school years. This is where my exploration into hedonic adaption began. This led me to discover that happiness in intrinsic to the *ātmā*.

Most of us believe successful people are the winners in the game of life. Five years back I might have said Steve Jobs. I wouldn't have been wrong either, he created something extraordinary. Jeff Bezos is successful too; just like so many technological creators I used to look up to. I mean, I still do, but not with the belief that success leads to happiness. Today, I have come to believe that the real winners in the game of life are those that don't play the game at all; those that rise above it and beyond it. Those few whose internal mental and spiritual state is at an equilibrium, who are self-aware, fulfilled, and need nothing more. My guru, Mahant Swami Maharaj is the embodiment of peace and happiness. He has no money or possessions. He has status, but it means nothing to him. He doesn't see himself in a position of status. He is in the same elevated state as he was thirty years ago, probably even sixty years ago. He is fulfilled. One who is peaceful inside and out, who views the world and all of God's creation with divinity, eventually lives in this state of happiness, this is *ānanda*.

Reconfigure, refresh, and reprogram.

Rewrite your story today.

Live The Keshav Way.

PART SIX

APPENDICE

Appendix A: The Brain

The human brain is split into centres, structures, and pathways. There are specific centres covering language, others that perceive information such as sight, and there are pathways that result in pleasure. Some perform multiple roles, and many work together as a team. It is a complex system at a high-level, and at the low-level too, with hormones, neuroreceptors, and neurotransmitters. The brain can also be looked at by how the different structs work in day-to-day life. In this way, it can be divided into six key areas. A number of therapy methods, such as CBT, are based around these six themes.

- Behavioural (responses)
- Cognitive (thoughts and beliefs)
- Dynamic (instincts and drive)
- Analytical (methods of thinking)
- Developmental (stages of maturity)
- Biological (physical state)

Specific Areas

Many consider the brain as a machine, made up of different areas, that perform functions in different ways, but I think that it is more than that. To give you an idea of how the brain works in action, we will look at an example, but before that, let me simplify the parts of the brain.

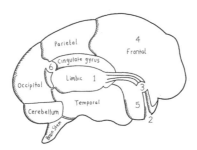

1. The **amygdala** is the head emotional centre in the limbic system.
2. The **orbitofrontal cortex** is a smaller area of the outer edge of the frontal lobe.
3. The **uncinate fasciculus** is the pathway that joins the amygdala to the orbitofrontal cortex.
4. The **dorsolateral prefrontal cortex** is part of the frontal lobe.
5. The **ventromedial prefrontal cortex** is the area encircling the the uncinate fasciculus.
6. The **cingulate gyrus** is part of the limbic system.

This diagram shows six specific numbered areas of the brain, and research shows that each play at least one specific role. For example, the amygdala has at least 17 different nuclei, each with its own specific role, mostly to do with emotional responses. The cingulate cortex (or gyrus) is responsible for memory formation, learning and decision-making. To keep it simple, we will assume one role for each area.

1. The amygdala is a fast-acting defence mechanism. It doesn't think, it simply responds.
2. The orbitofrontal cortex acts by attempting to control impulses and it uses moral judgements to keep us within social norms.
3. The uncinate fasciculus is a moral guide, providing us with a conscience.
4. The dorsolateral prefrontal cortex works analytically, using logic.
5. The ventromedial prefrontal cortex is empathetic and considers the feelings of others.
6. The cingulate cortex is involved in making decisions influenced by past experience.

Brain Functioning Example

Everyone's brain reacts differently. Let's look at Vinay's brain at work. Vinay has just been told that someone he knows has said negative stuff about him. This is how each part of his brain may react. The message arrives at a relay station called the thalamus. This structure sends the information to all of the six reps, but first it reaches the amygdala.

1. The amygdala is quick to react and immediately makes him angry. Vinay raises his voice, threatening to attack the person. The amygdala releases numerous chemicals to disable the other parts of the brain (for example, the dorsolateral prefrontal cortex is prevented from working) so that they don't interfere with its plans.

2. His orbitofrontal cortex desperately tries to warn Vinay that he must keep within socially accepted behaviour. It tries to contain his impulsive behaviours, telling him it would be immoral to attack someone and also that he mustn't become unpopular.

3. The uncinate faciculus acts as a conscience. It says, "I feel guilty. This is morally wrong." But it also adds, "However, if you can persuade me that this action is reasonable, then I won't mind adjusting my conscience and going along with it."

4. The dorsolateral prefrontal cortex is trying to establish and work with the facts but it is being overruled and even being fed misinformation by the amygdala.

5. The ventromedial prefrontal cortex asks what the other person feels. It has empathy and compassion for the other person who made the unpleasant remarks and wants to understand why they may have said what they did, and wants to then put things right.

6. The cingulate cortex draws on other structures and simply wants to remind Vinay of past experience. "If you shout, you might end up in trouble," or it may have learnt, "If you shout loud enough, you will get your way." It is a reminder to him from previous personal experiences of the consequences.

All of this happens in less than a second. This is just a brief overview of six areas that compete to give advice and take action. If we look more broadly, there are two teams in our brain. One team is powerful and quick to act. It is emotionally based, with irrational thinking. The other team is not as powerful, it is slower to act and is logically used, with compassion and guilt. Considering the frontal lobe alone, we can see more easily why there is a problem. The outer edge of the frontal lobe is called the cortex ,and it is in the cortex where thinking with interpretation occurs. Maybe this helps you understand why we say, "think before you act," or, "take a step back for a moment and breathe."

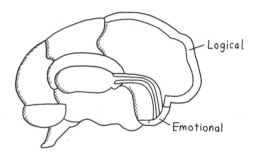

If the outer edge had just one area for thinking, there wouldn't be any issues. But, it is believed that there are at least two thinking and interpreting areas. The dorsolateral edge is interpreting in a rational way. The orbitofrontal cortex is interpreting by impression and feeling, and has direct links to the amygdala. This second way of thinking joins forces with the strongest emotional centre of the brain - the amygdala. What we now have, in effect, are two interpreting brains. One is virtually automatic and thinks on behalf of us, without our input and is based solely on emotion. The other is under our control, and allows us to think the way we want. The issue is that both brains don't think in the same way and don't agree on the interpretation of what is going on. This is merely a small part of the battle that continues in our brain.

The Real Pandemic

Technology may have sold economic problems of the past, but they have given us new psychological problems. The Internet has open-sourced information; but also open-sourced insecurity, anxiety, and self-doubt. I won't go all technical here, but there are four types of brainwaves; alpha, beta, theta, and delta. The average person opens up their phone 80 times a day. This is by design. Companies are putting in millions of dollars to understand why we do what we do. Picking up your phone the first thing in the morning when you wake up is a dangerous thing.

So right now you are in the beta state – awake. Delta is when you are fast asleep. In between those two states is theta and alpha. They are the most important states for learning. Theta is the state in and out of sleep – the creativity state, when we are usually the most creative. We have experienced this when we are in and out of sleep, our mind comes up with amazing ideas. Showers also put us in a theta state. You may notice that when you are in the shower, you come up with some of your best, and most creative ideas. When someone does something amazing, either in athletics, education, technology, or with the human body, there's always work behind it.

Above theta, there is the alpha state. This is the state where you are most aware and awake. Alpha is the state of learning - accelerated learning. It is the state of relaxed awareness. When we meditate, this is the state we go in. Your critical mind is set aside and you absorb information unconsciously. TVs put us in an alpha state. Have you noticed that if somebody is watching a football game, or watching their favourite series, they are literally hypnotised? As if they can't hear you? That is the alpha state, where information is going directly into your mind.

Now you know that you are in this alpha-theta state first thing in the morning, and the first thing you're picking up is your phone. This is reprogramming your brain. Doing this decreases your level of productivity and performance – you don't notice this, because it is affecting your mind directly. It is training you to become distracted, just like we are not focussed when having a conversation with somebody. So some form of mindfulness is important, whether that is through meditation, or another way. Don't see meditation as a way to achieve the Zen state, but see it as a mental exercise to improve your cognitive capabilities.

Your mind is the most amazing tool you have, you just need to learn to use it properly. It is the most powerful super-computer. Common sense is not common practice. Knowledge isn't power. But knowledge has the potential to become power when we use and apply it correctly. We've learnt a lot throughout this book, but it is time to put it into practice. Sometimes, we don't remember everything we learnt - we have heard about the learning curve, but there is a forgetting curve too. It says that if you learn something once, within 48 hours, 80% of it is gone. You watch a video, listen to a podcast, read a book, or go to a talk, and within two days it is gone. This is why memory is so important.

You should also know that most technological devices like your phone, laptop, and tablet emit blue light which inhibits the production of melatonin that helps you relax and go to sleep. Every single study has shown that the happiest people are the ones that feel like they control their own happiness, and not put it on to other people, places, or things.

So back to the point, don't keep touching your phone because it is distracting you and reprogramming your mind to become reactive. Especially when we wake up first thing, in the relaxed state of mind, as this will spoil your mood and thinking for the rest of the day. You're in that hypnotic state, where everything will become impressionable, and so you will never have a quality life.

We talk about concentration, and how we struggle to maintain it. This is one of the reasons. Concentration is your ability to maintain your awareness on one thing for an extended period of time. When you are speaking to someone, give them your undivided attention - train yourself. There is no quick-fix. We live in a world where we all want a quick-fix, but sadly it isn't that simple. I know people that have left their worldly lives to spend years, or even their entire lifetime, to discover their true self and the higher power.

Social media isn't bad if you know how to use it with discipline. But no matter how much we hear this, we are slaves to social media. We have lost. Most of us reading this form part of the addictive generation. It isn't entirely our fault though, it is by design. Recently we have come to know that many of the social media giants hire *attention engineers*. Their job is to make these products as addictive as possible, based on ideas from Las Vegas casinos - that is what social media is. They are designed to be addictive. Maximum addiction equals maximum profit. It has come to the point now where these tools, which were meant to help us, seem to be ripping up the very fabric of society.

Research tells us that if we spend extensive amounts of a day in a state of fragmented attention, like checking our phone again and again, this can permanently reduce your capacity for concentration. Again, it is dopamine that drives this addiction from within us. A Stanford study, by Robert Sapolsky, calls this the *magic of maybe* – when you look at your mobile phone *maybe* there is a text, or *maybe* there is not. That high you get when there is, that is dopamine – a 400 percent spike. That is roughly the same amount of dopamine that you get from cocaine. Today, a new highly addictive drug is being put into the hands of young children, with no age limits or restrictions.

We live our life for others. When we upload a picture to Instagram, our mind is vulnerable to see who likes the photo and who comments on it. When we get new likes, the application can notify you knowing that you will be vulnerable to that moment. Social media giants use algorithms to control how long and where your photo appears on other people's feeds - a unique orchestration, for you to keep coming back to see the new likes. This leads to the likes of *Facebook Depression*, where we compare our lives to the highlights of other people's lives, and thus we get less satisfaction from our life.

We curate our lives around this perceived sense of perfection, for the short-term rewards of likes, hearts, and shares. This is a false sense of happiness, that is short lived and will leave you feeling more empty than you did before. The more you use social media, the more likely you are to feel lonely or isolated. Our brains are not wired for the exposure of this type of stimuli for intermittent rewards. Let's assume that it is bad to keep pulling a slot machine at a casino, but today we carry a slot machine around us all day, and we keep pulling on it waiting for a reward. Studies have shown that this has several cognitive consequences, like anxiety.

Unfortunately, we do not have a global solution. The solution is down to you as an individual. Today, all the technological giants are in competition to maximise attention and persuasion. Social media isn't bad but don't become reliant on these short-term dopamine releases which are affecting all across society.

If you feed the beast, that beast will destroy you.

If you push back on it, you can control it.

ACKNOWLEDGEMENTS

I offer my sincere gratitude and heartfelt prayers to His Holiness Pramukh Swami Maharaj (1921-2016), whose life and teachings have been the foundation of how I aim to live my life. My spiritual guru, His Holiness Mahant Swami Maharaj (b. 1933), who has been a constant inspiration and example in living a life of humility, integrity, divinity, and perfected character. He is the embodiment of Param Ānanda. Without his blessings, love, support and guidance, this book would never have been possible. I am eternally grateful to my gurus.

Special thanks to Swamis of Neasden Temple, as well as the swamis and Sanskrit scholars of BAPS, for their continuous insights and support in ensuring clarity and authenticity, and for providing guidance in my times of need.

I'd like to thank Shiv for working with me in transforming my ideas into illustrative diagrams and drawings. Thanks to Dhwani and other editors for dealing with my endless stream of edits, reviews and changes to the text. A shoutout to Tilak for the cover design and theme.

Finally, I express my gratitude to you for the love, support, and blessings you haven given me. To evert one of my readers, family, friends, well-wishers, and supporters online. It is because of your enthusiasm and love that I even had the opportunity to put my thoughts onto paper. I hope that you enjoy my humble attempt to pass on the practical wisdom that I have shared with you.

To leave a review, or to get in touch with me, visit:
www.thekeshavway.com